CRIMINAL JUSTICE, LAW ENFORCEMENT AND CORRECTIONS

REVISITING AND ENFORCING THE CRIME VICTIMS' RIGHTS ACT

CRIMINAL JUSTICE, LAW ENFORCEMENT AND CORRECTIONS

Additional books in this series can be found on Nova's website at:

https://www.novapublishers.com/catalog/index.php?cPath=23_29&seriesp=Criminal+Justice%2C+Law+Enforcement+and+Corrections

Additional E-books in this series can be found on Nova's website at:

https://www.novapublishers.com/catalog/index.php?cPath=23_29&seriespe=Criminal+Justice%2C+Law+Enforcement+and+Corrections

CRIMINAL JUSTICE, LAW ENFORCEMENT AND CORRECTIONS

REVISITING AND ENFORCING THE CRIME VICTIMS' RIGHTS ACT

JORGE S. EHRLICH
EDITOR

Nova
Nova Science Publishers, Inc.
New York

For permission to use material from this book please contact us:
Telephone 631-231-7269; Fax 631-231-8175
Web Site: http://www.novapublishers.com

LIBRARY OF CONGRESS CATALOGING-IN-PUBLICATION DATA

Revisiting and enforcing the Crime Victims' Rights Act / Jorge S. Ehrlich.
p. cm.
Includes index.
ISBN 978-1-60741-231-1 (hardcover)
1. Victims of crimes--Legal status, laws, etc.--United States. 2. United States. Crime Victims' Rights Act of 2004. I. Title.
KF9763.E38 2009
344.7303'288--dc22

2009029247

Published by Nova Science Publishers, Inc. † New York

CONTENTS

PREFACE

To implement the Crime Victims' Rights Act (CVRA), the federal judiciary have, among other things, revised internal guidelines, trained the Department of Justice (DOJ) staff and judges, provided victims with emergency, temporary housing to protect them and proactively asked victims if they would like to speak in court. Mechanisms to ensure adherence to the CVRA include processes for victims to submit complaints against DOJ employees and assert their rights in court; however, the majority of victims reported they were not aware that these mechanisms exist. If victims are not aware of the complaint process or their ability to assert their rights in court, these mechanisms will not be effective at helping ensure that victims are afforded their rights. Thus, this book attempts to increase awareness of the CVRA and improve its implementation.

Chapter 1 - As part of the Justice For All Act of 2004, Pub. L. No. 108-405, 118 Stat. 2260 (effective Oct. 30, 2004), victims of federal crimes were given significantly ex-panded rights in the Scott Campbell, Stephanie Roper, Wendy Preston, Louarna Gillis, and Nila Lynn Crime Victims' Rights Act (CVRA). The CVRA set forth these rights in newly enacted 18 U.S.C. § 3771, which also placed on the federal courts a duty to ensure that victims are afforded those rights. Section 3771 effec-tively replaces 42 U.S.C. § 10606 ("Victims' Rights"), now repealed by the CVRA, which included a list of victims' rights but did not provide any means of enforcement.

Among the rights given to victims by the CVRA are the right to be present at public court proceedings involving the crime, section 3771(a)(2) and (3), and the right to be "reasonably heard at any public proceeding in the district court involv-ing release, plea, sentencing, or any parole proceeding," section 3771(a)(4). Up to now, victims have had a right to be heard only in limited circumstances. For example, Fed. R. Crim. P. 32(i)(4)(B) allows "any victim of a crime of violence or sexual abuse who is present at sentencing . . . to speak or submit any information about the sentence." (Note: Effective Dec. 1, 2008, a proposed amendment to Fed. R. Crim. P. 32(i)(4)(B) states that the sentencing court "must address any victim of the crime who is present at sentencing and must permit the victim to be rea-sonably heard.")

As did the prior statute, the CVRA directs Department of Justice personnel (and personnel of other agencies, as appropriate) to "make their best efforts to see that crime victims are notified of, and accorded, the rights described in subsection (a)." Section 3771(c)(1). However, under section 3771(d)(1), crime victims are now authorized to assert those rights independently. In addition, the federal dis-trict courts themselves are now directed, "[i]n any court proceeding involving an offense against a crime victim, [to] ensure that the crime victim is afforded the rights described in subsection (a)." 18 U.S.C. § 3771(b)(1).

In an amendment effective July 27, 2006, new section 3771(b)(2)(A) provides that "[i]n a Federal habeas corpus proceeding arising out of a State conviction, the court shall ensure that a crime victim is afforded" certain of the rights given to federal crime victims, namely: to be present at public court proceedings involving the crime; to be reasonably heard at any public proceeding involving release, plea, sentencing, or parole; to proceedings free from unreasonable delay; and to be treated with fairness and with respect for the victim's dignity and privacy. Al-though the state crime victim can enforce these rights in the same way as a federal crime victim, see section 3771(b)(2)(B)(i), no agency is charged with providing notice or other assistance to a state crime victim under this section. In fact, section 3771(b)(2)(C) specifically excludes any "Executive Branch" personnel from "any obligation or requirement" in such proceedings.

The CVRA included a process for congressional review of the new legisla-tion's effectiveness: "[T]he Administrative Office of the United States Courts, for each Federal court, shall report to Congress the number of times that a right estab-lished in [section 3771] is asserted in a criminal case and the relief requested is denied and . . . the reason for such denial." And within four years of the CVRA's effective date, the Comptroller General shall submit a report on "the effect and efficacy of the implementation of the amendments made by this title on the treat-ment of crime victims in the Federal system." See Pub. L. No. 108-405, Title I, § 104(a) and (b).

The expanded victims' rights under the CVRA may affect several stages of federal criminal proceedings, from a defendant's initial appearance through sen-tencing. The Center's *Benchbook for U.S. District Court Judges* has been revised to reflect section 3771 and the possible effects on court procedure. Part II below provides a quick guide to how various procedures covered in the *Benchbook* may be affected by the CVRA. Part III notes several other issues that courts may have to deal with under the CVRA, and Part IV contains summaries of cases that have addressed aspects of the CVRA. The complete text of 18 U.S.C. § 3771 is pro-vided in Part V.

Chapter 2 - According to the Department of Justice (DOJ), as of September 2008 there were approximately 750,000 crime victims in the federal criminal justice system with active cases. In general, for a crime to be prosecuted within the federal criminal justice system, it must be a violation of a federal law. The role for crime victims within the criminal justice process has changed over time. Since the middle of the nineteenth century, crime in the United States has been a public rather than private matter, where the philosophy has been that criminal prosecutions should serve societal interests of deterrence and retribution, as opposed to the individual interests of victims. As such, the American criminal justice system is comprised of two parties—a public prosecutor and the defense—who present their arguments to an impartial body (the judge and jury) for judgment. However, individuals advocating on behalf of crime victims have raised concerns that by focusing solely on the public interest, the criminal justice system has overlooked the individual interests and needs of victims and has limited victims' access to and participation in the prosecution of their cases.

In: Revisiting and Enforcing the Crime…
Editor: Jorge S. Ehrlich

ISBN: 978-1-60741-231-1

Chapter 1

The Crime Victims' Rights Act of 2004 and the Federal Courts

Jefri Wood

I. Overview of the Act

As part of the Justice For All Act of 2004, Pub. L. No. 108-405, 118 Stat. 2260 (effective Oct. 30, 2004), victims of federal crimes were given significantly ex-panded rights in the Scott Campbell, Stephanie Roper, Wendy Preston, Louarna Gillis, and Nila Lynn Crime Victims' Rights Act (CVRA). The CVRA set forth these rights in newly enacted 18 U.S.C. § 3771, which also placed on the federal courts a duty to ensure that victims are afforded those rights. Section 3771 effec-tively replaces 42 U.S.C. § 10606 ("Victims' Rights"), now repealed by the CVRA, which included a list of victims' rights but did not provide any means of enforcement.

Among the rights given to victims by the CVRA are the right to be present at public court proceedings involving the crime, section 3771(a)(2) and (3), and the right to be "reasonably heard at any public proceeding in the district court involv-ing release, plea, sentencing, or any parole proceeding," section 3771(a)(4). Up to now, victims have had a right to be heard only in limited circumstances. For example, Fed. R. Crim. P. 32(i)(4)(B) allows "any victim of a crime of violence or sexual abuse who is present at sentencing . . . to speak or submit any information about the sentence." (Note: Effective Dec. 1, 2008, a proposed amendment to Fed. R. Crim. P. 32(i)(4)(B) states that the sentencing court "must address any victim of the crime who is present at sentencing and must permit the victim to be rea-sonably heard.")

As did the prior statute, the CVRA directs Department of Justice personnel (and personnel of other agencies, as appropriate) to "make their best efforts to see that crime victims are notified of, and accorded, the rights described in subsection (a)." Section 3771(c)(1). However, under section 3771(d)(1), crime victims are now authorized to assert those rights independently. In addition, the federal dis-trict courts themselves are now directed, "[i]n any court proceeding involving an offense against a crime victim, [to] ensure that the crime victim is afforded the rights described in subsection (a)." 18 U.S.C. § 3771(b)(1).

In an amendment effective July 27, 2006, new section 3771(b)(2)(A) provides that "[i]n a Federal habeas corpus proceeding arising out of a State conviction, the court shall ensure that a crime victim is afforded" certain of the rights given to federal crime victims, namely: to be present at public court proceedings involving the crime; to be reasonably heard at any public proceeding involving release, plea, sentencing, or parole; to proceedings free from unreasonable delay; and to be treated with fairness and with respect for the victim's dignity and privacy. Al-though the state crime victim can enforce these rights in the same way as a federal crime victim, see section 3771(b)(2)(B)(i), no agency is charged with providing notice or other assistance to a state crime victim under this section. In fact, section 3771(b)(2)(C) specifically excludes any "Executive Branch" personnel from "any obligation or requirement" in such proceedings.

The CVRA included a process for congressional review of the new legisla-tion's effectiveness: "[T]he Administrative Office of the United States Courts, for each Federal court, shall report to Congress the number of times that a right estab-lished in [section 3771] is asserted in a criminal case and the relief requested is denied and . . . the reason for such denial." And within four years of the CVRA's effective date, the Comptroller General shall submit a report on "the effect and efficacy of the implementation of the amendments made by this title on the treat-ment of crime victims in the Federal system." See Pub. L. No. 108-405, Title I, § 104(a) and (b).

The expanded victims' rights under the CVRA may affect several stages of federal criminal proceedings, from a defendant's initial appearance through sen-tencing. The Center's *Benchbook for U.S. District Court Judges* has been revised to reflect section 3771 and the possible effects on court procedure. Part II below provides a quick guide to how various procedures covered in the *Benchbook* may be affected by the CVRA. Part III notes several other issues that courts may have to deal with under the CVRA, and Part IV contains summaries of cases that have addressed aspects of the CVRA. The complete text of 18 U.S.C. § 3771 is pro-vided in Part V.

II. *Benchbook* Sections Affected by the CVRA

Listed below are sections of the *Benchbook for U.S. District Court Judges* where the various provisions of section 3771 might come into play. Potential issues that may arise in a particular proceeding are also noted in some sections. Because of the right of victims to enforce their rights, courts may want to put on the record any matters pertaining to victims, such as inquiring whether the offense involved any victims, whether the government has provided the victims with adequate no-tice of all proceedings, and whether any victims wish to be "reasonably heard" where appropriate.

1.01 Initial Appearance

Section 3771(a)(2) to (4) may apply here. The victim has the right to be notified of and present at the defendant's initial appearance, and if bail is to be set or de-nied at the initial appearance, the victim has the right to be "reasonably heard." The district court may want to ask the prosecutor specifically if there are any vic-tims in the offense and if they have been properly informed of these rights. See

U.S. v. Turner in Part IV *infra* for a summary of a district court's actions to cor-rect inadequate notice to victims about a defendant's arraignment and bail hear-ing.

A few other points should be considered here. Because the CVRA does not distinguish between proceedings that occur before a plea or guilty verdict and proceedings that follow a plea or verdict, it seems that in all proceedings courts must treat alleged victims as if they were admitted or proven victims. Also, now that video teleconferencing is available under Fed. R. Crim. P. 5(f) for the defen-dant's initial appearance, it raises the issue of where a victim who wishes to "be present" would go. Note, too, that because the time between arrest and initial ap-pearance may be very brief, questions concerning what constitutes "reasonable . . . and timely notice" under section 3771(a)(2) may arise.

1.02 Assignment of Counsel or Pro Se Representation

If assignment of counsel is done in a public proceeding, as part of the defendant's initial appearance or separately, victims have the right to be notified and present.

1.03 Release or Detention Pending Trial

As noted for section 1.01, victims have a right to be reasonably heard when the court determines whether the defendant will be released before trial. Section 3771(a)(1) provides that crime victims have the right "to be reasonably protected from the accused."

Note that the statute does not in any way indicate what *weight* a court should give to a victim's statements. This may have to be decided on a case-by-case ba-sis, and may also depend on the proceeding involved or the other legal require-ments courts must consider, such as 18 U.S.C. § 3142 (for release) or the Sentenc-ing Guidelines (for sentencing).

The statute also does not specify whether the right to be "reasonably heard" requires the court to allow an oral statement or can be limited to a written submis-sion. One district court determined that, in a pretrial detention hearing, section 3771(a)(4) would be satisfied by a written statement under the particular circum-stances of the case. See *U.S. v. Marcello* in Part IV, *infra*.

1.04 Offense Committed in Another District

If the defendant is arrested and makes his or her initial appearance in a district that is different from the one in which the offense was committed, a victim has the right to be notified and present. If the defendant agrees to have the prosecution transferred to the different district and pleads guilty or nolo contendere under Fed. R. Crim. P. 20, a victim also has the right to be reasonably heard at that proceeding.

1.05 Commitment to Another District (Removal Proceedings)

If the defendant is arrested in a district that is different from the one in which the offense occurred, as above, and declines to have the prosecution transferred, the court must hold a removal hearing in order to send the defendant to the district in which the offense occurred. A victim has the right to be notified of and present at the removal hearing. Also, if the defendant is to be released on bail rather than held and transferred, a victim has the right to be reasonably heard.

Section 1.05 also covers commitment to another district after the arrest of a probationer or supervised releasee, which raises a question not answered by the text of section 3771. Are the victims of the original offense of conviction "vic-tims" under the CVRA with respect to the violation proceedings? If the conduct underlying the violation of release was the commission of a new federal crime, are the victims of that crime entitled to the rights under the CVRA for the pro-ceedings related to the violation? Or does the CVRA only apply to proceedings that result if new federal charges are brought for that underlying conduct?

1.06 Waiver of Indictment

A victim has the right to be notified of and present at a waiver of indictment hear-ing. If the release of the defendant becomes an issue, as when the defendant re-fuses to waive indictment and bail must be continued or modified, a victim has a right to be heard.

1.07 Arraignment and Plea

A victim has the right to be notified of and present at the defendant's arraignment, and has the right to be heard regarding the plea and the continuation or resetting of bail.

Note that, as with the initial appearance in section 1.01 *supra*, the defendant may agree to video teleconferencing for arraignment. Fed. R. Crim. P. 10(c). A victim's right to be present and reasonably heard must be accommodated if the court is in public session during the video teleconference.

1.08 Joint Representation of Codefendants

A victim has the right to be notified of and present at a hearing regarding joint representation of codefendants.

1.09 Waiver of Jury Trial

A victim has the right to be notified of and present at a hearing regarding waiver of a jury trial.

1.10 Speedy Trial Act

A victim has the right to be notified of and present at any public hearing regarding Speedy Trial Act issues. If a violation of the Speedy Trial Act could lead to dis-missal of the charges against the defendant and to his or her possible release, it appears that a victim would have the right to be reasonably heard in any public proceeding on that issue.

Section 3771(a)(7) states that victims have a right to "proceedings free from unreasonable delay." While that right may normally be compatible with a defen-dant's right to a speedy trial, there are several exceptions in the Speedy Trial Act, *see* 18 U.S.C. § 3161(h), that could authorize a delay that seems unreasonable to a victim. The question may arise whether a delay that is authorized under section 3161(h) is presumptively reasonable or possibly a violation of section 3771(a)(7).

A victim has the right to be notified of and present at any public hearing on a motion to delay the trial, but does not have the right to be reasonably heard unless the defendant is to be released upon a finding that his or her speedy trial rights were violated. If the defendant is not to be released, a victim can object to a delay only by filing a motion for relief under section 3771(d)(3). If a delay will be granted, the court may wish to explain to the victim, or ask the government to ex-plain, why such a delay is necessary and not unreasonable.

1.11 Delinquency Proceedings

The definition of "victim" in section 3771(e) is not limited to victims of adult of-fenders, so it appears that the CVRA applies to juvenile offenses and delinquency proceedings. However, because those proceedings are generally not public, the rights to be notified of and present at any public proceeding, and to be heard at certain public proceedings, would not be applicable. See the summary of U.S. v. L.M. in Part IV, *infra*, for a discussion of this issue.

1.12 Mental Competency in Criminal Matters

A victim has the right to be notified of and present at a public hearing to deter-mine the defendant's mental competency. If civil commitment of the defendant is at issue, it could be argued that the CVRA gives the victim a right to be heard.

2.01 Taking Pleas of Guilty or Nolo Contendere

Any victims have the right to be "reasonably heard" at the plea hearing.

One significant question not addressed in the CVRA, for a plea hearing or any other proceeding, is *when* the victim must be heard. For the right to be meaning-ful, it can be argued that the victim should be heard before the court makes a deci-sion, such as whether to accept a plea bargain or to release the defendant pending sentencing.

Note, however, that a victim's rights with respect to a plea agreement do not extend beyond being heard and, under section 3771(a)(5), "confer[ring] with the attorney for the Government." As the Second Circuit found in *In re W.R. Huff As-set Management Co., LLC*, summarized in Part IV, *infra*, "[n]othing in the CVRA requires the Government to seek approval from crime victims before negotiating or entering into a settlement agreement." And section 3771(d)(6) specifies that "[n]othing in this chapter shall be construed to impair the prosecutorial discretion of the Attorney General or any officer under his direction."

2.02 Taking Pleas of Guilty or Nolo Contendere (Organization)

As with a plea hearing for an individual defendant, a victim has the right to be reasonably heard at a plea hearing when the defendant is an organization. With organizations, there may be more of a chance that "the number of crime victims makes it impracticable to accord all of the crime victims the rights described in subsection (a)." In that case, "the court shall fashion a reasonable procedure to give effect to this chapter that does not unduly complicate or prolong the proceed-ings." Section 3771(d)(2).

2.03 Trial Outline (Criminal Case)

Note that 18 U.S.C. § 3510 already prohibits excluding victims from the trial merely because they may speak at the sentencing hearing. Section 3771(a)(3) now prohibits exclusion of victims from any covered proceeding "unless the court, after receiving clear and convincing evidence, determines that testimony by the victim would be materially altered if the victim heard other testimony at that proceeding." Even then, "the court shall make every effort to permit the fullest attendance possible by the victim and shall consider reasonable alternatives to the exclusion of the victim from the criminal proceeding." Section 3771(b). *See also* Fed. R. Evid. 615 ("This rule does not authorize exclusion of . . . a person authorized by statute to be present.").

If the defendant is found guilty, section 3771(a)(4) appears to give a victim the right to be heard regarding the decision whether the defendant will be released pending sentencing.

2.06 Standard Voir Dire Questions—Criminal

Victims have the right to notice of and to be present during jury selection, unless the courtroom is closed for all or part of voir dire.

2.09 Verdict—Criminal

Victims have the right to be notified that the jury has reached a verdict and that the court will be reconvening to hear it.

2.10 Trial and Post-trial Motions

If a motion for judgment of acquittal, Fed. R. Crim. P. 29, a motion for new trial, Fed. R. Crim. P. 33, or a motion for arrest of judgment, Fed. R. Crim. P. 34, will involve a public hearing, victims should be notified.

2.11 Release or Detention Pending Sentence or Appeal

If there is an issue whether the defendant may be released pending sentencing or appeal, victims must be notified of the hearing and provided an opportunity to be heard. As noted earlier, section 3771(a)(1) provides that crime victims have the right "to be reasonably protected from the accused." Under Fed. R. Crim. P. 46, the defendant has the burden of establishing that he or she does not "pose a dan-ger to any other person or to the community."

3.01 Death Penalty Procedures

The definition of "crime victim" in section 3771(e) states that, if the crime victim is deceased, "the representatives of the victim's estate, family members, or any other persons appointed as suitable by the court, may assume the crime victim's rights under this chapter."

Note that a defendant convicted of a capital offense will usually be sentenced by a jury. It seems that a victim's "right to be reasonably heard at . . . sentencing" would have to be before this jury to be meaningful.

4.01 Sentencing Procedure

A victim has the right to notice of the sentencing hearing and to be reasonably heard sometime during the hearing. As noted earlier for the plea hearing, courts will have to determine when during the hearing to allow a victim to be heard. Fed. R. Crim. P. 32(i)(4)(B) gives victims of a crime of violence or sexual abuse the right to make a statement and present information at sentencing. Court practice under Rule 32(i)(4)(B) may provide a model to follow. Note that a proposed amendment to Rule 32(i)(4)(B), to be effective December 1, 2008, states that the sentencing court "must address any victim of the crime who is present at sentenc-ing and must permit the victim to be reasonably heard." The Committee Note to Rule 32(i)(4)(B) adds that "[a]bsent unusual circumstances, any victim who is present should be allowed a reasonable opportunity to speak directly to the judge."

4.02 Revocation of Probation or Supervised Release

As noted above for section 1.05, courts may have to determine whether the vic-tims of the original offense may also have rights when probation or supervised release is revoked. The Supreme Court has held that "postrevocation penalties re-late to the original offense," so that "postrevocation sanctions [are] part of the penalty for the initial offense." *Johnson v.*

U.S., 495 U.S. 694, 700–01 (2000). Revocation of supervised release was at issue in *Johnson*, but the same reasoning could be applied to probation. If revocation proceedings are seen as "involving the [original] crime . . . of the accused," section 3771(a)(2), then the victims or the original offense may be entitled to the CVRA rights, including the rights to notice of any public court proceedings, to be present at such proceedings, and to be "rea-sonably heard" at sentencing.

Also, if the violation of probation or release involves not just a violation of the conditions of release but a new crime, even if not separately charged, could the revocation proceeding be considered to "involve" the new crime of the accused so as to entitle any victims of that offense to the CVRA rights?

III Other Issues That May Arise Under the CVRA

A. Large Numbers of Victims

Although section 3771(d)(2) provides courts with the flexibility to "fashion a rea-sonable procedure" when trying to accommodate the rights of large numbers of victims, it does not offer any specific ways to do so. How, for example, would the "right to be reasonably heard" be satisfied? Could the court select a group of rep-resentative victims to be heard in court, perhaps allowing the rest to submit writ-ten statements? If the number of victims who want to be present at a proceeding exceeds the capacity of the courtroom, how shall the court determine who is al-lowed to attend? And, while the prosecution is responsible for notifying and con-sulting with the victims, the court may be called upon to determine whether those efforts were adequate under the CVRA.

B. Alternative Means of Being "Heard"

May a court accommodate a victim's right to be reasonably heard by means other than in person? For example, a child victim is allowed under 18 U.S.C. § 3509(b) to testify on closed-circuit television or videotape if the court finds that the child could not testify in person because of fear, or that there is a substantial likelihood that the child would suffer emotional trauma. The CVRA does not specifically allow or prohibit such an alternative means of being "heard." A similar accom-modation might be considered in cases in which victims live far from the court-house, as may happen in a large, multi-state fraud case.

C. Weight to Give Victim's Statement

When a victim has the right to be heard at a proceeding, what weight, if any, must the court give to the victim's statement or other submission? Must the court somehow account on the record for the impact, if any, such submissions have on its decisions involving release, plea, sentencing, or parole?

D. Waiver of Rights by Victim

If a victim waives any of the rights granted by the CVRA—intentionally or sim-ply by a failure to respond to notice—would it be prudent to make a record of the waiver? Can a victim rescind an initial waiver and seek to enforce his or her rights later in the proceedings?

E. Act Applies to All Federal Offenses

The CVRA is not limited to felony offenses. A victim is defined, in part, in sec-tion 3771(e) as a person harmed "as a result of the commission of a federal of-fense," so it seems that the CVRA could apply to a misdemeanor offense or in-fraction.

F. Possible Confrontation Clause Issues

Does the defendant have any right to cross-examine a victim who makes an oral statement? To dispute written statements? To challenge any other evidence prof-fered by a victim? To give a rebuttal? The substance of a victim's statements or other submissions may raise Confrontation Clause issues.

G. Absent Defendant

Note that the CVRA does not require that the defendant be present for a victim to have the right to notice or to be heard. The victim would, for example, still have a right to be notified of an arraignment if the defendant waived his or her appear-ance under Fed. R. Crim. P. 10(b). And if the defendant escaped after conviction and was to be sentenced in absentia, it appears that the victim would retain the right to be heard at sentencing and to receive notice of any public court proceed-ing related to the escape itself.

H. Victims and Relevant Conduct

What about victims of related but uncharged, dismissed, or acquitted criminal conduct? If a defendant is, for example, charged with three counts involving sepa-rate but related offenses, each with different victims, and as part of a plea agree-ment one or two counts are dismissed, are the victims of the dismissed counts also "dismissed" from proceedings thereafter?

Or, because under the U.S. Sentencing Guidelines, relevant or related conduct that is considered at sentencing may involve victims who are not victims of the count or counts of conviction, could there be circumstances where such victims can be considered "directly and proximately harmed as a result of the commission of" the offense of conviction so as to qualify as victims under section 3771(e)? Similarly, can there be a CVRA "victim" in an ostensibly victim-less crime of conviction, such as an illegal weapon possession offense that involved an un-charged assault that may be considered at sentencing? See summaries of *In re An-trobus* and *U.S. v. Sharp* in Part IV, *infra.*

I. Motion for Relief—Procedures and Remedies

When a victim makes a "motion for relief" under section 3771(d)(3), the district court is to "decide any motion asserting a victim's rights forthwith." The statute does not further specify a time limit or a procedure for deciding the motion. Should the court hold a hearing? Should it allow submission of briefs or otherwise give the prosecution and defendant an opportunity to respond? If the claimed vio-lation relates solely to an action of the government, is the defendant entitled to notice and an opportunity to be heard on the motion?

What remedies are available for a violation? If a victim claims, for example, that the government is not reasonably conferring under section 3771(a)(5), could the court order the government to hold more frequent meetings with the victim, or perhaps provide written answers to questions the victim may have? What if the violation relates to the right to notice of and to be present at a proceeding that has already occurred?

J. Motion to Reopen A Plea or Sentence—Procedures

Section 3771(d)(5) states that under limited circumstances a victim "may make a motion to re-open a plea or sentence" when the right to be heard was denied. If the plea or sentence is reopened, then what? Could the defendant withdraw his or her plea? Could the defendant or government seek to renegotiate a plea agree-ment? Would sentencing have to begin anew? Or could the court simply give the victim an opportunity to be heard and re-accept the plea and/or reinstate the sen-tence? If the victim is given the opportunity to be heard, should the defendant and government be allowed to respond? What happens if the court decides, after the victim's statement, to disallow the plea or change the sentence?

K. Restitution

How will section 3771(a)(6)'s "right to full and timely restitution as provided in law" interact with the current restitution statutes, such as sections 3663, 3663A, and 3664? Since under section 3771(d)(1) each crime victim "may assert the rights described in subsection (a)," could a victim file a motion claiming that res-titution is not "full" or "timely" under the applicable restitution statute? Could a victim claim that the court did not adequately follow section 3572(b), which di-rects it to impose a fine "only to the extent that such fine . . . will not impair the ability of the defendant to make restitution"? Does a victim's right to restitution remain in force until the amount of restitution ordered is fully paid? (Note that section 3771 only imposes a time limit on motions "to re-open a plea or sen-tence.")

If payment of restitution is a condition of probation or supervised release, could a victim's complaint that restitution is not being paid be used to begin revo-cation proceedings? And would the victim then have the right to be present and possibly be heard at any revocation hearings?

L. Challenging A Victim's Status

Because a victim's rights under the CVRA seem to begin long before an actual guilty plea or conviction after trial, the status of "victim" may be based on allega-tions rather than proof. Does the defendant have the right to challenge whether a person should be considered a victim under section 3771(e)? If so, when and how? Would the victim and the government then be required to supply some modicum of proof that the person in question actually is a victim of the defen-dant's offense?

M. Oath or Affirmation by Victim

Should a victim be treated like a witness and required to take an oath or make an affirmation before being allowed "to be reasonably heard"? Should some form of affidavit be required for written submissions?

N. Potential Claims Against Government

Note that, although 42 U.S.C. § 10606 was repealed, section 10607 remains in effect. It outlines the specific "services to victims" that government personnel must supply, some of which are related to the rights set out in section 3771. Al-though section 10607(d) specifically states that it "does not create a cause of ac-tion" for failure to provide these services, a failure to satisfy section 10607 could be relevant to some claims under the CVRA, such as the government did not ade-quately consult with the victim, section 3771(a)(5), or the victim was not "treated with fairness and with respect for the victim's dignity and privacy," section 3771(a)(8).

O. Organizational "Victims"

Do companies or other organizations have rights under the CVRA? The definition of "victim" in section 3771(e) refers only to "a person," and the alternates who may assume the rights of an incapacitated victim are also individuals. However, organizations are not specifically excluded. A related statute, 42 U.S.C. § 10607(e), includes "an institutional entity" in its definition of a victim.

P. Habeas Corpus Proceedings

As noted above in Part I, section 3771(b)(2) was added in 2006 to give some rights to state crime victims when the defendant brings a habeas proceeding in federal court. The federal courts are again charged with "ensur[ing] that a crime victim is afforded the rights described" therein. However, this section does not require anyone to provide notice to state victims, as the government must for federal crime victims under section 3771(c)(1). As part of its obligation to "ensure" that victims are afforded their rights, should a court take any steps to see that state crime victims are notified?

Also, regarding the right to be heard at a public proceeding "involving release, plea, sentencing," how should "involving" be interpreted in the habeas context? In a regular federal criminal proceeding, "involving the plea" would refer to the plea colloquy and the taking of the defendant's plea. In the habeas context, the plea colloquy and plea occurred previously in the state court. The same is true of the sentencing hearing and imposition of sentence. If plea or sentencing is "involved" in habeas, it may only be as legal arguments about the validity of past pleas or sentences. Should section 3771(b)(2)(A) be read as allowing a victim to be heard during such arguments?

IV. Case Summaries

Note: Because there are still relatively few opinions available on the CVRA, this section will list unpublished opinions and orders as well as published cases. These are provided for informational purposes only, and their listing here should not be considered any indication of precedential value. In each section, published cases will be listed first, starting with the most recent.

A. Courts of Appeals

1. In re Dean, __ F.3d __ (5th Cir. May 7, 2008) (per curiam)

Victims from the *BP Products* case, *infra*, petitioned the appellate court for a writ of mandamus after the district court denied their motion to reject the plea agree-ment between the government and BP Products and their claim that their rights under the CVRA were violated. [Note: See the summary of *BP Products, infra,* at B.11, for details of the underlying case.] Although the appellate court agreed that their rights had been violated, it denied the petition because it did not meet the strict standards for granting a writ of mandamus.

The court first held that it agreed with *In re Antrobus*, *infra*, that the strict standards for obtaining a writ of mandamus apply, rather than the "ordinary ap-peal standards" used in *Kenna I* and *In re Huff, infra*. "A writ of mandamus may issue only if (1) the petitioner has 'no other adequate means' to attain the desired relief; (2) the petitioner has demonstrated a right to the issuance of a writ that is 'clear and indisputable;' and (3) the issuing court, in the exercise of its discretion, is satisfied that the writ is 'appropriate under the circumstances.'"

The court then found that, "under the specific facts and circumstances of this case, it was contrary to the provisions of the CVRA for the court to permit and employ the *ex parte* proceedings that have taken place—proceedings that have no precedent, as far as we can determine. . . . The district court acknowledged that '[t]here are clearly rights under the CVRA that apply before any prosecution is underway.' . . . Logically, this includes the CVRA's establishment of victims' 'reasonable right to confer with the attorney for the Government.' 18 U.S.C. § 3771(a)(5). . . . The government and the district court relied on the provision of the CVRA that states that '[i]n a case where the court finds that the number of crime victims makes it impracticable to accord all of the crime victims the rights described in subsection (a), the court shall fashion a reasonable procedure to give effect to this chapter that does not unduly complicate or prolong the proceedings.' 18 U.S.C. § 3771(d)(2). Here, however, where there were fewer than two hundred victims, all of whom could be easily reached, it is not reasonable to say that noti-fication and inclusion were 'impracticable.'"

As for the district court's concern that early notification could impair the plea negotiation or prejudice the case, "the court missed the purpose of the CVRA's right to confer. In passing the Act, Congress made the policy decision—which we are bound to enforce—that the victims have a right to inform the plea negotiation process by conferring with prosecutors before a plea agreement is reached. That is not an infringement, as the district court believed, on the government's independ-ent prosecutorial discretion . . . ; instead, it is only a requirement that the govern-ment confer in some reasonable way with the victims before ultimately exercising its broad discretion."

However, the petition would be denied "because a writ is not 'appropriate un-der the circumstances.' . . . [A]s we have explained, the victims were notified— albeit much too late in the process—and were allowed substantial and meaningful participation at the February 4 hearing. . . . The district court, therefore, has the benefit of the views of the victims who chose to participate at the hearing or by their various filings. . . . The decision whether to grant mandamus is largely pru-dential. We conclude that the better course is to deny relief, confident that the dis-trict court will take heed that the victims have not been accorded their full rights under the CVRA and will carefully consider their objections and briefs as this matter proceeds."

See also *In re Antrobus* and *BP Products, infra. Cf. Kenna I* and *In re Huff, infra.*

2. U.S. v. Eberhard, __ F.3d __ (2d Cir. May 5, 2008) (Jacobs, C.J.)

Shortly before passage of the CVRA, the defendant pled guilty to conspiracy, in-vestment advisor fraud, and obstruction of justice. The parties stipulated to a guidelines range of 97–121 months. The presentence report added an enhance-ment for a leadership role and calculated the guidelines range at 151–188 months, but recommended a below-range sentence of 96 months. Before sentencing, the district court issued a written opinion adopting the PSR's calculations, but indi-cated it planned to impose a sentence of 151 months. At the sentencing hearing, which occurred several months after the effective date of the CVRA, the court "heard from several victims, who urged a draconian sentence." The court sen-tenced the defendant to 160 months. The defendant appealed his sentence, in part on the ground that the CVRA "is unconstitutional as applied to him . . . [because,] as a consequence of § 3771(a)'s requirement that his victims be allowed the 'right to be reasonably heard' at his sentencing (and of their vindictive statements), he received a sentence nine months longer than otherwise, and that § 3771(a) thus violated his rights under both the *Ex Post Facto* and Due Process Clauses."

The appellate court found the defendant's claims were without merit and af-firmed. The court stated that, apart from the fact that courts were permitted to al-low victims to speak long before passage of the CVRA, "even if we assumed (as we do not) both that (1) the longer sentence was attributable to the victim state-ments and (2) the court was barred from considering victim impact statements prior to enactment of § 3771(a), Eberhard's *Ex Post Facto* rights would still be unimpaired. The *Ex Post Facto* Clause does not prohibit all retroactive laws that disadvantage defendants, . . . [and a] law requiring that victims be reasonably heard (if they request) after the defendant has already been convicted does not implicate the *Ex Post Facto* clause."

On the due process claim, the defendant argued "that the district court's appli-cation of § 3771(a) allowed or compelled the government to circumvent the agreement through 'victim-surrogates,' and thereby deprived Eberhard of the benefit of his plea agreement." The appellate court rejected this argument also, finding that "nothing in the [plea agreement] precluded the government from pre-senting victim impact testimony. There was no evasion of the contractual limita-tions on the government's legal arguments: the victims' pleas for a harsh sentence were incidental to presentation of facts. They were not allowed to argue as amici curiae." The defendant also claimed that "he received insufficient notice both of the identity of the victims who would address the sentencing court and of the na-ture of their statements. But the court afforded Eberhard an opportunity to re-spond after hearing from the victims. Eberhard neither objected to the victim statements nor requested additional time to prepare a more thorough response."

3. In re Antrobus, 519 F.3d 1123, 1124–26 (10th Cir. 2008)

The defendant pled guilty to the illegal transfer of a handgun to a juvenile. Sev-eral months after the sale, and after the juvenile had turned eighteen, the juvenile killed several people at a shopping center and was himself killed. The parents of one of the victims of that crime moved to have their daughter recognized as a vic-tim of the instant crime so that they, assuming her rights under section 3771(e), would be allowed to be heard at this defendant's sentencing. The district court held that the illegal gun sale was not a direct and proximate cause of the later murder and the daughter was not a "victim" of the illegal gun sale under the terms of section 3771(e); therefore, the parents did not have a right to be heard at sen-tencing. *U.S. v. Hunter,* No. 2:07CR307DAK (D. Utah Jan. 3, 2008) (Kimball, J.) (memorandum decision and order).

The parents petitioned for a writ of mandamus, but the court of appeals upheld the district court's decision and denied the writ. After first finding that the stan-dard of review for a writ of mandamus requires the petitioners to "show that their right to the writ is 'clear and indisputable,'" the court concluded that, under the facts of the case, "we cannot say that the district court was clearly wrong in its conclusion." In a later order denying the petitioners' request for a rehearing, the court more fully explained its decision to treat the petition under the stricter stan-dards for review of writs of mandamus rather than the standards that apply to re-view of interlocutory appeals, noting its disagreement on this issue with *In re Huff* and *Kenna I, infra*.

See also *In re Dean, supra,* and *Sharp, infra.*

4. U.S. v. Ausburn, 502 F.3d 313, 324 & n.17 (3d Cir. 2007)

The defendant pled guilty to an offense involving sex with a minor. He received a sentence of 144 months, approximately double the high end of the applicable guidelines range. On appeal, the defendant claimed that he should have received prior notice that the court was considering imposing a sentence so far above the guidelines range, and also that the sentence was unreasonable. As part of his claim of inadequate notice, the defendant "contends that he was subject to unfair surprise because he 'had no idea that the district court intended to double his sen-tence based upon victim statements,' and that 'had [he] received prior notice, he could have taken action to mitigate the victim statements.'"

The appellate court remanded, holding that the defendant's sentence was un-reasonable because the district court failed to adequately respond to his arguments for a lower sentence. However, the court rejected the defendant's argument that the victim statements unfairly surprised him. Noting that the CVRA gives victims the right to participate in criminal cases and to allocute at sentencing, the court added that "we perceive no violation of due process in the 'emotional appeal' pre-sented by the victim impact statements. While it may be true that the statements presented a compelling account of the harms allegedly wrought by Ausburn's conduct, this is inherent in the victim's right to attend court and present his or her own account of the crime and its impact. ... Nothing in the victim impact state-ments in this case was so unfairly prejudicial or inflammatory as to present a due process issue."

5. U.S. v. Moussaoui, 483 F.3d 220, 234–35 (4th Cir. 2007)

The defendant was convicted of offenses related to the September 11 terrorist at-tacks. Separate from the criminal prosecution, victims and family members of vic-tims of the attacks brought civil suits against the defendant and others. The civil plaintiffs filed a motion with the court handling the criminal case for access to virtually all non-public discovery materials provided by the government to the defendant. The district court, basing its decision partly on the CVRA, ordered the government to provide much of that material. A later order granted the court han-dling the civil suit the authority to determine what documents could be disclosed. The government appealed the orders.

In reversing this decision on several grounds, the appellate court found that the CVRA offered "no support for the district court's orders." "The rights codi-fied by the CVRA . . . are limited to the criminal justice process; the Act is there-fore silent and unconcerned with victims' rights to file civil claims against their assailants."

See also *Kenna II, Brock, Citgo,* and *Sacane, infra.*

6. In re Kenna, 453 F.3d 1136, 1136–37 (9th Cir. 2006) (per curiam) (Kenna II)

A victim in a fraud case filed a petition for a writ of mandamus, seeking an order to require the sentencing court to release to the victim the entire presentence re-port. Agreeing with the district court, the appellate court found no support "in ei-ther the language of the statute or the legislative history" for the victim's argu-ment that the CVRA conferred a general right for crime victims to access presentence reports. The district court had also found that the victim "has not demonstrated that his reasons for requesting the PSR outweigh the confidentiality of the report under the traditional 'ends of justice' test."

See also *Moussaoui, supra,* and *Brock, Citgo,* and *Sacane, infra.*

7. In re Mikhel, 453 F.3d 1137, 1139–40 (9th Cir. 2006) (per curiam)

In a multiple-murder case, the government moved to allow family members of the murder victims—including those who planned to testify—to observe the trial in its entirety. The district court ruled that non-witness family members could ob-serve the entire trial, but that witnesses would be excluded from the courtroom until after they had testified. The government then filed a petition for a writ of mandamus under section 3771(d)(3) to order the district court to allow the witness family members to observe the entire trial.

The appellate court granted the writ and remanded for reconsideration, after first finding that the family members would be considered to have "assume[d] the [deceased] crime victim[s'] rights" pursuant to section 3771(e). Although Fed. R. Evid. 615 allows a party to request that the court "order witnesses excluded so they cannot hear the testimony of other witnesses," the rule contains an exception for "a person authorized by statute to be present." The court concluded that sec-tion 3771(a)(3) provides just such an exception, and reading the rule and statute together, it held that the "mere *possibility* that a victim-witness may alter his or her testimony as a result of hearing others testify is therefore insufficient to justify excluding him or her from trial. Rather, a district court must find by clear and convincing evidence that it is *highly likely,* not merely *possible,* that the victim-witness will alter his or her testimony." On remand, the district court must "con-sider whether clear and convincing evidence proves that the victim-witnesses' tes-timony will be 'materially altered' if they are allowed to attend the trial in its en-tirety."

See also *Johnson, infra.*

8. Kenna v. U.S. Dist. Court for the Central Dist. of Calif., 435 F.3d 1011, 1015–16 (9th Cir. 2006) (Kenna I)

The defendants, a father and son, defrauded dozens of victims in an investment scheme. Several victims spoke at the father's sentencing. When the son was sen-tenced three months later, the court denied the victims the opportunity to speak, stating that it had heard the victims at the previous sentencing and did not think they could say anything that would impact the court's sentence because the court already considered the crime to be very serious, and that if anything had changed since the first sentencing, the prosecutor would inform the court. One victim filed a petition for mandamus, seeking an order vacating the defendant's sentence and ordering the court to allow the victims to speak at the resentencing.

The appellate court granted the petition, finding that, despite the use of the term "mandamus," the CVRA contemplates "routine interlocutory review of dis-trict court decisions denying rights asserted under the statute . . . [and] we must issue the writ whenever we find that the district court's order reflects an abuse of discretion or legal error." After determining that the statute "is ambiguous as to what it means for crime victims to be heard," the court turned to the legislative history of the CVRA for guidance. Reviewing the floor statements of the bill's sponsors, as well as an earlier Senate report, the court concluded that there was "a clear congressional intent to give crime victims the right to speak at proceedings covered by the CVRA." That right was not satisfied by the fact that the victims were allowed to speak at the father's sentencing three months earlier. The right to be heard at any public proceeding involving sentencing "means that the district court must hear from the victims, if they choose to speak, at more than one crimi-nal sentencing." It was left to the district court to decide whether it should con-duct a new sentencing hearing.

See also *Degenhardt* and *Marcello, infra.*

9. In re W.R. Huff Asset Management Co., LLC, 409 F.3d 555, 558–64 (2d Cir. 2005)

In what appears to have been the first appellate decision involving an action brought under the CVRA, a group of victims petitioned for a writ of mandamus, seeking to vacate a settlement agreement in a forfeiture action. The underlying case involved a large and complex securities fraud, and the government entered into a proposed settlement agreement that involved setting up a $715 million vic-tim compensation fund. To receive a distribution from the fund, victims would have to forgo most separate civil actions. Two sets of victims objected to the pro-posed settlement, claiming mainly that the compensation fund would be inade-quate and their right to "full and timely restitution" under section 3771(a)(6) would be violated. Victims also argued that the government did not adequately consult with the victims before entering the settlement, section 3771(a)(5), and that the victims were not "treated with fairness," section 3771(a)(8). The district court accepted the settlement agreement and ruled against the victims, finding that, in light of the complexity of the case and the many thousands of potential victims, the settlement was the sort of reasonable compromise envisioned by sec-tion 3771(d)(2) to avoid "unduly complicat[ing] or prolong[ing] the proceedings."

The appellate court, after first holding that "a district court's determination under the CVRA should be reviewed for abuse of discretion," denied the petition for mandamus. The right to full and timely restitution is qualified by the phrase "as provided in law." The court found that the relevant law was the Mandatory Victim Restitution Act, 18 U.S.C. § 3663A, which specifically allows for less than full restitution in a case with so many victims as to "make restitution imprac-ticable" and complex issues that could "complicate or prolong the sentencing process." The court also noted that the settlement agreement involved some de-fendants who were not convicted, as well as other individuals who had not been charged. "[T]he CVRA does not grant any rights against individuals who have not been convicted of a crime. Concomitantly, neither the Government nor the sen-tencing court are restricted by the CVRA from effecting reasonable settlement or restitution measures against non-convicted defendants."

As to the other claims, the appellate court held that "no petitioner has alleged that it asked the Government to confer with it and was denied the opportunity to do so. Nothing in the CVRA requires the Government to seek approval from crime victims before negotiating or entering into a settlement agreement. The CVRA requires only that the court provide victims with an opportunity to be heard concerning a proposed settlement agreement, and the court provided the victims with a full opportunity to do so in this case." The court also held that "the district court in no way treated the victims unfairly or without 'respect for [their] dignity and privacy,' 18 U.S.C. § 3771(a)(8), but rather took into consideration the numerosity of victims, the uncertainty of recovery, and the prospect of unduly prolonging the sentencing proceedings when adopting the settlement, factors which Congress has required the court to consider. See 18 U.S.C. § 3771(d)(2)."

10. In re Brock, No. 08-1086 (4th Cir. Jan. 31, 2008) (per curiam) (unpublished)

Prior to sentencing, the victim filed a motion requesting disclosure of several parts of the defendants' sentencing reports, including the calculation of their guideline ranges. The district court denied the motion, finding that the victim, who had already been given some documents relating to the defendants' sentenc-ing, had sufficient information to make a victim impact statement. The victim did, in fact, file a victim impact statement and speak at sentencing. After the sentenc-ing, however, he filed a mandamus petition, claiming that the district court did not sufficiently afford him the rights under section 3771(a)(4) and (8) "to be reasona-bly heard at . . . sentencing" and "to be treated with fairness and with respect for [his] dignity."

The appellate court denied the petition. "Based on the record before us, we cannot conclude that the district court abused its discretion or abridged Brock's rights under the CVRA by denying him access to portions of the PSR. Although Brock claims that, without the PSR, he had insufficient knowledge of the issues relevant to sentencing to meaningfully exercise his right to be reasonably heard, the record reveals that he was provided ample information concerning the appli-cable Sentencing Guidelines and other issues related to the defendants' sentenc-ing. And, of course, he did not need access to the PSR to describe the crime's im-pact on him." As for the calculation of the guideline ranges, the district court had stated that it would have imposed the same sentence, and in any event, the appel-late court noted that "the CVRA does not provide victims with a right to appeal a defendant's sentence by challenging the district court's calculation of the Guide-lines range."

See also *Moussaoui* and *Kenna II, supra,* and *Citgo* and *Sacane, infra.*

11. In re Jane Doe, No. 07-1705 (4th Cir. Aug. 9, 2007) (per curiam) (unpublished)

In a federal criminal prosecution of a pharmaceutical company, Purdue Frederick Company, Inc., and its corporate officers for misbranding the prescription drug OxyContin, the parties sought acceptance from the district court of a proposed plea agreement. The agreement would require the company to pay a significant amount of fines and penalties, and provide restitution to various entities affected by the misbranding conduct. However, the parties asked the court to limit the res-titution obligations to those provided in the plea agreement. An individual who had used OxyContin objected to the proposed limitation on restitution, claiming that under the CVRA, she, too, should receive restitution for harms suffered from using OxyContin to treat chronic pain. The district court denied her motion and accepted the guilty plea and plea agreement. The individual then petitioned the appellate court for a writ of mandamus under the CVRA, seeking to reopen the company's sentencing and enforce her claimed right to restitution.

In denying the petition, the appellate court first noted that the petitioner had to demonstrate a legal entitlement to restitution. The CVRA itself does not provide that entitlement; rather, it states that a victim has a right to full and timely restitu-tion "as provided in law." 18 U.S.C. § 3771(a)(6). The relevant law in this in-stance, as the petitioner acknowledged, is the Victim Witness and Protection Act (VWPA), 18 U.S.C. § 3663. Under the VWPA, restitution is limited to "victims" as defined in the statute. Section 3663(A)(2) states that "the term 'victim' means a person directly and proximately harmed as a result of the commission of an of-fense for which restitution may be ordered." Although "not unsympathetic" to the petitioner's problems, the court found that "we cannot conclude that they were 'directly and proximately' related to the conduct underlying Purdue's offense of conviction so as to justify restitution under § 3663. Purdue pleaded guilty to in-troducing a misbranded drug into interstate commerce with the intent to defraud or mislead. . . . In order to qualify as a victim under § 3663, Petitioner would have to demonstrate that her injuries flowed 'directly and proximately' from the con-duct underlying one of the elements of this offense." Because no evidence to that effect had been introduced, "we cannot conclude that the district court abused its discretion in denying [the] motion under the CVRA to seek such restitution."

B. District Courts

1. U.S. v. Sharp, 463 F. Supp. 2d 556, 561–67 (E.D. Va. 2006)

The defendant pled guilty to a conspiracy to possess with intent to distribute mari-juana. The former girlfriend ("Nowicki") of one of the defendant's customers claimed that her former boyfriend abused her at least in part because of his use of the marijuana sold by the defendant, and that she is therefore a victim of the de-fendant's offense, with the right to give a victim impact statement at the defen-dant's sentencing hearing.

After an extensive discussion of the meaning of "directly and proximately harmed," the standard under section 3771(e), the court concluded that she was not a victim of the defendant's offense under the CVRA. "Here, Nowicki is not a 'victim' as that term is used in the CVRA because she is not a person 'directly and proximately harmed' by the federal crime committed by the Defendant. The Defendant has pled guilty to conspiring to distribute marijuana. But linking this fact to Nowicki's abuse is too attenuated, either temporally or factually, to confer 'victim' status on Nowicki as that term is used in the statute. Nowicki is no doubt an alleged victim of her boyfriend's violent ways. But Nowicki cannot demon-strate the nexus between the Defendant's act of selling drugs and her former boy-friend's subsequent act of abusing her."

See also *Antrobus, supra.*

2. U.S. v. Heaton, 458 F. Supp. 2d 1271, 1272–73 (D. Utah 2006)

After charging the defendant with attempting to entice a minor into unlawful sex-ual activity, the government sought leave to dismiss the charge without prejudice, citing as its reason only that the dismissal would be "in the interest of justice." Apart from noting that the court should make its own determination whether dis-missal is warranted, it found that "[t]here is a particular need to examine the rea-sons for dismissal in this case to ensure that the crime victim's rights are fully protected. The indictment alleges a sexual offense against a young victim. Under the Crime Victims' Rights Act (CVRA), this victim has the broad right 'to be treated with fairness and with respect for [her] dignity and privacy.'"

"This victim's right to fairness extends to the court's decision regarding whether to dismiss an indictment even though no public proceeding will be held on the issue. Although some of the other rights in the Crime Victims' Rights Act (such as the right to be heard and the right to not be excluded) are limited to 'pub-lic proceedings,' the right to fairness is not so restricted."

"When the government files a motion to dismiss criminal charges that involve a specific victim, the only way to protect the victim's right to be treated fairly and with respect for her dignity is to consider the victim's views on the dismissal. . . . [B]efore granting any motion by the government . . . to dismiss charges involving a specific victim, the court must have the victim's views on the motion." In such cases, therefore, the government should consult with the victim and inform the court "that the victim has been consulted on the dismissal and what the victim's views were on the matter."

3. U.S. v. L.M., 425 F. Supp. 2d 948, 951–57 (N.D. Iowa 2006)

A juvenile defendant ("L.M.") was charged with multiple counts of heroin distri-bution, including counts of distribution resulting in death (of a juvenile, "T.L.") and in serious bodily injury (to a different juvenile). The government filed a mo-tion to transfer the juvenile defendant to adult status, but before that hearing was held the government asked the court for permission to notify T.L.'s family mem-bers of the proceedings and to allow them to attend any hearings related to this case. Because the defendant was still being treated as a juvenile at this stage, the court engaged in an extensive examination of how to protect the rights of the ju-venile while also taking into account the rights of the victims to be present under section 3771(a)(3) and (b)(1). The court considered whether the proceedings should be closed and what steps could be taken to allow victim participation.

The court first held that a juvenile proceeding was not by nature a closed pro-ceeding, but that the court has discretion to balance the interests of the public, the victims, and the defendant on a case-by-case basis. After reviewing the many competing factors in this case, the court granted the government's motion to no-tify T.L.'s family of the proceedings against L.M. and unseal the case, but only after certain redactions in the record to protect L.M.'s interests. The family would be allowed to attend any public proceedings, but the transfer hearing would be closed to the public. The court reserved ruling on whether other hearings would be open to the public. The court ordered the government to "inform all of the crime victims of their CVRA rights," including "their rights to appeal this order."

4. U.S. v. Degenhardt, 405 F. Supp. 2d 1341, 1343–45 (D. Utah 2005)

Prior to the sentencing hearing of a defendant in a multimillion dollar fraud case, the government informed the court that several victims planned to attend and wished to make a statement to the court. The district court had to determine whether the right of any federal crime victim to "be reasonably heard" at sentenc-ing conflicted with the narrower right to speak granted in Fed. R. Crim. P. 32(i)(4)(B), which is granted only to victims of certain violent or sexual crimes.

The court held that "a broad congressional mandate in a statute must take precedence over a narrower court rule, . . . [and] the limits in Rule 32 of the Fed-eral Rules of Criminal Procedure must give way to the CVRA's command that all victims have the right to allocute." The court also concluded that "the CVRA gives victims the right to speak directly to the judge at sentencing." The phrase "to be reasonably heard" is ambiguous, but the legislative history "makes it clear that the CVRA created a right to be heard in person." Finally, the court concluded that a victim's right to speak is mandatory, and is not subject to the discretion of the court unless such a large number of victims are involved that the court's abil-ity to function effectively would be threatened.

See also *Kenna I, supra,* and *Marcello, infra.*

5. U.S. v. Crompton Corp., 399 F. Supp. 2d 1047, 1051 (N.D. Cal. 2005)

In an antitrust case, the defendant company pled guilty to one count and was sen-tenced according to the terms of a plea agreement. In order to protect ongoing in-vestigations in which the defendant was assisting the government, the sentencing hearing was closed, the transcript of the sentencing was sealed, and the plea agreement was filed under seal. Later, the government moved to unseal the plea agreement and the transcript. The defendant did not oppose the motion, but re-quested that the name of one of its executives—who had not been indicted—be redacted from any documents before they were unsealed.

The district court granted the motion to unseal the documents, but denied the motion to redact the name of the executive. Apart from policy considerations and the fact that the plea agreement probably should not have been sealed in the first place, the court found that redacting the executive's name "would violate the Crime Victims' Rights Act." The defendant wanted to shield the executive from civil lawsuits filed against the company by victims of the offense. "[T]he plain-tiffs in the additional civil lawsuits filed against Defendant are those who were directly and proximately harmed as a result of the commission of the antitrust vio-lation. Therefore, the Court should be particularly sensitive to ensuring they are given full access to the proceedings and the Plea Agreement" in accordance with section 3771(a)(2)–(3), (b).

6. U.S. v. Ingrassia, 392 F. Supp. 2d 493, 495–98 (E.D.N.Y. 2005)

This case provides some examples of notice issues under the CVRA when multi-ple victims are involved. After the government had identified more than 200 vic-tims of the large securities fraud scheme at issue, it initially sought to provide no-tice solely through publication. The court rejected that request, and required the government to submit a proposed notice for the court's review and to then provide the approved notice to each identified victim by mail with return receipt re-quested. The court later removed the requirement for a return receipt and ap-proved a request by the government to supplement the mailing by including notice of the case in a national publication.

The notice mailed to the victims informed them about the case and their rights under the CVRA. It also stated that there was a pending trial date and that they could obtain current information about the case through the government's Victim Notification System (VNS); they were also given an identification number and a phone number to gain access to the VNS. The notice added that, because of the large number of victims, further information would most likely be provided only through the Internet or the VNS call center. A week later, the government sent a second mailing that informed victims that three of the defendants were going to plead guilty and provided the scheduled dates and times for the pleas, but it did not place this information on its website. At the same time, the government placed an advertisement in *USA Today* to notify unidentified potential victims about the case. The ad listed a government website that contained information concerning victims' rights, how to register as a victim, and how to obtain access to the VNS. The website also contained a link to provide updated information about the case. However, the information provided at that link was not current.

At issue in the instant decision was a report to the court by a magistrate judge relating to plea proceedings of the remaining defendants and whether the govern-ment's notification of victims met the requirements of the CVRA. The report con-cluded that notification through the VNS did not satisfy the CVRA, and "recom-mended that [the court] accept each guilty plea only after the government has provided notice by first-class mail or other reasonably equivalent method to all identified victims of the following: each defendant's plea, release status, sentenc-ing date, and notice of the victims' right to be heard with regard to the plea and sentence." The government agreed to do this, and "as an additional curative measure it . . . agreed not to object on the ground of timeliness to a victim's asser-tion of any rights the victim could have asserted under the CVRA at the plea pro-ceeding." The court accepted the magistrate judge's report, but upheld the gov-ernment's objection to the magistrate judge's order that the government provide a copy of its objections to the report to each victim by first-class mail (or reasonable equivalent) within ten days. The court concluded that such notification was "un-necessary and not required under the CVRA or the Federal Magistrates Act. The Report, the government's objections, and this Memorandum of Decision and Or-der are all available to the public on the Public Access to Court Electronic Re-cords (PACER) service."

See also *Turner, Saltsman,* and *Stokes, infra.*

7. U.S. v. Marcello, 370 F. Supp. 2d 745, 746–50 (N.D. Ill. 2005)

At a pretrial detention hearing for two defendants accused of murder, the govern-ment moved to allow the son of the murder victim to give an oral statement in court, under section 3771(a)(4), opposing release of the defendants. The district court allowed only a written statement, concluding that "heard" is a term of art that includes written statements and that under the facts of this case—the murder occurred over twenty years ago, the son had no personal knowledge of the crime, and the judge had already determined that the defendants would not be released pending trial—a written statement would allow the victim to be "reasonably heard." The court acknowledged that "reasonable minds may differ" on this issue.

See also *Kenna I* and *Degenhardt, supra.*

8. U.S. v. Turner, 367 F. Supp. 2d 319, 321–28 (E.D.N.Y. 2005)

After discovering at the defendant's bail hearing that the victims in the case had not received adequate notice of either the initial hearing or the bail hearing, the court concluded the bail hearing, ordered that the defendant be detained, and or-dered the government to provide all alleged victims of the offense with a written summary of the proceedings to that point and notification of their rights under the CVRA with respect to future proceedings. After complying with the court's order, the government reported that none of the victims wished to attend or be heard at a later hearing regarding the defendant's application for release. The court then "di-rect[ed] the government to provide the court with sufficient information about the victims in this case to fulfill its independent obligation to ensure that those vic-tims are afforded their rights," including name and contact information, while al-lowing for the exclusion of such information under certain circumstances. The parties later filed a joint request to exclude a period of delay for purposes of com-puting Speedy Trial Act time limits. After noting that a public hearing on this matter would require further notice to the victims, but that a written submission would not, the court allowed the parties to submit a joint written waiver form and then approved the waiver in a written order.

Note: This opinion contains an extended discussion of many of the CVRA's provisions, the legislative history, potential problems that courts may face, and actions courts may take in attempting to balance the various interests involved.

See also *Ingrassia, supra,* and *Saltsman* and *Stokes, infra.*

9. U.S. v. Johnson, 362 F. Supp. 2d 1043, 1055–56 (N.D. Iowa 2005)

In a murder case involving five victims, the district court approved the govern-ment's request to allow seventeen "victim witnesses," who were family members of the deceased, to be present during the guilt phase of the trial. The court found that the defendant had made no attempt to show under section 3771(a)(3) that any of the witnesses' testimony would be "materially altered" by hearing the other testimony, and there was no other evidence to that effect, so the victim witnesses could not be excluded from the trial.

10. U.S. v. Visinaiz, 344 F. Supp. 2d 1310, 1314 (D. Utah 2004)

In a case that focused on the issue of lost income awards in homicide cases under the Mandatory Victims Restitution Act (MVRA) and the possible effect of *Blakely v. Washington,* 124 S. Ct. 2531 (2004), on the MVRA, the court also noted that the passage of the CVRA reinforced its decision to award lost income. The court cited legislative history that endorsed an "expansive definition of resti-tution" and the intention that the "right to full and timely restitution as provided in law" under the CVRA "means that existing restitution laws will be more effec-tive."

11. U.S. v. BP Products of North America, Inc., No. H-07-434 (S.D. Tex. Feb. 21, 2008)

A large explosion at a BP Products refinery in Texas in 2005 resulted in a large number of victims, extensive media coverage, and civil and criminal litigation. Over two years later, before criminal charges were actually filed, the government sought and obtained ex parte a sealed order from the district court allowing it to reach a plea agreement with BP Products before notifying the victims of the agreement. The government was concerned that it would be impracticable to con-fer with the large number of victims during negotiations and that premature pub-licity could impair the negotiations and possibly prejudice the case if no agree-ment were reached. After an agreement was reached, the government was obligated to provide prompt notice to the victims, allow an extended period of time to ensure that notice was received, and delay the plea hearing to allow vic-tims to exercise their rights to attend the hearing and be heard. Within days, the government filed a criminal information, which was sealed, and then the parties signed a binding plea agreement. After the agreement was signed, the information was unsealed and notification of the victims began.

Prior to the plea hearing on February 4, 2008, "[l]awyers for the victims filed motions and extensive briefs with supporting materials in opposition to the pro-posed plea agreement. One hundred and thirty-four individuals filed victim-impact statements." At the hearing, BP

Products entered a guilty plea and "the court heard from all those present who wanted to speak, whether represented by counsel or not and whether they had previously indicated an intent to appear or not. Ten individuals spoke in open court. The lawyers representing the victims presented arguments on the asserted grounds for asking the court to reject the proposed plea agreement." The day after the hearing, the victims filed a motion urging rejection of the plea agreement on the grounds that the government vio-lated its obligations under the CVRA, specifically "that the October 18, 2007 *ex parte* motion and order granting it, and the government's failure to answer the two letters [questioning the restitution calculation] later sent by one of the lawyers representing the victims, violated the CVRA 'reasonable right to confer' with the prosecutors and to be treated with fairness and breached the government's obliga-tion to use its best efforts to notify the victims of these rights."

In a lengthy opinion that surveyed virtually all CVRA cases to date, the dis-trict court held that the government adequately met its obligations to the victims and denied the motion to reject the plea agreement. First, "[t]he notices of the right to appear and be heard at court proceedings met the section 3771(a)(2) re-quirements." The government sent out three mailings to inform victims of court hearings, set up a website and telephone number, and made a victim-witness co-ordinator available. As noted above, many victims participated in the plea hearing personally, through their attorneys, or in writing.

Second, the court found that the "right to confer" was subject to differing in-terpretations based on case law, legislative history, and Department of Justice guidelines. However, "[e]ven under an expansive approach, the reasonable right to confer on a proposed plea agreement and the government's obligation to pro-vide notice of that right is subject to the limit that the CVRA not impair prosecu-torial discretion. The right to confer is not a right to approve or disapprove a pro-posed plea in advance of the government's decision. . . . The right to confer is a right to obtain and provide information and to express opinions. The right to con-fer about a proposed plea and the obligation to provide notice of this right are also subject to the multiple-victim provisions." In light of the circumstances of the case, including the delay of the plea hearing to allow victim participation, the court found that the government adequately conferred with the victims.

The court also held that "[t]he government did not violate the CVRA by seek-ing judicial permission for the approach it wanted to take to giving notice to the victims, and which included delaying notice until after the charging instrument was filed and after the plea negotiations had concluded. The CVRA contemplates judicial supervision over a[n alternative] procedure used under section 3771(d)(2). Filing a motion *ex parte* because of a need for confidentiality is not in itself im-proper. . . . The court's October 18, 2007 order made specific findings that justi-fied the use of the procedure under the CVRA. The order made it clear that after the proposed plea agreement and information were made public, the victims would be given notice of their CVRA rights and the hearing on the proposed plea agreement and sentence would be deferred so that the victims could fully exercise their rights to attend and be heard. That procedure was followed and the well-represented victims have taken full advantage of the rights afforded."

But see In re Dean, supra (denying a petition for writ of mandamus by the victims in this case but disagreeing with the district court on some issues).

12. U.S. v. Patkar, No. 06-00250 JMS (D. Haw. Jan. 28, 2008) (Seabright, J.) (unpublished order)

The defendant was accused of "transmitting in foreign commerce threats to injure the reputation of another." During the course of discovery, some potentially em-barrassing e-mails were placed under a protective order so as to avoid harm to the victim's reputation. The Associated Press (AP) sought an order to dissolve the protective order and release the e-mails, claiming that they should be part of the public record of the case or that it should be allowed to seek access to the e-mails from the defendant.

The court denied the motion to dissolve the protective order, relying on a vic-tim's "right to be treated with fairness and with respect for the victim's dignity and privacy" under section 3771(a)(8). The court recognized that this section's "broad language will undoubtedly lead to litigation over the extent to which courts must police the way victims are treated inside and outside the courtroom. Nevertheless, the Senate sponsors of the law were clear in their articulation of the overall import of the provision: to promote a liberal reading of the statute in favor of interpretations that promote victims' interest in fairness, respect, and dig-nity. . . . In order to protect [the victim]'s statutory right to be treated with fairness and with respect to his privacy, good cause exists to limit disclosure of these ma-terials." The court added that even though the defendant has pled guilty and been sentenced, the victim "retains his right to be treated with fairness and with respect to his privacy." In response to the AP's argument that the public interest favored disclosure, the court stated that the victim had not been accused of any wrongdo-ing and, under the circumstances of the case, "the crime victim's right to be treated with fairness and respect for his privacy clearly outweighs any public in-terest in disclosure."

See also *Kaufman, infra.*

13. U.S. v. Saltsman, No. 07-CR-641 (NGG) (E.D.N.Y. Nov. 27, 2007) (Garaufis, J.) (unpublished memorandum and order)

Section 3771(d)(2) of the CVRA provides that in cases involving a large number of victims, "the court shall fashion a reasonable procedure to give effect to this chapter that does not unduly complicate or prolong the proceedings." In a large securities fraud case, the government estimated that there were potentially tens of thousands of victims, "only some of whom it has yet been able to identify, locate, and notify. It is thus impracticable in this case for the Government to attempt to identify and locate all of the potential alleged crime victims and provide them with reasonable, accurate and timely notice by mail. . . . The Government has proposed that published notice shall direct potential alleged victims to the website for the United States Attorney's Office in the Eastern District of New York or a website maintained by the Department of Justice, where hyperlinks will provide updates about the status of the case."

Relying on section 3771(d)(2), the court concluded that "the Government's proposal is a reasonable one. . . . Given the large number of potential alleged crime victims, notification by publication is a reasonable procedure that will both give effect to the CVRA and not unduly complicate or prolong the proceedings." The court also noted "victims' rights under the

CVRA begin well before a convic-tion; thus, the status of 'victim' may be based on allegations rather than proof."

See also *Ingrassia* and *Turner, supra,* and *Stokes, infra.*

14. U.S. v. Citgo Petroleum Corp., CR. No. C-06-563 (S.D. Tex. Aug. 8, 2007) (Rainey, J.) (unpublished order)

After the disposition of the case, the government moved to unseal its submission to the United States Probation Office in aid of sentencing. The court noted two reasons the government gave for disclosure: "(1) to aid in the discharge of its du-ties under the Crime Victims' Rights Act, 18 U.S.C. § 3771; and (2) to counter certain CITGO publications. While the Government's submission is not a presen-tence report, it contains information of the same type and character that is nor-mally contained in a presentence report. For this reason, the same considerations that apply to the disclosure of a presentence report also apply to the Government's submission."

The court noted that there is a general presumption against granting third par-ties access to presentence reports absent a "compelling, particularized need for disclosure." In this case, the Court found that such a need "has not been demon-strated. . . . [T]he Court acknowledges that the CVRA confers a duty upon the Government to make 'best efforts' to notify crime victims. 18 U.S.C. § 3371(c)(1). However, the Act does not require the disclosure of presentence in-vestigation reports or other documents of a similar nature."

See also *Kenna II* and *In re Brock, supra,* and *Sacane, infra.*

15. U.S. v. Stokes, No. 3:06-00204 (M.D. Tenn. June 22, 2007) (Echols, J.) (unpublished order)

In an embezzlement case, the government sought authorization to provide notice to a large number of victims by various means. The estimated number of victims was 35,000 individuals employed by approximately 1,000 companies, and "[g]iven the time-line of this case, it will not be practical for the government to identify and locate all the victims and provide them with reasonable, accurate, and timely notice by mail in advance of defendant's trial or further court appear-ances." The government proposed to provide notice by a combination of a web-site, a toll-free telephone number, direct notice by letter for some victims, notice to the employers for other victims, and a blanket notice by publication for all vic-tims.

The court agreed with the government's plan, finding "

(1) that the 'multiple victim' provisions of 18 U.S.C. § 3771(d)(2) apply to the above-captioned case;

(2) that it is impractical for the Government to identify all of the direct and proximate victims of the charged offenses on an individual basis at this time to provide the individuals with reasonable, accurate, and timely notice in advance of defendant's trial or further court appearances; and (3) [that] notice in the manner proposed by the government is consistent with precedent and practice in other ju-risdictions and is a 'reasonable procedure' to give effect to the provisions of 18

U.S.C. § 3771." See also *Ingrassia, Turner,* and *Saltsman, supra.*

16. U.S. v. Sacane, Crim. No. 3:05cr325(AHN) (D. Conn. Mar. 28, 2007) (Nevas, J.) (unpublished order)

The victims, a group of investment funds, moved for an order requiring more de-tailed financial disclosures from the defendant in advance of a restitution hearing. They claimed they needed the information to enforce their right to "full and timely restitution" under the CVRA. The court denied the motion, noting that other courts have found that victims have no right to information contained in a presentence report. "If the CVRA does not provide crime victims with a right to disclosure of the presentence report, then a fortiori it would not provide crime vic-tims with a right to obtain such disclosures directly from a defendant. . . . If the [victims] believe that additional financial disclosures are necessary, then pursuant to the CVRA they may enlist the assistance of the government; but they are not permitted to bypass the government and discover information directly from Sacane."

See also *Moussaoui, Kenna II, In re Brock,* and *Citgo, supra.*

17. U.S. v. Kaufman, No. CRIM.A. 04-40141-01 (D. Kan. Oct. 17, 2005) (Belot, J.) (unpublished memorandum and order)

In a case involving, among other things, Medicare fraud, civil rights violations, and abuse of mentally ill patients, a local television station filed a motion to allow a sketch artist to be present in the courtroom during trial. Apart from the First Amendment issues presented, the court had to account for the rights of each vic-tim who would be testifying at the trial, specifically the right under section 3771(a)(8) of the CVRA to "be treated with fairness and with respect for the vic-tim's dignity and privacy." Some of the evidence in the case involved sexually graphic videos of the abuse of the victims, and the court had previously ruled, in light of section 3771(a)(8), that "these videos be displayed on a screen that is visible to the jury, the court, and the parties, but not to people seated in the gal-lery."

The court agreed to allow a sketch artist, but held that none of the victims may be sketched. Section 3771(a)(8) "requires that sketch artists' activities in the courtroom be restricted under the circumstances of this case. First, there is a com-pelling government interest in protecting the dignity, as well as the physical and psychological well-being, of mentally-ill alleged crime victims . . . . Most, if not all, of the witnesses entitled to protection under 18 U.S.C. § 3771 suffer from forms of schizophrenia. The court has already viewed the testimony of two men-tally ill witnesses and observed the distress that these individuals exhibited trying to concentrate on the questions and formulate answers. If that distress was com-pounded with concerns that the witness' picture was going to be shown on televi-sion as one of those 'victims' who appeared in the graphic videos, the victim un-doubtedly would not only face considerable additional distress and loss of dignity, but . . . might not even be able to testify, thereby damaging the truth-seeking func-tion of a criminal trial." The court concluded, "18 U.S.C. § 3771 proscribes all forms of identification of the victims in this case, including, but not limited to, sketching for purposes of television," the station has to find out from the parties' counsel when a victim will appear as a witness, and "no sketching materials of any kind will be visible in the courtroom" when a victim appears.

See also *Patkar, supra.*

18. U.S. v. Tobin, No. 04-CR-216-01-SM (D.N.H. July 22, 2005) (unpublished order)

The defendant was accused of conspiring to interfere with the right to vote by jamming phone lines set up to facilitate "get out the vote" efforts by the New Hampshire Democratic Party (NHDP) and a firefighters' association. When the defendant and the prosecutor jointly moved to continue the trial for ninety days, the NHDP claimed it was a "victim" under section 3771(e) and filed an objection to the motion, arguing that the continuance would violate the "right to proceed-ings free from unreasonable delay" under section 3771(a)(7). Assuming, without deciding, that the NHDP can be considered a victim, the court ruled that the con-tinuance was reasonable—it did not violate the Speedy Trial Act and the extra time was needed to allow a "full and adequate opportunity to prepare for trial." However, in light of the rights of the ostensible victims, "and taking into account the court's statutory obligation to 'ensure that [all] crime victim[s][are] afforded the rights described,'" the court stated that "the parties are hereby put on notice that no further continuance will be granted in the absence of extraordinary cir-cumstances."

Cf. Turner, 367 F. Supp. 2d at 321 (court notes that it allowed the parties to exclude a period of delay in computing the time within which an indictment must have been filed by simply filing with the court a written waiver form signed by counsel for both parties, an action that did not require notice to the victims).

19. U.S. v. Guevara-Toloso, No. M 04-1455 (E.D.N.Y. May 23, 2005) (unpublished order)

In a case involving the initial appearance of a defendant arrested for illegally re-entering the United States after being convicted of a felony and subsequently de-ported, the court asked whether any victim of the predicate crimes had been given notice pursuant to the CVRA. The prosecutor stated that he did not think notice was required, and the court agreed, concluding that, because the previous convic-tions were for *state* offenses, any victims of those crimes did not meet the defini-tion in section 3771(e), which does not include victims of state offenses. The opinion also includes some discussion of the legislative history of the CVRA.

V. TEXT OF 18 U.S.C. § 3771

§ 3771. Crime Victims' Rights

(a) Rights of crime victims.—A crime victim has the following rights:

(1) The right to be reasonably protected from the accused.
(2) The right to reasonable, accurate, and timely notice of any public court proceed-ing, or any parole proceeding, involving the crime or of any release or escape of the ac-cused.

(3) The right not to be excluded from any such public court proceeding, unless the court, after receiving clear and convincing evidence, determines that testimony by the victim would be materially altered if the victim heard other testimony at that proceeding
(4) The right to be reasonably heard at any public proceeding in the district court involving release, plea, sentencing, or any parole proceeding.
(5) The reasonable right to confer with the attorney for the Government in the case.
(6) The right to full and timely restitution as provided in law.
(7) The right to proceedings free from unreasonable delay.
(8) The right to be treated with fairness and with respect for the victim's dignity and privacy.

(b) Rights afforded.—

(1) **In general.**—In any court proceeding involving an offense against a crime victim, the court shall ensure that the crime victim is afforded the rights described in subsec-tion (a). Before making a determination described in subsection (a)(3), the court shall make every effort to permit the fullest attendance possible by the victim and shall con-sider reasonable alternatives to the exclusion of the victim from the criminal proceeding. The reasons for any decision denying relief under this chapter shall be clearly stated on the record.

(2) **Habeas corpus proceedings.—**
(A) **In general.**—In a Federal habeas corpus proceeding arising out of a State conviction, the court shall ensure that a crime victim is afforded the rights described in paragraphs (3), (4), (7), and (8) of subsection (a).

(B) **Enforcement.—**
(i) **In general.**—These rights may be enforced by the crime victim or the crime victim's lawful representative in the manner described in paragraphs (1) and (3) of subsection (d).
(ii) **Multiple victims.**—In a case involving multiple victims, subsection (d)(2) shall also apply.

(C) **Limitation.**—This paragraph relates to the duties of a court in relation to the rights of a crime victim in Federal habeas corpus proceedings arising out of a State conviction, and does not give rise to any obligation or requirement applicable to per-sonnel of any agency of the Executive Branch of the Federal Government.
(D) **Definition.**—For purposes of this paragraph, the term "crime victim" means the person against whom the State offense is committed or, if that person is killed or incapacitated, that person's family member or other lawful representative.

(c) Best efforts to accord rights.—

(1) **Government.**—Officers and employees of the Department of Justice and other departments and agencies of the United States engaged in the detection, investigation, or prosecution of crime shall make their best efforts to see that crime victims are notified of, and accorded, the rights described in subsection (a).
(2) **Advice of attorney.**—The prosecutor shall advise the crime victim that the crime victim can seek the advice of an attorney with respect to the rights described in subsec-tion (a).
(3) **Notice.**—Notice of release otherwise required pursuant to this chapter shall not be given if such notice may endanger the safety of any person.

(d) Enforcement and limitations.—

(1) **Rights.**—The crime victim or the crime victim's lawful representative, and the attorney for the Government may assert the rights described in subsection (a). A person accused of the crime may not obtain any form of relief under this chapter.
(2) **Multiple crime victims.**—In a case where the court finds that the number of crime victims makes it impracticable to accord all of the crime victims the rights de-scribed in subsection (a), the court shall fashion a reasonable procedure to give effect to this chapter that does not unduly complicate or prolong the proceedings.
(3) **Motion for relief and writ of mandamus.**—The rights described in subsection (a) shall be asserted in the district court in which a defendant is being prosecuted for the crime or, if no prosecution is underway, in the district court in the district in which the crime occurred. The district court shall take up and decide any motion asserting a vic-tim's right forthwith. If the district court denies the relief sought, the movant may petition the court of appeals for a writ of mandamus. The court of appeals may issue the writ on the order of a single judge pursuant to circuit rule or the Federal Rules of Appellate Pro-cedure. The court of appeals shall take up and decide such application forthwith within 72 hours after the petition has been filed. In no event shall proceedings be stayed or sub-ject to a continuance of more than five days for purposes of enforcing this chapter. If the court of appeals denies the relief sought, the reasons for the denial shall be clearly stated on the record in a written opinion.
(4) **Error.**—In any appeal in a criminal case, the Government may assert as error the district court's denial of any crime victim's right in the proceeding to which the appeal relates.
(5) **Limitation on relief.**—In no case shall a failure to afford a right under this chap-ter provide grounds for a new trial. A victim may make a motion to re-open a plea or sen-tence only if—
    (A) the victim has asserted the right to be heard before or during the proceeding at issue and such right was denied;
    (B) the victim petitions the court of appeals for a writ of mandamus within 10 days; and

(C) in the case of a plea, the accused has not pled to the highest offense charged.

This paragraph does not affect the victim's right to restitution as provided in title 18, United States Code.

(6) **No cause of action.**—Nothing in this chapter shall be construed to authorize a cause of action for damages or to create, to enlarge, or to imply any duty or obligation to any victim or other person for the breach of which the United States or any of its officers or employees could be held liable in damages. Nothing in this chapter shall be construed to impair the prosecutorial discretion of the Attorney General or any officer under his direction.

(e) Definitions.—

For the purposes of this chapter, the term "crime victim" means a person directly and proximately harmed as a result of the commission of a Federal offense or an offense in the District of Columbia. In the case of a crime victim who is under 18 years of age, incompetent, incapacitated, or deceased, the legal guardians of the crime victim or the representatives of the crime victim's estate, family members, or any other persons appointed as suitable by the court, may assume the crime victim's rights under this chapter, but in no event shall the defendant be named as such guardian or representative.

(f) Procedures to promote compliance.—

(1) **Regulations.**—Not later than 1 year after the date of enactment of this chapter, the Attorney General of the United States shall promulgate regulations to enforce the rights of crime victims and to ensure compliance by responsible officials with the obliga-tions described in law respecting crime victims.

(2) **Contents.**—The regulations promulgated under paragraph (1) shall—

(A) designate an administrative authority within the Department of Justice to re-ceive and investigate complaints relating to the provision or violation of the rights of a crime victim;

(B) require a course of training for employees and offices of the Department of Justice that fail to comply with provisions of Federal law pertaining to the treatment of crime victims, and otherwise assist such employees and offices in responding more effectively to the needs of crime victims;

(C) contain disciplinary sanctions, including suspension or termination from employment, for employees of the Department of Justice who willfully or wantonly fail to comply with provisions of Federal law pertaining to the treatment of crime vic-tims; and

(D) provide that the Attorney General, or the designee of the Attorney General, shall be the final arbiter of the complaint, and that there shall be no judicial review of the final decision of the Attorney General by a complainant.

THE FEDERAL JUDICIAL CENTER

Board

The Chief Justice of the United States, *Chair*
Judge Susan H. Black, U.S. Court of Appeals for the Eleventh Circuit
Judge David O. Carter, U.S. District Court for the Central District of California
Magistrate Judge Karen Klein, U.S. District Court for the District of North Dakota
Judge Loretta A. Preska, U.S. District Court for the Southern District of New York
Judge Philip M. Pro, U.S. District Court for the District of Nevada
Judge Stephen Raslavich, U.S. Bankruptcy Court for the Eastern District of Pennsylvania
Judge William B. Traxler, Jr., U.S. Court of Appeals for the Fourth Circuit
James C. Duff, Director of the Administrative Office of the U.S. Courts

Director

Judge Barbara J. Rothstein

Deputy Director

John S. Cooke

About the Federal Judicial Center

The Federal Judicial Center is the research and education agency of the federal judicial system. It was established by Congress in 1967 (28 U.S.C. §§ 620–629), on the recommendation of the Judi-cial Conference of the United States.

By statute, the Chief Justice of the United States chairs the Center's Board, which also includes the director of the Administrative Office of the U.S. Courts and seven judges elected by the Judi-cial Conference.

The organization of the Center reflects its primary statutory mandates. The Education Division plans and produces education and training programs for judges and court staff, including satellite broadcasts, video programs, publications, curriculum packages for in-court training, and Web-based programs and resources. The Research Division examines and evaluates current and alterna-tive federal court practices and policies. This research assists Judicial Conference committees, who request most Center research, in developing policy recommendations. The Center's research also contributes substantially to its educational programs. The two divisions work closely with two units of the Director's Office—the Systems Innovations & Development Office and Communica-tions Policy & Design Office—in using print, broadcast, and on-line media to deliver education and training and to disseminate the results of Center research. The Federal Judicial History Office helps courts and others study and preserve federal judicial history. The International Judicial Rela-tions

Office provides information to judicial and legal officials from foreign countries and assesses how to inform federal judicial personnel of developments in international law and other court sys-tems that may affect their work.

Federal Judicial Center Thurgood Marshall Federal Judiciary Building
One Columbus Circle N.E., Washington, DC 20002-8003

In: Revisiting and Enforcing the Crime Victims…
Editor: Jorge S. Ehrlich

ISBN: 978-1-60741-231-1

Chapter 2

CRIME VICTIMS' RIGHTS ACT: INCREASING AWARENESS, MODIFYING THE COMPLAINT PROCESS, AND ENHANCING COMPLIANCE MONITORING WILL IMPROVE IMPLEMENTATION OF THE ACT

United States Government Accountability Office

ABBREVIATIONS

AOUSC	Administrative Office of the United States Courts
ATF	Bureau of Alcohol, Tobacco, Firearms, and Explosives
AUSA	Assistant U.S. Attorney
BOP	Bureau of Prisons
CM/ECF	Case Management/Electronic Case Filing system
CTS	Counterterrorism Section
CVRA	Crime Victims' Rights Act
DEA	Drug Enforcement Agency
DOJ	Department of Justice
EOUSA	Executive Office of the United States Attorneys
FBI	Federal Bureau of Investigation
FJC	Federal Judicial Center
GPRA	Government Performance and Results Act
LIONS	Legal Information Office Network System
NAC	National Advocacy Center
NCVLI	National Crime Victims Law Institute
OIG	Office of the Inspector General
OJP	Office for Justice Programs
OVA	Office for Victims Assistance
OVC	Office for Victims of Crime
OVT	Office of Justice for Victims of Overseas Terrorism

USAO	U.S. Attorneys Offices
USMS	U.S. Marshals Service
USPC	U.S. Parole Commission
USPIS	U.S. Postal Inspection Service
VNS	Victim Notification System
VRO	Victims' Rights Ombudsman

December 15, 2008 December 15, 2008

The Honorable Patrick J. Leahy The Honorable Patrick J. Leahy
Chairman Chairman
The Honorable Arlen Specter The Honorable Arlen Specter
Ranking Member Ranking Member
Committee on the Judiciary Committee on the Judiciary
United States Senate United States Senate

The Honorable John Conyers, Jr. The Honorable John Conyers, Jr.
Chairman Chairman
The Honorable Lamar Smith The Honorable Lamar Smith
Ranking Member Ranking Member
Committee on the Judiciary Committee on the Judiciary
House of Representatives House of Representatives

The Honorable Joseph R. Biden, Jr. The Honorable Joseph R. Biden, Jr.
Chairman Chairman
The Honorable Lindsey Graham The Honorable Lindsey Graham
Ranking Member Ranking Member
Subcommittee on Crime and Drugs Subcommittee on Crime and Drugs
Committee on the Judiciary Committee on the Judiciary
United States Senate United States Senate

The Honorable Robert C. "Bobby" Scott The Honorable Robert C. "Bobby" Scott
Chairman Chairman
The Honorable Louie Gohmert The Honorable Louie Gohmert
Ranking Member Ranking Member
Subcommittee on Crime, Terrorism, and Homeland Security Subcommittee on Crime, Terrorism, and Homeland Security
Committee on the Judiciary Committee on the Judiciary
House of Representatives House of Representatives

According to the Department of Justice (DOJ), as of September 2008 there were approximately 750,000 crime victims in the federal criminal justice system with active cases. In general, for a crime to be prosecuted within the federal criminal justice system, it must be a violation of a federal law. The role for crime victims within the criminal justice process has changed over time. Since the middle of the nineteenth century, crime in the United States has been a public rather than private matter, where the philosophy has been that criminal prosecutions should serve societal interests of deterrence and retribution, as opposed to the individual interests of victims. As such, the American criminal justice system is comprised of two parties—a public prosecutor and the defense—who present their arguments to an impartial body (the judge and jury) for judgment. However, individuals advocating on behalf of crime victims have raised concerns that by focusing solely on the public interest, the criminal justice system has overlooked the individual interests and needs of victims and has limited victims' access to and participation in the prosecution of their cases.

In April 1982, President Reagan formed the President's Task Force on Victims of Crime (Task Force) to investigate the treatment of crime victims within the criminal justice system. The Task Force concluded that, in general, many crime victims were neglected by the criminal justice system, and in its final report (issued in December 1982) the Task Force presented multiple recommendations for how executive and legislative branches of federal and state governments, as well as the private sector, could help improve the treatment of crime victims. According to the National Conference of State Legislatures, 33 states have incorporated victims' rights into their state constitutions, and all 50 states and the District of Columbia have some form of legislation affording rights to crime victims. At the federal level, the government implemented many of the Task Force's recommendations by passing laws that both afforded certain rights to federal crime victims and made funding available to provide a range of services to them.

Most recently, on October 30, 2004, the Justice for All Act was signed into law.[1] Title I of this act—the Scott Campbell, Stephanie Roper, Wendy Preston, Louarna Gillis, and Nila Lynn Crime Victims' Rights Act (CVRA)— established eight rights for federal crime victims, including, among others, the right to be notified of any public court proceeding, the right not to be excluded from such proceedings, and the right to be heard at certain public court proceedings related to the crime. The law requires officers and employees of DOJ, which includes prosecutors, investigative agents, and victim-witness professionals—individuals who are responsible for providing services to crime victims and witnesses—to make their best efforts to see that crime victims are notified of and accorded their rights under the CVRA. Since most federal crimes are prosecuted by DOJ's U.S. Attorneys Offices (USAO), staff in these offices have primary responsibility for assisting crime victims during the prosecution phase of a case. The federal courts also have responsibilities for ensuring that crime victims are afforded their CVRA rights, such as by generally not excluding victims from certain public court proceedings.

The CVRA also established mechanisms to enforce crime victims' rights. Specifically, to ensure that DOJ employees are complying with CVRA requirements, the act directs DOJ to establish a process for receiving and investigating victim-related complaints against DOJ employees, and to require training or impose disciplinary sanctions on any DOJ employees who fail to comply with federal law pertaining to the treatment of crime victims. The CVRA also enables victims to assert their rights in district court by filing a motion for relief[2]—a formal request made to a judge for an order or ruling—with the district court regarding the provision of their rights.[3] If the district court denies victims the relief they are seeking—such as a request that the judge allow the victim to be heard at a court proceeding—the victim can petition the court of appeals for a writ of mandamus, in which case the court of appeals may instruct the district court to grant the victim the relief sought.[4]

Section 104(b) of the Justice for All Act directs GAO to evaluate the "effect and efficacy of the implementation of the [CVRA] on the treatment of crime victims in the federal system." To address this mandate, we sought answers to the following questions:

1. **What efforts have been made to implement the CVRA, what factors have affected these implementation efforts, and how have these factors been addressed?**
2. **What mechanisms are in place to ensure adherence to the CVRA, and how well are these mechanisms working?**
3. **To what extent does DOJ monitor its performance and the performance of its employees regarding the provision of CVRA rights?**
4. **What are the key issues that have arisen as courts interpret and apply the CVRA in cases?**
5. **What are the perspectives of various participants in the federal criminal justice system regarding the effect and efficacy of CVRA implementation?**

Our approach for evaluating the effect and efficacy of CVRA implementation was comprised of various evaluation methods. First, we surveyed by mail a stratified random probability sample of federal crime victims whose cases became active on or after January 1, 2006, and were closed no later than November 30, 2007. We selected the start date because the DOJ guidance and regulations for implementing the CVRA were effective as of December 19, 2005. The case-closed date was selected because we drew our sample in February 2008 and wanted to offer DOJ officials sufficient time to update the database from which we drew our sample for cases closed by the end of November 2007. We surveyed only victims whose cases were closed in order to obtain victims' perspectives over the duration of the criminal justice process. We selected our sample of federal crime victims from DOJ's Victim Notification System (VNS), which is used to notify crime victims of proceedings related to their cases. Of the 1,179 victims we surveyed, 248 (21 percent) returned completed questionnaires. Due to the relatively low response rate to our survey, we cannot generalize the survey results to all federal crime victims in our study period; instead, the discussion of survey results is limited only to the victims who responded. However, these results provided us with an indication of the range of views held by federal crime victims who responded.

Second, we conducted a Web-based survey of all 201 victim-witness professionals who were located in each of the 93 U.S. Attorneys Offices as of April 2008, which is when we issued the survey, to obtain their perspectives about CVRA implementation. We received responses from 174 (87 percent) of them.

Third, we visited nine federal judicial districts. We visited the District of Arizona and the District of Maryland during the design phase of our review due to the long-standing history of victims' rights enforcement in these states. Because CVRA enforcement mechanisms—including victims' ability to file motions in court and petition for writs of mandamus—is an expansion of other federal crime victims statutes, we visited locations where these enforcement mechanisms had been employed. We selected a nonprobability sample of seven federal judicial districts, in six different federal circuits, to visit because these districts either had multiple instances in which individuals asserted CVRA rights in court or a judge, on his or her own initiative, based a case-related decision on the CVRA.[5] In addition, one of these districts is where several victim complaints against DOJ employees were investigated. We met with district or magistrate judges, Federal Public Defenders or Assistant Federal Public Defenders, and U.S. Attorneys Office staff—including Criminal Division Chiefs, Assistant U.S. Attorneys, and victim-witness professionals—who were involved in cases where crime victims filed CVRA-related motions or petitioned for writs of mandamus. In addition, we met with investigative agents and victim-witness professionals at Federal Bureau of Investigation (FBI) field offices and at U.S. Postal Inspection Service (USPIS), Bureau of Alcohol, Tobacco, Firearms and Explosives (ATF), and Drug Enforcement Agency (DEA) offices if located in the jurisdictions we visited. Because we used nonprobability sampling to select federal judicial districts to visit, the information we obtained from these visits cannot be generalized to other districts. However, the visits provided us with information on the perspectives of various participants in the federal judicial system about CVRA.

In addition to the surveys and site visits, we employed other methodologies to address each individual objective. To address our first objective, we reviewed CVRA-related written guidance and training materials made available to DOJ employees and federal judges. We interviewed DOJ headquarters officials—including Executive Office of the United States Attorneys (EOUSA) staff who oversee the victim-witness program for U.S. Attorneys Offices, USAO staff, investigative agency field staff, and federal judiciary officials from the Administrative Office of the United States Courts (AOUSC), the Federal Judicial Center (FJC), and various federal judges. Also, we reviewed the timeliness of notification letters sent by select U.S. Attorneys Offices—three large, three medium- sized, and three small USAOs—over specified 30-day periods.[6] Because we selected a nonprobability sample of USAOs and notification letters from these offices, the results of this analysis cannot be generalized either to other USAOs or to all notification letters sent by the offices we selected. However, this analysis provided us with informative examples of the timeliness of notification letters sent by USAOs.

To address the second objective, we reviewed files related to 141 of the 144 victim complaints received by DOJ's Victims' Rights Ombudsman (VRO) from December 2005 to April 2008[7] to obtain information on the nature of the complaints and the VRO's decisions as to whether the DOJ office or employees cited in the complaints had not afforded victims their CVRA rights. We selected December 2005 as the start date for our review of victim complaints because this was when the first person filed a complaint with the VRO. While DOJ's regulations regarding the complaint process did not take effect until December 19, 2005, the VRO accepted a complaint filed before the effective date and responded to it after the regulations took effect.[8] We chose April 2008 as the end date of our review to allow us enough time to analyze the complaint information prior to issuing our report. We also reviewed internal guidelines about the victim complaint process and met with the VRO and the five DOJ employees who had investigated victims' complaints. We compared DOJ's victim complaint investigation process to professional ombudsman standards as well as the practices used by other offices that conduct similar investigations.[9] Also, we reviewed various DOJ components' brochures and Web sites to determine what complaint process information was being provided to crime victims. We also obtained information on instances where the CVRA was addressed in court, including motions or petitions for writs of mandamus filed by victims. We identified CVRA-related cases using legal search engines, court dockets, interviews, and case compilations generated by the FJC and the National Crime Victims Law Institute (NCVLI). We also interviewed judges and prosecutors involved in cases where victims asserted their rights.

For the third objective, we reviewed DOJ's 2007-2012 Strategic Plan as well as the strategic plans of DOJ components with victim-related responsibilities to determine the extent to which the department and relevant components had developed CVRA-related objectives and measures. We assessed the contents of these documents against the requirements of the Government Performance and Results Act (GPRA). We also reviewed the annual compliance reports prepared by each DOJ component agency with victim-related responsibilities. Lastly, we reviewed the work plans and performance appraisal criteria for all DOJ employees.

To address objective four, we reviewed and analyzed CVRA-related motions and petitions for writs of mandamus and cases in which the CVRA was otherwise mentioned to identify key CVRA provisions that are being interpreted by the courts and any differences in the courts' interpretations. However, we are not in a position to make an evaluative judgment on the courts' decisions. In addition, we interviewed judges, prosecutors, defense attorneys, and victim attorneys who were involved in cases that addressed the CVRA. We also analyzed DOJ CVRA-related policies and interviewed DOJ officials about these policies.

For the final objective, we used our victim survey to assess the extent to which respondents were aware of and satisfied with the provision of their CVRA rights, and the extent to which they exercised these rights. As stated previously in this chapter, given our survey's low response rate, these results cannot be generalized to all victims in our study period. However, these results provided us with an indication of the range of views held by federal crime victims who responded. We obtained victim-witness professionals' perspectives about the effect and efficacy of CVRA implementation through the Web-based survey and site visits. In our site visits, we also interviewed federal judges, federal prosecutors, and federal defenders about the CVRA's overall impact. In addition, we talked with representatives of national crime victim advocacy associations—such as the National Center for Victims of Crime—about the effect and efficacy of the CVRA, and interviewed representatives from defendant rights advocacy organizations, such as the American Civil Liberties Union. We identified these organizations based on publications they had issued regarding crime victims' rights.

We conducted this performance audit from May 2007 to December 2008 in accordance with generally accepted government auditing standards. Those standards require that we plan and perform the audit to obtain sufficient, appropriate evidence to provide a reasonable basis for our findings and conclusions based on our audit objectives. We believe that the evidence obtained provides a reasonable basis for our findings and conclusions based on our audit objectives. Appendix I contains more details about our scope and methodology.

Results in Brief

DOJ and the federal judiciary have made various efforts to implement the CVRA—from revising internal guidelines and developing training materials for DOJ staff and judges to providing victims with emergency, temporary housing in some cases to protect them from the accused offender and proactively asking victims if they would like to speak in court—as well as taken actions to address four factors that have affected CVRA implementation. These factors include the characteristics of certain cases, the increased workload of some USAO staff, the scheduling of court proceedings, and diverging interests between the prosecution and victims. First, the characteristics of certain cases, such as the number of victims involved and the location of the victims, make it difficult to afford victims certain CVRA rights. For instance, USAO staff stated that it can be difficult to provide timely notification of court proceedings to victims located on Indian reservations because the victims may not have access to a mailbox, telephone, or the Internet. To address this challenge, victim-witness personnel told us that they have driven to Indian reservations to personally inform victims of upcoming court proceedings. Second, due to CVRA requirements, particularly notification requirements, USAO victim-witness staff face an increased workload—about 45 percent of staff who responded to our survey reported working an average of about 6 additional hours per week in order to meet CVRA requirements. DOJ has made efforts to address this issue by providing funding to 41 of the 93 USAOs to hire contractors to assist with clerical duties related to victim notification. Third, inherent characteristics of the criminal justice process, such as the short period of time over which pretrial proceedings are scheduled and take place, make it difficult to provide timely notice to crime victims and afford them their right to be heard. When faced with this challenge, USAO victim-witness personnel told us that they have notified victims of court proceedings by telephone rather than mail, which may not arrive in enough time to enable the victim to attend the proceeding. Fourth, diverging interests between the prosecution and victims may affect the way in which the government affords victims their CVRA rights. For instance, according to DOJ, it is not always in the interest of a successful prosecution for victims to be notified of and attend a plea hearing for a cooperating defendant who agrees to testify against or provide information about other defendants in the case in exchange for a lesser sentence because public knowledge of the defendant's cooperation could compromise the investigation, as well as bring harm to the defendant and others. DOJ's efforts to address this issue include requesting that the court close plea agreement proceedings and proposing legislation to revise the CVRA to allow for an exception to victims' notification rights in these instances.

Mechanisms in place to ensure adherence to the CVRA include processes for victims to (1) submit complaints against DOJ employees who have allegedly violated or not provided rights to a crime victim and (2) assert their rights in court; however, the majority of victims who responded to our survey reported that they were not aware that these mechanisms exist. In addition, the lack of independence among investigators involved in the complaint investigation process impedes impartiality. Specifically, 129 of the 235 victims who responded to our survey question regarding the complaint process reported that they were not aware of it, and 51 did not recall whether they were aware. USAOs have been directed to take reasonable steps to provide notice to victims of the complaint process, and they generally do so through a brochure provided to victims at the beginning of the case. However, DOJ has opportunities to enhance victim awareness of the complaint process, such as by making greater use of office Web sites to publicize the process or, when appropriate, personally informing victims. If victims are not aware of the complaint process, it becomes an ineffective method for ensuring that the responsible DOJ officials are complying with CVRA requirements and that corrective action is taken when needed. Furthermore, the lack of independence within the complaint investigation process could compromise impartiality of the investigation. Professional ombudsman standards for investigatingcomplaints against employees, as well as the practices of other offices that investigate complaints, suggest that the investigative process should be structured to ensure impartiality. For example, in practice, the investigators are generally not located in the same office with the subject of the investigation, in order to avoid possible bias. DOJ's Office of Professional Responsibility, which investigates other types of complaints against DOJ employees, also does not use investigators who are located in the same office with the subject of the complaint. However, under DOJ's victim complaint investigation process, the two are generally located in the same office. In addition, in some instances the DOJ victim complaint investigator has been the subordinate or peer of the subject of the complaint. According to DOJ officials, the department structured the victim complaint investigation process as such due to resource constraints and the perception that complaints could be resolved more quickly if addressed locally. However, this structure gives the appearance of bias in the investigation, which raises questions as to whether DOJ employees' violation of victims' rights will be overlooked and employees will not receive appropriate training on the treatment of crime victims or disciplinary sanctions. The results of our survey also suggest that victims lack awareness of their ability to file a motion to assert their CVRA rights in district court. Specifically, 134 of the 236 victims who responded to our survey question regarding victim motions reported that they were not aware of their ability to file a motion to assert their rights in district court, and 48 did not recall whether they were aware. DOJ generally does not inform victims of their ability to assert their rights in court. While the CVRA does not explicitly require DOJ to do so, the law does direct DOJ to inform victims of their eight CVRA rights and their ability to seek the advice of an attorney. In addition, DOJ's guidelines state that responsible officials should provide information to victims about their role in the criminal justice process, which could include their ability to file motions with regard to their CVRA rights. If victims are not aware of their ability to assert their rights in court, it will reduce the effectiveness of this mechanism in ensuring adherence to victims' rights and addressing any violations.

DOJ has an overall departmental objective to uphold the rights of crime victims, but it does not have performance measures in place to assess the extent to which this objective is met. While DOJ components with victim- related responsibilities have made efforts to collect information regarding their provision of victims' rights, these efforts have not been timely or standardized, thus limiting the usefulness of the information in assessing overall performance across DOJ. Furthermore, not all relevant DOJ components have incorporated adherence to victims' rights in the performance appraisal criteria for all their employees with victim-related responsibilities. In the absence of performance measures, agencies may not be able to determine how well they are performing related to the provision of victims' rights, nor can they identify or address deficiencies in performance. Federal law requires DOJ's Office for Victims of Crime to monitor the department's compliance with internal guidelines regarding fair treatment of victims and witnesses. In response, the Office for Victims of Crime is to collect compliance information from components with victim-related responsibilities, including DOJ's 4 investigative agencies, such as the Federal Bureau of Investigation, 8 litigation divisions, such as the USAOs, and 2 corrections divisions, such as the Bureau of Prisons. However, until August 2008, the office had not yet analyzed and reported on the compliance information collected since implementation of the CVRA—although internal guidelines state that this information is supposed to be reported annually—thus preventing DOJ from identifying and addressing deficiencies related to the provision of victims' rights in a timely manner, as recommended by standards for internal control in the federal government.

Officials in this office said that they lacked the resources to analyze and report the compliance information. However, in August 2008, Office for Victims of Crime officials stated that they had received funding and begun analyzing the compliance data submitted to them by the various DOJ components. The office may be hindered in its analysis, however, because it has not required that components with similar victim-related functions submit the same type of data—which we have previously recommended for federal agencies in general, thus making it difficult to determine overall department compliance. Finally, DOJ guidelines require that all components with victim-related responsibilities incorporate information on adherence to victims' rights requirements into their work plans and into the performance appraisals for their employees. We found that 8 of the 14 relevant DOJ components have complied with this requirement for all responsible employees, and as of October 2008 officials from 5 of the remaining 6 components told us that they were in the process of fulfilling this requirement. According to the Director of the FBI's Office for Victim Assistance, it is not necessary to incorporate references to victims' rights in the performance appraisals for FBI investigative agents and victim specialists because adherence to victims' rights requirements is included in the performance appraisals for the special agents-in-charge, who generally are responsible for the activities of an entire FBI field office. However, considering that investigative agents are responsible for identifying victims and victim specialists help ensure victims receive needed services, incorporating victims' rights requirements into their performance appraisals could better ensure that these employees are aware of and held accountable for their CVRA responsibilities.

Several key issues have arisen as courts interpret and apply the CVRA in cases, including (1) when in the criminal justice process CVRA rights apply, (2) what it means for a victim to be "reasonably heard" in court proceedings, (3) which standard should be used to review victim appeals of district court decisions regarding CVRA rights, and (4) whether the CVRA applies to victims of local offenses prosecuted in the District of Columbia Superior Court. First, the courts have issued varied decisions regarding whether CVRA rights apply to victims of offenses that have not been charged in court by DOJ, stating that the law applies in some circumstances and not in others. On the other hand, DOJ has specified in its guidelines that CVRA rights do not apply unless charges have been filed against a defendant, based on its initial interpretation of the law, but is reviewing its policy in response to a court ruling in 2008.[10] As of September 2008, DOJ could not provide an estimated date of when the review of its policy would be completed. Second, the courts have issued varied rulings that interpret the meaning of the right to be "reasonably heard" at court proceedings, with, for example, one court ruling that the right to be heard gave victims the right to speak and another ruling that the right could be satisfied by a written statement, given the specific facts of the case. Third, the courts have differing interpretations regarding which standard should be used to review victim appeals of district court decisions regarding CVRA rights, with U.S. courts of appeals using two different standards, one of which is stricter than the other, to review these appeals. As typically occurs when new legislation is enacted, the courts are interpreting and applying provisions of the CVRA through rulings on individual cases that come before them, which helps to further develop the law. However, DOJ and D.C. Superior Court officials stated that a statutory change would be beneficial in resolving the issue of CVRA applicability to the D.C. Superior Court.[11] The CVRA is not explicit about whether the law applies to victims of local offenses prosecuted in this court. As a result, judges in the D.C. Superior Court have differing interpretations on this issue. In July 2005, DOJ proposed legislation to clarify whether the CVRA applies to cases in the D.C. Superior Court, but no legislation had been passed as of October 23, 2008. Without clarification on this issue, the question of whether the D.C. Superior Court has responsibility to implement the CVRA will remain and judges in the D.C. Superior Court may continue to differ in whether they apply the law in their cases.

Perceptions are mixed regarding the effect and efficacy of the implementation of the CVRA, based on factors such as awareness of CVRA rights, victim satisfaction, participation, and treatment, as well as regarding potential conflicts of the law with defendants' interests. For example, while a majority of federal crime victims who responded to our survey reported that they were aware of most of their CVRA rights, less than half reported that they were aware of their right to confer with the prosecutor. In addition, victims who responded to our survey reported varying levels of satisfaction with the provision of individual CVRA rights. For instance, 132 of the 169 victims who responded to the survey question regarding satisfaction with their right to notice of public court proceedings reported being satisfied with the provision of this right. In contrast, only 72 of the 229 victims who responded to the survey question regarding satisfaction with the right to confer with the prosecutor reported being satisfied with the provision of this right. The general perception among the criminal justice system participants we spoke with and surveyed is that CVRA implementation has improved the treatment of crime victims, although many also believe that victims were treated well prior to the act because of the influence of well-established victims' rights laws at the state level. Furthermore, while 72 percent of the victim-witness personnel who responded to our survey perceived that the CVRA has resulted in at least some increase in victim attendance at public court proceedings, 141 of the 167 victims who responded to our survey question regarding participation reported that they did not attend any of the proceedings related to their cases, primarily because the location of the court was too far to travel or they were not interested in attending. Finally, defense attorneys and representatives of organizations that promote the enforcement of defendants' rights expressed some concerns that CVRA implementation may pose conflicts with the interests of defendants. For example, victims have the right not to be excluded from public court proceedings unless clear and convincing evidence can be shown that their testimony would be materially altered if they heard the testimony of others first. However, 5 of the 9 federal defenders and 6 of the 19 district judges we met with said that it would be very difficult, if not impossible, to provide such evidence that the victim's testimony would be materially altered.

We are making several recommendations to assist DOJ in its efforts to effectively implement the CVRA. These include making efforts to increase victims' awareness of the complaint process and their ability to assert their rights in court to help ensure that these are effective mechanisms for promoting CVRA compliance; restructuring the complaint investigation process to ensure greater independence and impartiality among complaint investigators; and identifying performance measures regarding victims' rights, collecting standard compliance data, and incorporating references to adherence with victims' rights in the work plans and performance appraisals for investigative agents and victim specialists to help ensure accountability for the provision of victims' rights. We also believe that Congress should consider revising the language of the CVRA to clarify whether the CVRA applies to victims of local offenses prosecuted in the District of Columbia Superior Court. We provided a draft of this chapter to DOJ and AOUSC for review. DOJ and AOUSC both provided technical comments that we incorporated as appropriate. DOJ, in its written comments, generally concurred with the recommendations in the report and stated that the department intends to convene a working group to consider the extent and manner in which they are implemented. The full text of DOJ's comments is provided in appendix VI.

BACKGROUND

Victims of Federal Crimes

According to DOJ, as of September 2008, over 750,000 crime victims with active cases were registered with the Victim Notification System—the electronic system DOJ uses to notify federal crime victims of events related to their cases. In general, for a crime to be prosecuted within the federal criminal justice system, it must be a violation of a federal law. Almost half of the federal criminal cases that commenced between March 2006 and March 2007 in the federal criminal justice system were related to immigration and narcotics violations, which generally do not involve any victims. The most common types of cases prosecuted in the federal criminal justice system during the same 12 month period that did involve victims include: fraud; burglary, larceny and theft; sex offenses; and robberies.

Evolution of Crime Victims' Rights

In colonial America, crime was primarily resolved privately. Crimes were generally investigated and prosecuted at the initiative and cost of the victim, who usually hired a private investigator and attorney to handle the case. However, a shift in perspective occurred in the late 1800s, after which crime was perceived to affect not only individual victims but society in general. As a result, the government assumed responsibility for investigating and prosecuting criminal activity, and crime victims lost their status as parties in the criminal justice process. In the 1960s, individuals advocating on behalf of crime victims claimed that by not being acknowledged as a formal party, crime victims were not treated fairly within the criminal justice system and their interests were ignored. In response to these concerns, in April 1982 President Reagan formed the President's Task Force on Victims of Crime. The Task Force concluded that crime victims had been overlooked by the criminal justice system and in its final report issued in December 1982, the Task Force outlined 45 recommendations for the executive, legislative, and judicial branches of government for improving the treatment of crime victims. The recommendations that are applicable to the federal government are provided in table 1 below.

The recommendations of the President's Task Force on Victims of Crime provided the basis for subsequent attempts to amend the U.S. Constitution, as well as the enactment of statutes regarding the role of the crime victim in the criminal justice process. According to the Congressional Research Service, between 1996 and 2003 there were nine hearings held in the U.S. House of Representatives and U.S. Senate on the issue of amending the Constitution to incorporate victims' rights, but the legislation proposing to amend the Constitution was never brought up for a vote in either chamber of Congress. The federal government did, however, enact statutes that implemented many of the Task Force's recommendations by both affording certain rights to federal crime victims and making funding available to provide a range of services to crime victims.

Table 1. Recommendations of the 1982 President's Task Force on Victims of Crime

Legislative Recommendations
• Legislation should be enacted to ensure that addresses of victims and witnesses are not made public or available to the defense, absent a clear need as determined by the court. • Legislation should be enacted to abolish parole and limit judicial discretion in sentencing. • Legislation should be enacted to provide for the protection of victims and witnesses from intimidation. • Legislation should be enacted to require restitution in all cases, unless the court provides specific reasons for failing to require it. • Legislation should be enacted to ensure that sexual assault victims are not required to assume the cost of physical examinations and materials used to obtain evidence. • Congress should enact legislation to provide federal funding to assist state crime victim compensation programs. • Congress should enact legislation to provide federal funding...to assist in the operation of federal, state, local, and private victim/witness assistance agencies that make comprehensive case information available to all victims of crime.
Prosecutorial Recommendations
• Prosecutors should assume ultimate responsibility for informing victims of the status of a case from the time of the initial charging decision to determinations of parole. • Prosecutors have an obligation to bring to the attention of the court the views of the victims of violent crime on bail decisions, continuances, plea bargains, dismissals, sentencing, and restitution. They should establish procedures to ensure that such victims are given the opportunity to make their views on these matters known. • Prosecutors should strongly discourage case continuances.
Judiciary Recommendations
• Judges should allow victims and witnesses to be on call for court proceedings. • When ruling on requests for continuances, judges should give the same weight to the interests of victims and witnesses as that given to the interests of defendants. • Judges should allow for, and give appropriate weight to, input at sentencing from victims of violent crime. • Judges should order restitution to the victim in all cases in which the victim has suffered financial loss, unless they state compelling reasons for a contrary ruling on the record. • Judges should allow the victim and a member of the victim's family to attend the trial, even if identified as witnesses, absent a compelling need to the contrary.

Source: GAO analysis of the final report of the President's Task Force on Victims of Crime.

Since 1982, the federal government has passed a number of laws that address the role of the crime victim in the criminal justice system, including the Victim and Witness Protection Act of 1982,[12] Victims of Crime Act of 1984,[13] Victims' Rights and Restitution Act of

1990,[14] Violent Crime Control and Law Enforcement Act of 1994,[15] Mandatory Victims Restitution Act of 1996,[16] Victim Rights Clarification Act of 1997,[17] and Crime Victims' Rights Act of 2004.[18]

Several of these statutes provided crime victims with rights, but they also directed federal officials to provide victims with various services, such as notification of certain public court proceedings.

In particular, the Victims' Rights and Restitution Act of 1990 identified crime victims' rights, delineating seven such rights and requiring federal officials to make their best efforts to see that crime victims are accorded these rights.[19] The 1990 law also included a separate provision, codified at 42 U.S.C. § 10607, that requires federal officials to identify crime victims and provide them information about their cases and about services that may be available to them.[20] For example, it requires officials to provide victims with the earliest possible notice of the status of the investigation of the crime, to the extent that it is appropriate to inform the victim and to the extent that it will not interfere with the investigation, as well as notice of the arrest of the suspected offender, the filing of charges against the suspected offender, the scheduling of certain court proceedings, the release or detention status of the offender, the acceptance of a plea or the rendering of a verdict, and the sentence imposed on the offender. The law also requires officials to inform victims of a place where they may receive emergency medical and social services, to inform victims of programs that are available to provide counseling, treatment, and other support to the victim, and to assist victims in contacting persons who can provide such services. Further, the law requires officials to arrange for victims to receive reasonable protection from a suspected offender and ensure that victims are provided a waiting area removed from and out of the sight and hearing of the defendant and defense witnesses during court proceedings.

On October 30, 2004, the Crime Victims' Rights Act, as a component of the Justice for All Act, was signed into law.[21] The CVRA left in place 42 U.S.C. § 10607—the provision requiring federal officials to inform victims about their cases and about services available to them—but the CVRA modified the provision from the 1990 law regarding crime victims' rights and identified eight rights for federal crime victims, some of which were similar to the rights from the 1990 law and others of which were new. The CVRA provided that crime victims have the following rights:

- **the right to be reasonably protected from the accused;**
- **the right to reasonable, accurate, and timely notice of any public court proceeding, or any parole proceeding, involving the crime or of any release or escape of the accused;**
- **the right not to be excluded from any such public court proceeding, unless the court, after receiving clear and convincing evidence, determines that testimony by the victim would be materially altered if the victim heard other testimony at that proceeding;**
- **the right to be reasonably heard at any public proceeding in the district court involving the release, plea, sentencing, or any parole proceeding;**
- **the reasonable right to confer with the attorney for the government in the case;**
- **the right to full and timely restitution as provided in law;**
- **the right to proceedings free from unreasonable delay; and**

- **the right to be treated with fairness and with respect for the victim's dignity and privacy.**[22]

As shown in appendix II, earlier statutes included provisions that may be considered precursors to or foundations for the rights established by the CVRA.

Mechanisms for Federal Crime Victims to Ensure Adherence to the CVRA

The CVRA also established two mechanisms to ensure adherence to victims' rights under the law, neither of which had been available under previous statutes. Specifically, to ensure that DOJ employees are complying with CVRA requirements, the law directed DOJ to designate an administrative authority to receive and investigate complaints relating to the provision or violation of crime victims' rights.[23] To comply with this provision in the statute, DOJ issued regulations creating the Victims' Rights Ombudsman.[24] The VRO is a position within the Executive Office of United States Attorneys—the DOJ division responsible for facilitating coordination between USAOs, evaluating USAO performance, and providing general legal interpretations and opinions to USAOs, amongst other things. Federal crime victims may submit written complaints to the designated point of contact for the DOJ division that is the subject of the complaint, who then investigates the complaint and reports the results of the investigation to the VRO. Victims may also submit complaints directly to the VRO. If the VRO finds that an employee failed to afford a CVRA right to a victim, the VRO must require that employee to undergo training on victims' rights. If based on an investigation the VRO determines that an employee willfully and wantonly failed to provide a victim with a CVRA right, the VRO must recommend a range of disciplinary sanctions to the official authorized to take action on disciplinary matters for the relevant office. The CVRA does not require DOJ employees to provide relief to victims whose rights have been violated, but the VRO guidelines do require investigators, to the best of their ability, to resolve complaints to the victims' satisfaction.

The CVRA also enables victims to assert their rights in district court, by filing a motion—which they can do either verbally or per a written request—with the court.[25] Unlike the complaint process, this mechanism allows victims to assert their rights and seek relief from the court, and can be employed not only when victims believe that a DOJ employee violated their rights, but when they have general concerns regarding the provision of their rights. If the district court denies the victim's request regarding the provision of CVRA rights—such as a request to be heard at a hearing—the victim can petition the court of appeals for a writ of mandamus. Thus, if the court of appeals grants the victim's petition, it may direct the district court to take actions to afford CVRA rights to the victim. Petitions for writs of mandamus can be filed at any point in the case. The CVRA requires the court of appeals to take up and decide petitions for writs of mandamus within 72 hours after they are filed. A victim may also request to reopen a plea or sentence, but only if (a) the victim has asserted the right to be heard before or during the proceeding at issue and such right was denied; (b) the victim petitions the court of appeals for a writ of mandamus within 10 days; and (c) in the case of a plea, the accused has not pled to the highest offense charged. However, the CVRA states that a failure to afford victims their rights under the law will not provide grounds for a new trial.[26]

Federal Officials Responsible for Implementing the CVRA

The CVRA requires DOJ officers and employees—which includes prosecutors, investigative agents, corrections officials, and victim-witness professionals—to make their best efforts to see that crime victims are notified of and accorded their rights under the CVRA,[27] and furthermore requires that prosecutors inform victims of their ability to seek the advice of an attorney.[28] The 2005 Attorney General Guidelines on Victim and Witness Assistance (Attorney General Guidelines) provide guidance for DOJ employees on how to implement these best efforts. Table 2 lists the DOJ component agencies responsible for implementing the CVRA by type (investigative, prosecutorial, and corrections/parole).

Table 2. Department of Justice Component Agencies Responsible for Implementing the CVRA

Investigative
• Federal Bureau of Investigation • Drug Enforcement Administration • Bureau of Alcohol, Tobacco, Firearms and Explosives • U.S. Marshals Service • Office of the Inspector General
Prosecutorial
• U.S. Attorneys Offices • Antitrust Division • Civil Division • Civil Rights Division • Criminal Division • Environment and Natural Resources • National Security Division • Tax Division
Corrections/Parole
• Federal Bureau of Prisons • U.S. Parole Commission

Source: DOJ Attorney General Guidelines for Victim and Witness Assistance and DOJ Strategic Plan 2007-2012 for prosecutorial divisions.

Investigative and prosecutorial components in DOJ have victim specialists and victim-witness coordinators who were already in place prior to the CVRA. Their role is to assist investigative agents, litigation divisions within DOJ, and prosecutors in dealing with crime victims so that agents and prosecutors can focus their efforts on successfully investigating and prosecuting criminal cases. (Approximately 90 percent of federal crimes are prosecuted by the USAOs.) As shown in figure 1, according to a report issued by DOJ's Office of the Inspector General, as of October 2007, the FBI had worked with more crime victims registered in the Victim Notification System (51 percent) than any other federal investigative and corrections agency, either within or outside DOJ, including the U.S. Postal Inspection Service (27 percent), the U.S. Secret Service (5 percent), the Internal Revenue Service (4 percent), the Bureau of Prisons (2 percent), the Food and Drug Administration (2 percent), Department of Labor components (2 percent), and others (7 percent).

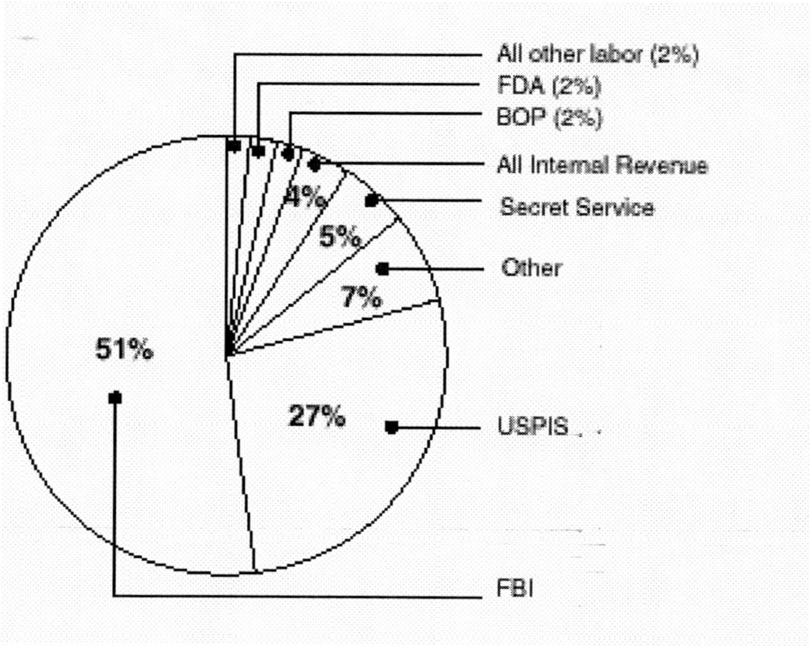

Figure 1. Percentage of Crime Victims Registered in the Victim Notification System by Federal Investigative Agency, as of October 2007. N=1 ,564,667
Source: DOJ Office of Inspector General.

The federal courts, primarily through district court judges, also have responsibility for ensuring that crime victims are afforded their rights under the CVRA. In addition, the CVRA requires the Administrative Office of the U.S. Courts—which provides administrative, legal, and other support to the federal judiciary—to annually report to Congress instances in which CVRA rights were asserted in a criminal case and the court denied the victim's request for relief, as well as the results of petitions for writs of mandamus that were brought before the court.

Authorization of Funding to Support CVRA Implementation

The CVRA authorized appropriations for fiscal years 2005, 2006, 2007, 2008, and 2009. Funds that may have been appropriated under the CVRA were likely appropriated in a lump sum with funds for other victim assistance and grant programs, making it unclear exactly how much was appropriated for CVRA-specific purposes. The authorized amounts, years, and purposes are listed in table 3.

Table 3. Funding Authorized by the CVRA

Purpose	Amount and fiscal years
For U.S. Attorneys Offices for Victim-Witness Assistance Programs	$2 million for 2005, $5 million annually for 2006-2009
For the Office for Victims of Crime for enhancement of the Victim Notification System	$2 million for 2005, $5 million annually for 2006-2009
For the Office for Victims of Crime for staff to administer the appropriation for the support of organizations that provide legal counsel to federal crime victims	$300,000 for 2005 and $500,000 annually for 2006-2009
For the Office for Victims of Crime for the support of organizations that provide legal counsel to federal crime victims	$7 million for 2005 and $11 million annually for 2006-2009
For the Office for Victims of Crime for the support of training and technical assistance to states and tribal jurisdictions to craft state-of-the-art victims' rights laws, and training and technical assistance to states and tribal jurisdictions to design a variety of compliance systems, which shall include an evaluation component	$5 million for 2005 and $7 million annually for 2006-2009
For grants to state, tribal, and local prosecutors' offices, law enforcement agencies, courts, jails, and correctional institutions, and to qualified public or private entities, to develop and implement state-of-the-art systems for notifying victims of crime of important dates and developments relating to the criminal proceedings at issue in a timely and efficient manner	$5 million annually for 2005-2009

Source: GAO analysis of section 103(b) of the Justice for All Act of 2004.

Multiple Efforts Have Been Made to Implement the CVRA, and DOJ and Federal Courts Have Taken Actions to Address Various Factors that Have Presented Challenges for Affording CrimeVictims Their Rights

DOJ and the federal judiciary have made multiple efforts to implement the CVRA and afford federal crime victims their CVRA rights, including making revisions to internal guidelines and providing training to investigative agents, prosecutors, victim-witness staff, and judges. They have also taken steps to address various factors—namely, the type of criminal case, the location of victims, the number of victims, the workload of USAO staff, and the scheduling of court proceedings—that, in some cases, have made it difficult for DOJ and federal courts to afford victims their CVRA rights. DOJ has also made efforts to provide victims their CVRA rights even in circumstances when there are diverging interests between the prosecution and victims, such as when a victim who is also a witness wants to observe the entire trial, which could cause the jury to question the credibility of the victim's testimony, thus potentially jeopardizing the success of the prosecution.

DOJ and the Federal Judiciary Have Made Efforts to Implement the CVRA and Afford Federal Crime Victims Their CVRA Rights

DOJ has made several efforts to implement the CVRA, including.

- Revision of the Attorney General Guidelines for Victim and Witness Assistance and Accompanying Materials. **DOJ issued these revised guidelines in May 2005 in response to the enactment of the CVRA in October 2004. The guidelines summarize victims' rights under the CVRA and specify which prosecutorial, investigative, and correctional components within DOJ have responsibilities to enforce the rights. The guidelines were updated from a previous version to include provisions for implementing the CVRA, such as directing prosecutors to file motions in district court requesting the court to fashion "reasonable procedures" for enforcing victims' rights in cases with large numbers of victims, such as the right to be reasonably heard at any public court proceeding. The guidelines also discuss services to be provided to victims and witnesses, restitution procedures, and guidelines to be used for certain classes of victims such as children and victims of domestic or sexual abuse, terrorism, human trafficking, and identity theft. In addition, an accompanying video was produced and made available to DOJ employees.·**

- Enhancement and Expanded Use of the Victim Notification System. **The CVRA affords victims the right to be notified of all public court proceedings related to their cases. According to EOUSA officials, before the enactment of the CVRA, DOJ notified victims of up to 58 events related to their cases, whereas now DOJ is responsible for notifying victims of up to 93 events. Additional events include competency hearings, post trial hearings, and pretrial motion hearings. In fiscal years 2005 through 2007, DOJ expended $2,250,320 to enhance the Victim Notification System to accommodate the additional notifications required by CVRA.**

- CVRA Training. **DOJ components have made several efforts to train employees on CVRA implementation. The FBI, DEA, ATF, and Bureau of Prisons (BOP) have all issued training materials for employees concerning the overall provision of victims' rights, as well as training materials that provide guidance for dealing with victims of certain types of crimes, such as child abuse or terrorism. According to a DOJ official, the DEA holds annual mandated training on the victim-witness program, which includes the CVRA, is developing mandated electronic training on the CVRA, and is revising the DEA Agents Manual to**

include details on the CVRA. The ATF has provided in-person training to all 25 field divisions, required all special agents to complete a 2-hour training on the CVRA, and developed an online training course on the CVRA. EOUSA has held 40 training sessions at the National Advocacy Center (NAC)[29] for prosecutors, victim-witness coordinators, and other victim-witness personnel from the individual USAOs. EOUSA staff and victim-witness coordinators also hold regional and local training for prosecutors, agents, and victim-witness personnel from other DOJ components. Victim-witness staff hold training sessions for new Assistant United States Attorneys on office-specific policies for affording victims their CVRA rights, such as the procedures prosecutors should use to coordinate with victim-witness professionals to make sure victims are correctly notified of case events. The Attorney General Guidelines also require that all employees whose primary responsibilities include contact with crime victims receive at least 1 hour of training concerning victims' rights within 60 days of assuming those responsibilities.

The federal judiciary has also made a number of efforts to implement the CVRA. Specifically, the AOUSC, Judicial Conference, and FJC have developed guidance and provided training on the statute to the courts. The Judicial Conference is the national policy-making body of the federal courts and the FJC is the principal education, training, and research resource for federal judges. The federal judiciary's efforts include:

- Memoranda about CVRA Rights and Requirements. **AOUSC issued a memorandum in December 2004 to all judges and clerks in the district and appellate courts informing them of the enactment of the CVRA. The memorandum summarized, among other things, victims' rights under the CVRA, the courts' responsibility to afford victims their rights, the ability of victims to assert their rights in court, and AOUSC's requirement to report to Congress instances in which victims asserted their rights in court and the relief requested was denied. AOUSC issued two additional memoranda to the courts, in July 2005 and February 2006. The first was a reminder of AOUSC's reporting requirement under the CVRA and the second summarized the CVRA's provisions and provided additional reporting instructions to the courts.**

- Revisions to the Benchbook for U.S. District Court Judges (Benchbook). **The purpose of the Benchbook is to provide a practical guide to help judges with situations they are likely to encounter on the bench. The guidance in the Benchbook is recommended but not required. According to the judges we interviewed, it is primarily used by newer judges. The September 2007 edition of the Benchbook was revised to incorporate victims' rights under the CVRA. According to FJC officials, the Benchbook contains 54 references to victims' rights under the law. Most of the CVRA-related revisions address the victims' rights to notice and not to be excluded from public court proceedings. Specifically, the revised Benchbook states at the beginning of applicable sections that under the CVRA, any victim of the offense has the right to notice of public court proceedings and to attend that proceeding. It advises judges to ask the**

prosecutor if there are any victims involved in the case and if so, whether the government has notified them of the proceeding. The Benchbook makes judges aware of other CVRA rights and issues by, for example:

- advising the court to give any victims present in the courtroom the opportunity to be reasonably heard in release or detention hearings;
- referencing the victim's right to be reasonably protected from the accused when considering release or detention pending trial;
- stating that the victim's right to proceedings free from unreasonable delay may have to be considered when contemplating granting a continuance—or postponement—of proceedings; and
- noting that it is unclear whether the CVRA would apply to hearings regarding revocation of probation or supervised release, and any subsequent sentencing hearings.

- CVRA Discussions in Judicial Workshops and Orientations. **According to FJC officials, the CVRA was discussed in orientations for newly appointed district court judges. In addition, officials stated that 90- minute CVRA breakout sessions were held at the National Workshops for Magistrate Judges[30] in April and July 2008, which featured a panel discussion on the CVRA and relevant case law. The Director of the FJC Education Division also stated that a 2-hour CVRA session was held at the National Sentencing Policy Institute in June 2008.[31]**

- CVRA Guidance Document. **The FJC prepared a guidance document entitled "The Crime Victims' Rights Act and the Federal Courts" in October 2005, which provides an overview of the CVRA, highlights issues that may arise in implementing the act, and summarizes CVRA-related cases. The guidance was updated in March 2008 and June 2008. According to FJC officials, it was distributed at orientation sessions for newly appointed district and magistrate judges, national workshops for district and magistrate judges, and other judicial education programs. The guidance document can also be accessed on the FJC Web site. According to officials, the guidance will be updated in January 2009 to coincide with and highlight the new criminal rules of procedure implementing the CVRA that are mentioned later in this section. They stated that the FJC will continue to distribute the document at appropriate educational programs as part of its ongoing efforts to educate new judges and magistrate judges and to keep the judiciary informed of developments in the law relating to the CVRA.**

- CVRA Training Video. **The FJC produced a 22-minute CVRA educational video entitled "The Rights of Crime Victims in Federal Courts." The video contains an overview of the act and interviews with judges and a U.S. Attorney regarding their responsibilities under the CVRA and issues they have encountered, such as in cases with a large number of victims. The video was broadcast on the Federal Judiciary Television Network to all federal court houses, as well as court**

administrative offices and the U.S. Sentencing Commission. It aired in March 2008 and was repeated 24 times as of October 23, 2008. According to FJC officials, the video is also available to judges on the center's internal Web site.

- Amendments to the Federal Rules of Criminal Procedure. **The Federal Rules of Criminal Procedure govern the conduct of all criminal proceedings in federal courts. The amendments, which took effect December 1, 2008, revised five criminal rules and created a new stand-alone rule to implement the CVRA. For instance, the revisions incorporate the CVRA's definition of a crime victim, provide that a victim's address and telephone number should not be automatically provided to the defendant when an alibi defense is raised, and require the court to consider the convenience of victims in setting the place for trial within the district. The new stand-alone rule incorporates several of the CVRA rights verbatim, such as the rights to notification, not to be excluded, and to be reasonably heard, as well as other provisions in the law.**

In addition to DOJ and the federal judiciary's overarching efforts to implement the CVRA, ederal investigative agencies, USAO staff, DOJ litigation divisions, district court judges, and corrections officials work to afford victims their individual CVRA rights in a number of ways. Table 4 provides examples of these efforts listed by each of the eight CVRA rights. The efforts listed are compiled from site visit interviews and are not a comprehensive list of all efforts made to implement the CVRA.

Table 4. Examples of Efforts to Afford Federal Crime Victims Their CVRA Rights that Were Made by Federal Investigative Agencies, U.S. Attorneys Offices, and Federal Courts GAO Visited during Site Visits

The right to be protected from the accused.

Federal investigative agencies and USAOs have helped victims secure their residences by:

- arranging for police patrols near victims' residence,
- helping victims change their locks, and
- developing a safety plan for the victims.

Federal investigative agencies have coordinated with USAOs to assist certain victims, such as those who live with the accused, with changing residences by:

- providing assistance to victims who are also witnesses and are the subject of a threat or a perceived threat through the Emergency Witness Assistance Program, which makes funding available to help such victims cover moving costs, including transportation and a security deposit and first month's rent for a new apartment; and
- in some cases, arranging for emergency temporary housing for victims, including hotels and shelters.

Regarding the courts:

- judges, per the prosecutor's request, have issued protective orders and no contact orders as a condition for release of the accused;
- courts have designated separate waiting rooms for victims and defendants;
- victim-witness professionals and federal investigative agents have accompanied victims to court to help victims feel more comfortable; and

Table 4. (Continued)

The right to be protected from the accused.
• prosecutors have ensured that victims' personal information, such as phone numbers and addresses, are redacted from publicly available court documents
The right to reasonable, accurate, and timely notice of all public court proceedings, or any parole proceeding, involving the crime or of any release or escape of the accused.
Federal investigative agencies and USAOs have: • used various people-search Web sites to obtain updated contact information for victims, and • set up Web sites that include information on the status of the case and provide victims with contact information for DOJ employees investigating and prosecuting the case. DOJ has employed a contractor to enter victim information into VNS in cases with a large number of victims. One USAO has an office policy of notifying victims at least 5 days in advance of a proceeding. One USAO's victim-witness coordinator sent weekly e-mails to all prosecutors reminding them about the process for collecting and forwarding victim information back to her. A district court clerk has notified the USAO immediately of any changes in the schedule for court proceedings. Federal judges have asked prosecutors whether the victims for a case have been given notice of particular proceedings.
The right not to be Excluded from any such Public Court Proceeding, Unless the Court, after Receiving Clear and Convincing Evidence, Determines that Testimony by the Victim would be Materially Altered if the Victim heard other Testimony at that Proceeding.
Judges have considered victims' availability when scheduling court proceedings. USAO and investigative agency staff have made transportation arrangements for victims to attend court proceedings.
The Right to be Reasonably Heard at any Public Proceeding in the District Court Involving the Release, Plea, Sentencing, or any Parole Proceeding.
USAO staff have: • personally called victims in sensitive cases (e.g., involving murder or child pornography) to inform them that they can speak at certain court proceedings and • sent victims a form on which to write and submit a victim impact statement. Judges have: • asked if any victims are present in the courtroom and wish to make a statement; • refused to cut off victims when they make statements in court, regardless of the length of the statement; and • closed a segment of a court proceeding so that the victim in a terrorism case who wished to remain anonymous from the public was still able to make a statement before the court in person
The Right to Confer with the Attorney for the Government in the Case.
A federal investigative agent provided victims with prosecutors' phone numbers, as appropriate. USAO staff have: • consulted with victims regarding proposed plea agreements when victims have expressed an interest in learning more about the case or if there is concern that the victim may disapprove of some concessions being made to the defendant and

Table 4. (Continued)

The Right to Confer with the Attorney for the Government in the Case.
A federal investigative agent provided victims with prosecutors' phone numbers, as appropriate. USAO staff have: • consulted with victims regarding proposed plea agreements when victims have expressed an interest in learning more about the case or if there is concern that the victim may disapprove of some concessions being made to the defendant and • for a violent crime case, met with victims in their home after each court proceeding, to discuss what transpired at the proceeding and inform them of what the prosecution planned to submit as evidence for upcoming proceedings, particularly if the evidence was potentially disturbing for the victim. A federal judge required prosecutors to confer with the victims regarding any plea agreements that were reached.
The Right to Full and Timely Restitution as Provided in Law.
Investigative agents and USAO victim-witness professionals have obtained information on victims' losses and input that information into a spreadsheet, which they then provided to the prosecutor and the court. Courts have held evidentiary hearings to determine an appropriate restitution amount in circumstances where calculating restitution may be complex
The **Right to Proceedings Free from Unreasonable Delay.**
In cases where the defendant has filed for several continuances (or delays in proceedings), USAO staff have met with victims who become frustrated with the delays to explain the rationale for why they are occurring
The Right to be Treated with Fairness and with Respect for the Victim's Dignity and Privacy.
Investigative agents and USAO staff have: • ensured that victim contact information is protected and not released to the public, • redacted (or removed) victim contact information in documents sent to defense counsel, and • used initials for victims in place of their full names in court filings. Judges have ensured that victim contact information is not revealed in court.

Source: GAO analysis of information obtained from DOJ, USPIS, and federal court officials during site visits.

DOJ and Federal Courts Are Addressing Challenges in Affording Victims Certain CVRA Rights and Ensuring CVRA Rights Are Afforded Amidst Diverging Interests

In some cases, several factors—specifically, the number of victims, the location of victims, the workload of USAO staff, and the scheduling of court proceedings— have made it difficult for DOJ and federal courts to afford federal crime victims their rights to be notified of, not to be excluded from, and to be heard at court proceedings. While most of these factors are inherent to the criminal justice system and generally are not within DOJ's or the court's control, DOJ and federal courts have made efforts to overcome the challenges that these factors have presented. In addition, DOJ has made efforts to ensure that crime victims are afforded their rights even when the interests of the prosecution and victim diverge. Many of the efforts have only recently been implemented; therefore, it is too soon to evaluate how effective these efforts have been at addressing CVRA implementation challenges.

Challenges Providing Notice in Large-Victim Cases

Staff at USAOs we met with found it challenging to afford victims their notification right in cases where there were large numbers of victims, such as corporate fraud and identity theft cases which can involve thousands of victims.[32] However, DOJ has taken a number of actions to address the challenges associated with such cases. The Attorney General Guidelines allow for victim-witness professionals to send each victim in the case one notification letter, which instructs the victim, from that point forward, to access VNS by phone or on the Internet to obtain updates on future court proceedings or the status of their case. To further address the challenge of reaching a large number of victims, USAOs have used various media outlets in an attempt to notify victims; used teleconferencing when courtrooms prove too small; and encouraged victims to submit written victim impact statements, or asked that large classes of victims choose a smaller number of victims to speak on everyone's behalf.

Challenges Providing Notice Due to the Victim's Location

Staff at the USAOs and investigative agency field offices we visited reported challenges in affording victims who live on Indian reservations their rights because such victims may not have access to a mailbox, telephone, or the Internet.[33] To address this issue, USAO or investigative agency staff may drive (sometimes for several hours each way) to the reservation to personally inform victims about upcoming proceedings related to their cases. Additionally, staff at USAOs and investigative agency offices we spoke with stated that it is difficult to afford victims who do not live in the United States their rights to be notified of and to participate in court proceedings. FBI noted that some foreign governments place restrictions on victims' receipt of mail from the United States government. To address this challenge, federal prosecutors and investigative agents coordinate with FBI Legal Attachés, DOJ's Office of International Affairs, and State Department officials located in U.S. embassies and consulates to facilitate notification.[34] In addition, federal courts have used teleconferencing to enable victims who do not reside in the United States, or who live in the United States but may not be able to travel to the court, the opportunity to participate in court proceedings related to their cases.

Challenges Affording Rights Due to Increased Workload of USAO Victim-Witness Staff

According to EOUSA officials and victim-witness professionals who responded to our survey, enactment of the CVRA led DOJ to a 60 percent increase in the number of possible notifications a victim could receive regarding his or her case. USAO victim-witness staff reported experiencing:

- **additional work hours—an average of 6 per week—in order to comply**
- **with CVRA requirements, specifically those related to notification;**[35]
- **an increased workload due to additional clerical duties related to notification;**
- **a great increase in the percentage of time spent preparing and sending notifications to victims and tracking down victims' contact information;**
- **a great increase in the percentage of time spent responding to victims' questions or concerns about the case; and**
- **a moderate or great increase in the percentage of time spent providing other types of assistance included in our survey, such as referring victims for services and accompanying victims to court proceedings, since the CVRA's enactment.**

DOJ has taken steps to alleviate the workload of victim-witness professionals. First, EOUSA developed a Memorandum of Understanding with AOUSC to link the courts' Case Management/Electronic Case Filing system (CM/ECF) with VNS,[36] thus eliminating the need to manually transfer schedule information from one system to another.[37] As of August 2008, EOUSA and AOUSC were conducting pilots in two judicial districts to test the link between VNS and CM/ECF. The final decision as to whether to utilize the linked systems will be up to individual courts. Second, EOUSA made funds available to 41 of the 93 USAOs to hire a contractor to assist with notification responsibilities. The funds were awarded based on the average number of cases and victims per victim- witness personnel, as well as the total number of approved VNS notifications. Based on our analysis of the districts that received funds, we determined that resources went to 20 of the USAOs with the highest ratio of cases per victim-witness personnel, 16 of the USAOs with a ratio that fell within the middle range, and 5 of the USAOs with the lowest ratio.[38]

Challenges Providing Notification and Participation Rights to Victims Due to Scheduling of Proceedings

The short period of time over which pretrial proceedings (such as arraignments and detention hearings[39]) are scheduled and take place, along with unexpected changes in the schedule of court proceedings in general, make it difficult to provide timely notice to victims and afford them their rights to participate in proceedings. According to the investigative agents, USAO staff, and one magistrate judge with whom we met, a detention hearing typically takes place within a few days of an arrest (as generally required by federal law), and in certain situations, can occur within hours of an arrest. In addition, as shown in figure 2, victim-witness professionals who responded to our survey also identified challenges in providing victims timely notice of pretrial hearings, particularly detention and plea hearings.

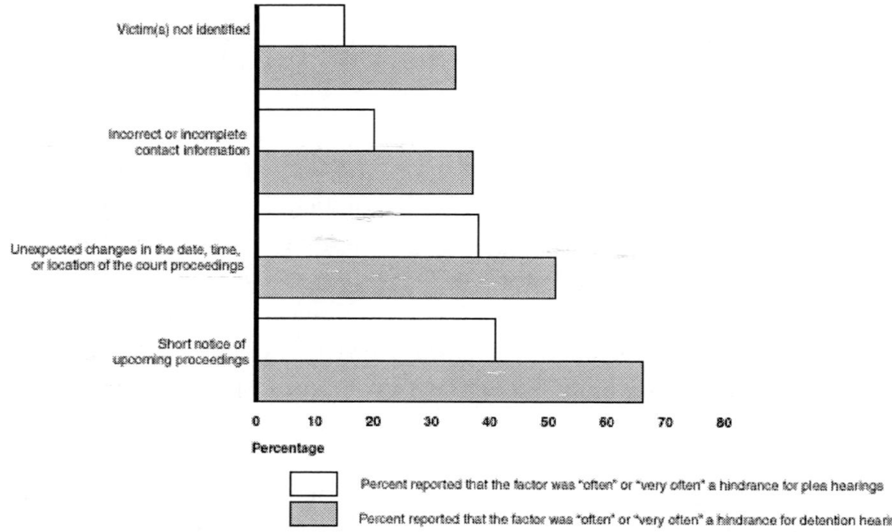

Figure 2. Extent to which Factors Often or Very Often Hindered Victim-Witness Professionals' Ability to Send Timely Notice to Victims of Pretrial Proceedings
Source: GAO analysis of victim-witness professional survey responses.

We also reviewed all notification letters sent to victims by three large, three mid-sized, and three small USAOs during the months of February, March, and April of 2008 to measure the timeliness of notification efforts.[40] The 106 victims who responded to our survey question regarding timeliness of notifications reported that, on average, they needed 16 days advance notice to be able to attend a proceeding. While DOJ provided more than 16 days advance notice of the proceeding for most of the letters we reviewed, this was not generally the case for pretrial proceedings. Specifically, the arraignment, detention, and initial appearance letters we reviewed were typically not sent in advance of the proceeding. In addition, the plea hearing letters we reviewed were sent a median of 5.5 days prior to when the proceeding was scheduled to take place. To address the challenge of notifying victims of pretrial proceedings in a timely manner, the USAO staff we met with said they attempt to contact victims by phone to inform them of when pretrial hearings will take place, as opposed to contacting victims by mail which may not arrive soon enough. Prosecutors also may request a delay in detention hearings to provide additional time for victim notification, and some of the judges with whom we spoke stated that they may consider the victim's schedule when setting court proceeding dates.

Challenges in Affording Participation and Notification Rights When There Are Diverging Interests between the Prosecution and Victims

According to USAO staff, district judges, and EOUSA officials we spoke with, it may be in the interest of a successful prosecution that a victim who intends to testify be excluded from trial, so as not to give the jury the impression that the victim's testimony was influenced by the testimony of the other witnesses. The Attorney General Guidelines state that if the prosecution prefers that the victim not attend the trial, the prosecutor should consider explaining the reasons to the victim in an effort to obtain voluntary compliance. In addition, in order to avoid the perception that a victim's testimony was influenced by other testimony, prosecutors may change the order in which they call their witnesses so that the victim testifies first. However, the prosecutors may still encounter this perception in cases where they call the victim back to the stand after others have testified.

Also, according to DOJ officials, it is not always in the interests of a successful prosecution for victims to be notified of and attend a plea hearing for a cooperating defendant who agrees to testify against or provide information about other defendants in the case in exchange for a lesser sentence because public knowledge of the defendant's cooperation could compromise the prosecutor's efforts in both current and future cases, as well as bring harm to the defendant and his or her family and associates. DOJ officials stated that this issue occurs frequently in gang- related prosecutions, where for instance, the victim is a member of the defendant's rival gang, but may occur in organized crime, sexual molestation, and other cases as well. EOUSA officials stated that some districts currently protect cooperating defendants and ensure investigation efforts are not hindered by closing proceedings or postponing the court's acceptance of the plea agreement. However, DOJ officials stated that closing proceedings may be impractical because the department's policy requires the express authorization of the Deputy Attorney General before a prosecutor may seek such closure. In addition, they stated that federal judges are frequently reluctant to close proceedings, as there is a general presumption in favor of keeping court proceedings open to the public. Hence, in DOJ's written responses to questions following a 2006 congressional hearing on the implementation of the CVRA, the department proposed that Congress revise the CVRA to allow for an exception to a victim's right to notification, such that notice should not be provided to victims if it "may endanger the safety of any person or compromise an ongoing investigation."[41] Currently, the CVRA only allows for this exception with regard to notification of release if it endangers the safety of any person. However, the victim advocates we spoke with expressed concerns with DOJ's proposed revision to the CVRA. Specifically, they stated that the language is overly broad and that exempting DOJ from the CVRA notification requirement in instances where notification "may" endanger a person or be perceived to compromise an investigation creates a potentially expansive opt-out provision in the law. They stated that any policy or revisions to the law need to be framed much more narrowly to pertain to specific situations and contain explicit standards, such as "clear and convincing evidence" that an individual would be endangered. In addition, victim advocates we spoke with stated that there may be preferable alternatives to revising the law, such as the methods that DOJ currently employs to protect cooperating defendants. One victim advocate stated that closing proceedings is preferable because a request by any party to close proceedings requires a hearing and therefore allows DOJ to present its reasons for doing so and opposing parties to raise challenges, if any. In addition, the advocate stated that the parties' arguments and basis for the decision would be documented on the court record.

Complaint Process and Victims' Ability to File Motions are Intended to Ensure Adherence to CVRA, but Some Victims are not Aware of these Enforcement Mechanisms and the Complaint Process Could Be Restructured to Ensure Independence

As directed by the CVRA, DOJ established a designated authority—the Victims' Rights Ombudsman—to receive and investigate complaints regarding employee compliance with the CVRA. Few victims have filed written complaints since the enactment of the CVRA, and the majority of victims who responded to our survey noted that they were unaware that the complaint process existed. In addition, the lack of independence in the structure of the complaint review process compromises the impartiality of the individuals investigating the complaints, which may generate bias or give the perception that there is bias in decisions regarding whether DOJ employees complied with the provisions of the CVRA pertaining to the treatment of crime victims. Also, inconsistent with internal VRO guidelines, complaint investigators were not consistently contacting victims as part of their investigations; however, the VRO told us that she has made efforts to address this issue. The other mechanism established by the CVRA to help ensure victims are afforded their rights—allowing victims to file motions and petitions for writs of mandamus to assert their rights in court—has also been used infrequently. Similar to the complaint process, the majority of victims who responded to our survey were not aware of their ability to assert their rights in court. In addition, while some appellate judges with whom we spoke expressed concern with the CVRA's requirement for petitions for writs of mandamus to be decided within 72 hours, efforts have been made by the courts to meet this requirement. Finally, AOUSC has reported to Congress information relating to instances in which CVRA rights were asserted in court and the relief requested was denied, as required by the law.

Few Victims have Filed Complaints Regarding their CVRA Rights, and Many Victims who Responded to our Survey Reported not being Aware of their Ability to do so

Of the more than 750,000 federal crime victims who, as of September 2008, were identified in DOJ's Victim Notification System as having active cases, the Victims' Rights Ombudsman—DOJ's designated authority to receive and investigate federal crime victim complaints regarding employee compliance to the CVRA—received 144 written complaints from December 2005 to April 2008, 141 of which we reviewed.[42] The VRO closed 130 of these complaints following a preliminary investigation for a number of reasons, including:

- **Statute of limitations: The alleged misconduct occurred prior to the enactment of the CVRA, or the complaint was not submitted within 60 days of the victim's knowledge of a violation and less than 1 year after the actual violation.[43]**
- **Jurisdiction: The complaint was filed by a defendant (who is not afforded rights under the CVRA)[44] or against private citizens, members of the judiciary, or**

against federal employees working in agencies other than the Department of Justice (who are not subject to the CVRA's complaint process). The VRO does not have authority to recommend training or disciplinary sanctions against these employees.

- **Not a federal crime victim: The complaint was filed by an individual who was unable to establish that he or she was a "crime victim" in a federal case, as defined by the Attorney General Guidelines.[45] The VRO operates under the Attorney General Guidelines, which provide that the CVRA applies to victims of a federal offense if the offense is charged in a federal court.**
- **State or local offense: The complaint was filed against state or local law enforcement officials.[46]**

Figure 3 displays why the 130 crime victims' complaints were closed.

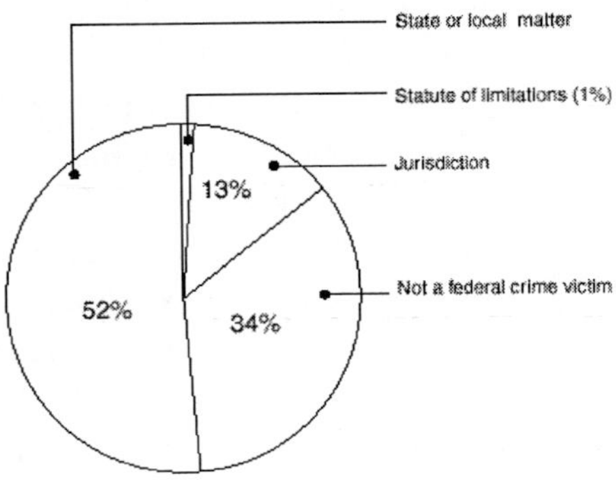

Figure 3: Reasons Why the VRO Closed 130 Complaints
Source: GAO analysis of letters sent by the Victims' Rights Ombudsman regarding closed complaints.

The VRO determined that the remaining 11 submitted complaints we reviewed warranted further investigation because they were filed by federal crime victims, as defined by the Attorney General Guidelines, submitted in accordance with time frames established by DOJ regulations,[47] and within the VRO's jurisdiction. (See app. III for a summary of these complaints.) Ten complaints were investigated by USAO employees located in the same office as the subjects of the complaints, and 1 was investigated by an employee within a U.S. Marshals Service field office. Investigators provided the VRO with the results of their investigations, and the VRO determined that in no instance did a DOJ employee or office fail to comply with the provisions of the law pertaining to the treatment of these federal crime victims. In this chapter, we will not be making a judgment on the reasonableness of the VRO's rationale for dismissing these complaints because we did not conduct an independent investigation of each complaint.

A number of factors likely contributed to the low number of complaints filed by federal crime victims against DOJ employees. First, DOJ officials believe few victims have filed complaints because victims are generally satisfied with DOJ's efforts to afford them their rights. Second, USAO officials we spoke with have made efforts to resolve complaints directly before they reached a point where a victim would file a formal complaint with the VRO. Third, lack of victim awareness about the complaint process may also explain why so few federal crime victims filed complaints. The CVRA does not require DOJ to inform victims about the complaint process. However, the VRO's internal guidelines for handling victims' complaints suggest that DOJ components should be taking reasonable steps to provide notice to victims of the complaint process through an office Web site or other means likely to accomplish actual notification to all victims. Officials have taken actions to inform victims about the complaint process using various methods:

- **During the investigative stage of the case, FBI and DEA officials told us that they provide victims with brochures that list their eight CVRA rights and provide information on the complaint process, including directions for filing a complaint. ATF provides victims with an informational brochure, but does not include information about the complaint process.**
- **EOUSA and the VRO have developed victim brochures in English and Spanish, which, according to DOJ officials, are mailed to victims after charges have been filed in a case. The brochure includes information about each of the eight CVRA rights and directs victims to contact their local USAO office if they believe a DOJ employee failed to provide them with one or more of their CVRA rights.**
- **Other DOJ divisions have created brochures that include information on how to file a complaint. The Criminal Division provides victims with a brochure that mentions the complaint process. The Antitrust Division told us that they e-mail victims, most of whom are organizations and state and federal agencies, a link to the division's online Victim Witness Handbook. This handbook provides information to victims on the complaint process as well as a link to the VRO's Web site. The Bureau of Prisons and the Civil Division developed pages on their Web sites explaining Victims' Rights Complaint procedures. The Bureau of Prisons posted to its Web site the CVRA rights and provided links to complaint forms for complaints alleging failure of a DOJ employee to provide rights to a crime victim under the CVRA. The Civil Division provided a link directly to the VRO Web site. The Tax Division and the Environmental and Natural Resources Division do not have their own document to inform victims of their rights under the CVRA, since they generally do not prosecute cases involving victims who are covered under this act. If these divisions happen to prosecute a case that involves victims, they provide victim brochures created by EOUSA, which mention the complaint process.**
- **The VRO stated that she has also met with representatives of victim advocacy groups to exchange ideas on effective programs, and participated throughout the country in training sessions for victim-witness coordinators, prosecutors, and agents.**
- **The VRO has created a Web page that includes downloadable English and Spanish complaint forms within the EOUSA Web site. The Web page provides instructions on how and where to file complaints; however the link to this Web page is not listed in the brochure developed by EOUSA.**

While DOJ has several mechanisms in place to inform victims about the complaint process, these mechanisms may not be achieving actual notification, given that 129 of the 248 victims who responded to our survey question regarding the complaint process stated that they were not aware that they could file a written complaint against a DOJ employee regarding their rights, and 51 victims could not recall if they were aware.[48]

Victims are required to submit their complaint in writing on a standard complaint form. According to the VRO, she has worked to ensure that all USAOs have information about her office on their Web sites, in both English and Spanish. However, based on our review, as of June 2008, 36 of the 93 USAO Web sites provided a downloadable English version of the complaint forms, and 21 USAO Web sites provided the Spanish version of the forms. The VRO noted that victims can also obtain hard copies of the complaint form from the victim-witness staff or points of contact located in the USAOs or other DOJ components, as well as from the VRO.

USAO victim-witness personnel, who have the most direct interaction with victims, are not required to personally inform victims about the complaint process. According to EOUSA officials, it would be awkward for victim- witness personnel to inform all victims about the complaint process. Specifically, these officials stated that victim-witness personnel are trying to develop a trusting relationship with the victim, and informing victims about the possibility that DOJ officials may violate their rights could hinder their relationship. Further, EOUSA officials noted that it is not feasible for victim-witness personnel to verbally inform all victims of the complaint process in large-victim cases. The VRO stated that she primarily relies on victim-witness personnel in the USAOs to exercise their best judgment about how and when to inform victims about the complaint process. Of the 174 victim-witness professionals who responded to our survey, 5 percent reported that they personally inform all victims about the complaint process. Forty percent of victim-witness personnel stated that they have personally informed victims about the complaint process only when victims had raised concerns about the provision of their CVRA rights. Fifty-seven percent of the victim-witness personnel reported that they have not personally informed any victims about the complaint process, primarily because they believe the victims' brochure and Web site are sufficient.[49] However, EOUSA officials stated that they are uncertain whether all USAOs are providing all victims with the brochures and, when brochures are provided, they are uncertain whether victims actually read them.

While DOJ has made efforts to inform victims about the complaint process, there are opportunities to increase victim awareness—such as through greater use of Web sites, brochures, and when appropriate, personal notification. The complaint process generally must be initiated by victims or their representatives. If victims are not aware of it, the complaint process becomes an ineffective method for ensuring that responsible officials are complying with CVRA requirements, and DOJ will not be able to effectively ensure that corrective actions are taken against those officials who do not comply with the law.

Lack of Independence among Investigators Could Inhibit DOJ's Ability to Conduct Impartial Investigations of Victim Complaints

The characteristics of DOJ's victim complaint investigation process differ from professional standards of practice—namely, independence and impartiality—that have been adopted by ombudsman associations and state victims' rights enforcement offices. The American Bar Association Standards for the Establishment and Operation of Ombuds Offices state that a key indicator of independence is whether anyone subject to the ombudsman's jurisdiction can (1) control or limit the ombudsman's performance of assigned duties, (2) eliminate the office, (3) remove the ombudsman for other than cause, or (4) reduce the office's budget or resources for retaliatory purposes. Similarly, the U.S. Ombudsman Association advocates that the ombudsman should be appointed by an entity not subject to the ombudsman's jurisdiction and which does not have operational or administrative authority over the programs or agencies that are subject to the ombudsman's jurisdiction. These standards maintain that independence and impartiality are important when addressing complaints because they establish confidence that the process is fair and credible. According to these standards, the VRO— though located in EOUSA, which provides administrative support and policy guidance to the U.S. Attorneys Offices—is nevertheless relatively independent from the DOJ components and offices that are likely to be the subjects of victims' complaints. However, the individuals who investigate victim complaints are not independent of the offices that they may investigate. Specifically, complaint investigators are typically located in the same offices that they are responsible for investigating and are thus located in the same offices with the individuals who are cited in the complaints. In addition, two of the five complaint investigators we spoke with had investigated their superiors. Moreover, complaint investigators may be in positions where they themselves could potentially be the subject of a victim complaint.

EOUSA officials stated that funding limitations as well as the desire to resolve complaints locally led to DOJ's decision to allow complaint investigators to be located in the same office with those whom they are investigating. According to EOUSA officials, they could only fund one full- time position to carry out complaint investigation duties. Further, officials told us that, in their opinion, the VRO's use of local managers to investigate complaints, as opposed to individuals in a central office, enables the VRO to resolve the complaint as quickly as possible for the victim.[50] However, the lack of independence of the complaint investigators raises questions about their impartiality and hence their ability to conduct credible, unbiased investigations. For example, according to an official who investigated 7 of the 11 federal crime victim complaints we reviewed, he felt awkward investigating his colleagues and found it difficult to remain objective while conducting the investigation since he has grown to respect his colleagues' judgment and decision-making capabilities over the years. However, other complaint investigators, including one who investigated his superior, did not think the current structure of the complaint investigation process compromised his impartiality. One stated that had he identified misconduct and disciplinary action was warranted for the superior whom he investigated, he would have referred the issue to the U.S. Attorney. In this investigation, however, the investigator determined the complaint should be closed after learning, through discussions with the subject of the complaint, that the complainant was satisfied.

The VRO told us that for the most part, officials are not put in a situation where they are called upon to investigate a superior. However, as stated previously, two of the five individuals who investigated the federal victim complaints we reviewed investigated their superiors. Although the VRO stated that DOJ has a process for addressing conflicts of interest among complaint investigators, the underlying theme of existing professional ombudsman standards is that an ombudsman should have both actual and apparent independence from individuals who may be the subject of a complaint. Therefore, although actual conflicts of interest among complaint investigators may be addressed by DOJ's internal procedures, the appearance of a conflict of interest remains given that investigators are located in the offices they are responsible for investigating.

While DOJ is not required to comply with ombudsman standards, the standards can serve as a guideline for implementing the core principles of an effective ombudsman. In addition, it is common practice among other entities that investigate external complaints against employees—including many of the state victims' rights offices that we reviewed—to adhere to the principles of independence and impartiality by, for example, ensuring that complaint investigators are located in separate departments or branches of government from those officials they investigate. For example, DOJ's Office for Professional Responsibility, which addresses complaints made by external parties against department employees, does not allow investigators to be located in the same office with the subject of the complaint.[51] However, for complaints filed by one department employee against another, the Office of Professional Responsibility allows a supervisor who is located in the same office with the subject of the complaint to determine the seriousness of the complaint and whether it should be referred to the Office of Professional Responsibility for further investigation. State victims' rights enforcement offices that we reviewed generally do not use officials who may be located in the same office with the subject of the complaint to conduct investigations. We reviewed two separate studies of state victims' rights enforcement offices that are responsible for addressing victim complaints against state officials.[52] Of the eight offices included in these studies,[53] three are structured such that investigators are not located in the same office with the state officials who are the subjects of the victims' complaints, whereas officials in three other offices may receive complaints against colleagues, but there are procedures in place to prohibit colleagues from actually investigating one another. These practices generally avoid a conflict of interest between the investigator and the individual under investigation. Officials in the other two offices may receive and investigate complaints regarding their own staff or someone they know. However, in these offices, complaints are investigated by the head of the state victim enforcement office.

When asked about the feasibility of having individuals who are not located in the same office with the subject of the complaint conduct investigations, EOUSA officials raised two concerns. First, they stated that DOJ did not make funding available to hire additional staff within the VRO's office to conduct investigations, thus the need to assign complaint investigations as a collateral duty for existing DOJ staff. Second, they stated that it would be difficult to resolve the complaint quickly to the victim's satisfaction if the investigator were not located in the same office with the subject of the complaint. Resource constraints are an important factor in determining an appropriate structure for the victim complaint review process; however, there may be low-cost adjustments available to DOJ that could help ensure both the independence and impartiality of complaint investigators. For example, it may be possible for DOJ to assign those who currently investigate complaints to investigate individuals in other offices, instead of having them review complaints against colleagues and superiors located in the same office. Also, the CVRA states that the complaint process is intended to ensure that responsible officials comply with federal law regarding the treatment of crime victims. Thus, while it is reasonable for DOJ to seek the victim's satisfaction when addressing the complaint, it is also important for DOJ to ensure that—regardless of the victim's satisfaction—the complaint investigation process is structured in such a way that any violation of CVRA rights would be identified. Therefore, based on the ombudsman standards and the practices of other offices that perform similar functions, it is important for the structure of the complaint process to ensure the independence of complaint investigators in order to maintain impartial investigations, as well as to maintain the appearance of impartiality during investigations, to not only ensure that they are being fair, but to also uphold the credibility of the complaint process. If a DOJ employee has violated a victim's rights, and the complaint investigation process is biased, then the Victims' Rights Ombudsman risks not making an informed determination about the complaint. Further, such a situation would impede the subjects of complaints from receiving appropriate training or disciplinary sanctions, when necessary, in order to prevent the violation from occurring again.

Complaint Investigators Had Generally Not Contacted Victims during the Investigation Process as Required, but the VRO Is Taking Action to Address this Issue

DOJ officials who investigated federal crime victim complaints were not consistently following internal procedures that direct them to speak with victims during an investigation, which could have affected the comprehensiveness of their investigation by excluding the victims' perspectives. However, the VRO is taking steps to address this issue. From December 2005 to April 2008, three of the four USAO officials who investigated complaints submitted by federal crime victims did not speak with the victim during the course of the investigation, as directed by VRO internal guidelines for handling complaint investigations. In one instance, the subject of the complaint contacted the victim to resolve the complaint, and then relayed his discussion with the victim to the investigator. The investigator recommended to the VRO that, since the victim was satisfied, the complaint should be closed prior to completing the investigation to determine whether a violation occurred. The VRO agreed to close the complaint without further action and later explained to us that having the subject of the complaint contact the victim and make efforts to obtain the victim's satisfaction was preferable to awaiting the completion of the complaint investigation, which may not have resulted in immediate relief being given to the victim. However, as stated previously in this chapter, while it is reasonable for DOJ to seek the victim's satisfaction, it is important that the complaint investigation be conducted in such a way as to ensure that any violation of victims' CVRA rights is identified, regardless of the victim's satisfaction.

The VRO guidelines direct complaint investigators to contact victims in an effort to resolve the complaint reasonably and to the victim's satisfaction. Similarly, 7 of the 8 state victims' rights enforcement offices whose procedures we reviewed direct investigators to speak with victims during the course of an investigation. It is also important for investigators to consistently contact victims so they may provide the VRO with the information necessary to determine the outcome of the complaint, especially when the complaint forms do not include narrative explaining why the victims thought their rights were violated, as was the case in 3 of the 11 federal victim complaints we reviewed. Therefore, contacting the victim would have been a reasonable approach for the investigator to independently obtain this information.

Officials investigating complaints by victims provided reasons for not contacting victims. For example, one investigator stated that he did not contact the victim because he could make his determination regarding the victim's complaint that her right to full and timely restitution was violated by reading the case file and the restitution order. After reviewing this information, he determined that no further information needed to be collected and that no violation had occurred on the part of the USAO. A second official, who investigated seven complaints, stated that he would only contact victims if his initial communications with the subject of the complaint left him uneasy or if unanswered questions remained about the complaint.

The VRO noted that between April 2008 and September 2008 she received eight additional complaints submitted by federal crime victims. In response to our inquiries as to whether complaint investigators were contacting victims, she asked each of the investigators that they personally contact the victims upon receipt of the complaint, after which they may determine, with the victim's consent, that it would be appropriate for other staff, such as victim-witness personnel or prosecutors, to speak with the victim to resolve the complaint. The VRO's continued emphasis on investigators contacting victims as part of their investigations will help ensure that investigators are collecting needed information for the VRO to make an informed decision regarding the complaint.

Few Victims Have Asserted CVRA Rights in Court, and Many Victims Who Responded to Our Survey Reported Not Being Aware of Their Ability to Do So

Among the hundreds of thousands of federal court cases filed in the U.S. district courts in the nearly 4-year period since the CVRA was enacted and June 30, 2008, we found 43 instances in which victims, or victims' attorneys or prosecutors on behalf of victims, asserted CVRA rights by filing a motion—either verbally or in writing—with the district court.[54] We also found 20 petitions for writs of mandamus that were filed with the appellate courts, the majority of which were in response to motions previously denied in the district court. Table 5 summarizes the number of times CVRA rights were asserted in the district and appellate courts and how the courts ruled in those instances. Appendix IV includes summaries of all cases we identified in which a court issued a decision based on the CVRA.

Victim attorneys and federal judicial officials gave several potential reasons for the low number of victim motions, including victims being satisfied with how they were treated and victims either being intimidated by the judicial process or too traumatized by the crime to assert their rights in court. However, the most frequently cited reason for the low number of motions was victims' lack of awareness of this enforcement mechanism. The results from our victim survey provide some support for this assertion. Of the 236 victims who responded to our survey question regarding victim motions, 134 reported that they were not aware of their ability to file a motion to enforce their rights in district court, and 48 victims did not recall whether they were aware of it.[55] DOJ generally does not inform victims of their ability to file a motion or petition for a writ of mandamus. This information is not included in the department's brochures and notification letters. It is also not included in the vast majority of USAO Web sites—6 of the 93 USAO Web sites mention this enforcement mechanism, but typically only when the entire text of the CVRA has been posted. Furthermore, in our survey of USAO victim-witness professionals, we asked whether they have personally informed victims of their ability to file a motion to assert their CVRA rights. In response, 42 percent reported that they had not informed any victims and 48 percent reported that they informed only those who raised concerns. EOUSA officials expressed concerns with the potential for providing victims with legal advice if USAO staff were to personally inform victims of their ability to assert CVRA rights in court. Specifically, officials anticipated that victims would request legal advice from prosecutors after being informed of this ability. If questions arise, however, USAO staff could inform victims, as required by the CVRA, that they can seek the advice of an attorney with respect to their rights.

Table 5. Number of Times CVRA Rights Were Asserted in District Courts and Courts of Appeals and How the Courts Ruled in Those Instances, as of June 30, 2008

Court ruling					
	Granted	Denied	Granted in part	Decision not based on the CVRA	Total
Number of motions (written and verbal) filed in district court[a]	**11**[b]	**26**	**1**	**5**	**43**
• Filed by victim or victim's attorney	3	20		2	25
	Granted	Denied	Granted in part	Decision not based on the CVRA	Total
•Filed by prosecutor on victim's behalf	8	6	1	3	18
Number of petitions for writs of mandamus filed in the court of appeals[c]	**1**	**17**	**1**	**1**	**20**

Source: GAO analysis of court cases in which the CVRA was raised.

[a]The number of motions includes four civil claims filed under the CVRA, one motion filed by the defendant in the case, and instances in which victims asserted CVRA rights in response to a motion or other action by another party. Also, three of the motions were filed not in district courts, but in the District of Columbia Superior Court, the local trial court for the District of Columbia.

[b]The victims' motion in United States v. Moussaoui was granted by the U.S. District Court for the Eastern District of Virginia; however, the government appealed the decision and it was reversed by the U.S. Court of Appeals for the Fourth Circuit. The victims did not rely on the CVRA in their arguments at the appellate level.

[c]The number of petitions for writs of mandamus includes eight petitions that did not arise out of criminal prosecutions in district courts.

While the law does not designate the responsibility to inform victims of their ability to assert CVRA rights to either DOJ or the courts, it does assign DOJ most of the other notification responsibilities, including informing victims of their eight CVRA rights and their ability to seek the advice of an attorney. Moreover, the Attorney General Guidelines state that responsible officials should provide information to victims about their role in the criminal justice process, which could encompass their ability to assert their rights in court. DOJ is already required to carry out these responsibilities without providing legal advice to victims and could do the same when informing victims of their ability to assert CVRA rights in court. In contrast to DOJ, it is impractical for the courts to effectively inform victims of their ability to file motions and petition for writs of mandamus. The courts currently do not have contact information for all victims and are not administratively equipped to inform victims of the CVRA's provisions, in the opinion of Federal Judicial Center officials. In addition, the courts do not interact with victims as early in the criminal justice process as DOJ. Judges stated that victims are rarely present at court proceedings other than sentencing hearings, which occur toward the end of the criminal justice process. Therefore, DOJ is in a better position to inform victims of their ability to assert CVRA rights in court either personally or through the same brochures and initial notification letters that inform victims of their eight CVRA rights. Victims cannot independently enforce their rights in court if they are not aware of their ability to do so. Considering that victims or their attorneys generally initiate such efforts, lack of awareness of their ability to file motions and petition for writs of mandamus in court will reduce the effectiveness of this enforcement mechanism in ensuring adherence to victims' rights and addressing any violations. Counsel for Legal Initiatives for EOUSA told us that the absence of a means to inform victims of their ability to file a motion is a legitimate concern and it is reasonable for DOJ to make some efforts to do this.

Some Judges Have Expressed Concerns Regarding the 72-Hour Requirement for Deciding Mandamus Petitions, but Courts Have Made Efforts to Help Ensure that the Requirement Is Met

We spoke with three appellate judges who presided over 4 of the 20 petitions for writ of mandamus that we reviewed (one judge presided over 2 cases). While all three of the appellate judges expressed concerns about the CVRA's requirement for petitions for writs of mandamus to be decided within 72 hours of filing, none indicated that the courts could not meet it under the present circumstances, in which only a small number of petitions are filed. In addition, some U.S. courts of appeals have established rules and procedures to help address the challenges with meeting the requirement. Nonetheless, all three of the appellate judges and several victim attorneys we spoke with stated that meeting the 72-hour requirement is difficult. The judges and others said that it may not provide enough time to decide on complex issues, produce well-thought-out opinions, and allow parties to respond to the petition. Furthermore, federal judiciary officials stated that the judiciary opposes all such time- limit requirements because, among other reasons, they can be detrimental to the handling of other vital matters before the court. Specifically, the requirements give certain cases priority over others that could be deemed to be of equal or greater importance, such as death penalty cases. However, the Chief of the Rules Committee Support Office noted that, to his knowledge,[56] the CVRA's 72-hour requirement has not prevented the courts from deciding any vital matters to date. Federal judicial officials stated that concerns regarding the requirement are largely theoretical at this point in time because of the small number of cases, but could potentially have negative consequences if the number increases. One of the three appellate court clerks we spoke with also made a similar point. AOUSC and FJC officials, as well as one appellate judge, also stated that it is unclear how to compute time for the 72-hour requirement. They stated that court deadlines are typically specified in days and that there is currently no guidance regarding when the clock starts ticking on the 72- hour requirement, or whether it applies to business or calendar days. Two of the three appellate judges and one of the three appellate court clerks we spoke with expressed concerns about petitions received on Fridays. The clerk stated that it is challenging to assemble a panel of judges and provide them with the necessary case documents during the weekend. To help address some of these concerns, the Judicial Conference Advisory Committee on Appellate Rules proposed an amendment to the Federal Rules of Appellate Procedure.[57]

We are aware of one case where the court did not meet the 72-hour requirement.[58] The case was heard in the U.S. Court of Appeals for the Ninth Circuit in 2006 and, according to one of the judges on the panel that reviewed the petition, the court was not aware of the requirement at the time. In the case's published decision, the court discussed its failure to consider the victim's petition for a writ of mandamus within the CVRA's time limits and apologized to the victim for the delay.[59] As a result of the case, the U.S. Court of Appeals for the Ninth Circuit enacted a local rule to help ensure that it complies with the 72-hour requirement in future cases. The local rule requires the petitioner to clearly label CVRA petitions for writs of mandamus and to call the clerk's office in advance to inform them that a petition will be filed. In addition, according to a judge in the Ninth Circuit, that court treats CVRA petitions for writs of mandamus as emergency motions, such that a rotating panel of judges is available to immediately review these petitions. He stated that the panel also has staff attorneys on hand to do research on the case, if necessary. U.S. courts of appeals in other circuits have also adopted similar rules and procedures to help ensure that the courts meet the 72-hour requirement. For instance, the U.S. Court of Appeals for the Fourth Circuit enacted a local rule and the U.S. Court of Appeals for the Third Circuit issued a standing order, both similar to the Ninth Circuit rule. In addition, according to the Clerk of the Court, the U.S. Court of Appeals for the District of Columbia Circuit also treats CVRA petitions for writs of mandamus as emergency motions.

AOUSC Has Reported to Congress Information Relating to Instances in which CVRA Rights Were Asserted in Court and the Relief Requested Was Denied, as Required

The CVRA requires AOUSC to annually report instances in which a CVRA right was asserted in a criminal case and the relief requested was denied. AOUSC is required to report both the number of denials and the reason for the denials. In addition, it is required to report the number of times a petition for writ of mandamus is filed with the court of appeals and the result of the petition. To meet this reporting requirement, AOUSC issued annual memoranda to all judges and clerks in the district and appellate courts requiring them to submit information on these instances. The 2004 to 2006 memos directly cite the language in the CVRA when outlining the reporting requirement. In addition, the 2006 memo required the courts to submit hearing transcripts if CVRA rights were asserted orally and the denial occurred without a written order. It also required court clerks to inform AOUSC if there were no cases to report. AOUSC officials stated that they review the cases submitted by the courts and call them to discuss if there are any questions. They added that they also contact the courts if AOUSC does not receive either a submission or a statement indicating that there were no cases to report by the deadline specified in its memo. According to AOUSC officials, the office does not conduct its own searches to identify cases that potentially may fall under the CVRA's reporting requirement but were not submitted by the courts. They stated that the responsibility to identify and submit applicable cases rests with the individual courts because it would not be feasible for AOUSC to search through the thousands of criminal cases that are prosecuted in the courts every year. According to the Judicial Business of the United States Courts' 2007 Annual Report of the Director, approximately 81,500 criminal cases were filed in the federal district and appellate courts for that fiscal year. In addition, AOUSC officials stated that they are dependent on the courts to identify and report unpublished orders and verbal denials of relief requested under the CVRA that occur without a written order because these could not necessarily be found through legal searches. Officials stated that AOUSC also coordinates with the National Crime Victims Law Institute, which compiles and summarizes cases that discuss or cite the CVRA, to help ensure that all reportable cases are identified. According to AOUSC officials, the NCVLI provides them with a list of cases that it believes should be included in the annual report to Congress. They added that if AOUSC discovers a case that potentially should have been submitted but was not, they would contact the court to discuss it.

A total of 20 cases were included in three AOUSC reports submitted to Congress for fiscal years 2005 to 2007. In our review of cases that discussed the CVRA, we identified three denials of victim motions under the CVRA that were not reported. Whether these cases should have been reported is not clear because there are different judicial interpretations of the CVRA language that requires the courts to report denials of "relief requested." Victims either asserted or invoked CVRA rights in all 3 of the cases. In the first case, the district court denied the prosecutor's motion to allow the victim to speak at the defendant's detention hearing but allowed the victim to submit a written victim impact statement.[60] When asked why this case was not submitted to AOUSC, a court official stated that the court had not denied the victim the right to be heard; rather, it had outlined the manner in which the victim could exercise this right. In the second case, the district court denied the victims' motion requesting that the court order DOJ to allow them to enter the United States to attend and participate in the defendant's sentencing hearing. As an alternative, the court allowed the victims to submit their views in writing and participate in the hearing via teleconference.[61] When asked why this case was not submitted, the judge stated that because the court fashioned an alternative means to accommodate the victim, the classification of the ruling is uncertain and may be considered to be denied in part and granted in part. In the third case, the district court denied the corporate victim's request to appear at a hearing to respond to the defendant's motion regarding whether the defense should be allowed to contact and interview the victim's employees.[62] When asked why this case was not submitted, a court official stated that although the victim was not allowed to appear, the victim was not denied the purpose for which the appearance was sought; that is, the court stated that the victim could still challenge in court any alleged contact with a represented employee. One judge, who denied one of the motions included in the fiscal year 2007 report to Congress, stated that clarification of the reporting requirement for situations where the specific relief requested was denied but not the right asserted under the CVRA would be beneficial. However, AOUSC officials stated that the 3 cases discussed above involve judicial interpretation of the statute and as such, determining whether they fall under the CVRA's reporting requirement would best be delegated to the individual courts. They added that if it is determined in the future that the courts are not submitting applicable cases because they are unclear about the requirement, AOUSC could issue additional guidance to clarify. Based on our compilation and review of CVRA-related cases, apart from the 3 cases in question, AOUSC has included all cases required under the statute in their reports to Congress for fiscal years 2005 to 2007.

DOJ Generally Has Not Evaluated Overall Department Performance Related to Victims' Rights, but Most Component Agencies Have Made Efforts to Evaluate Their Employees' Adherence with Victims' Rights Requirements

Although DOJ has a strategic objective in place focused on ensuring that victims' rights are provided, it has not developed performance measures to assess progress in meeting this objective. One component agency has a related performance measure in place; however, the measure does not demonstrate whether the agency has made progress in achieving the victims' rights objective. DOJ component agencies have collected data regarding the provision of victims' rights, but lack of timely and standard data collection and analysis limits the usefulness of the data in making meaningful assessments of overall performance. Most of the DOJ components with victim-related responsibilities have, however, incorporated references to the adherence to victims' rights into their employees' work plans and performance appraisals, as required by internal guidelines.

DOJ Has a Strategic Objective to Uphold Victims' Rights, but Has Not Developed Performance Measures to Assess Progress in Meeting this Objective

The DOJ Strategic Plan for Fiscal Years 2007-2012 includes a strategic objective to "uphold the rights and improve services to America's crime victims." Among the strategies listed to achieve that objective is to "increase participation of victims in the justice process." In addition, DOJ revised the Attorney General Guidelines for Victim and Witness Assistance, which includes actions that can be taken by DOJ component agencies to help ensure that victims are afforded their CVRA rights. The Government Performance and Results Act of 1993 (GPRA) requires that federal agencies produce annual performance measures to assess progress towards the objectives included in their strategic plans. In addition, standards for internal control in the federal government state that activities need to be established to monitor performance measures, and that controls aimed at both organizational and individual performance need to be implemented.[63] However, DOJ has not identified any agency- wide annual performance measures to assess progress towards its strategic objective to uphold victims' rights. DOJ's FY 2008 Performance Budget does include performance measures related to the funding of victims programs, but these measures focus primarily on services provided to federal victims—such as the ratio of victims who received services funded by the Crime Victims Fund to the total number of victimizations— but not the provision of rights.[64] There was a general consensus among the DOJ officials with whom we met that evaluating how effective the department has been at affording victims their CVRA rights is difficult, considering that most of the CVRA rights do not lend themselves to quantitative analysis. However, without performance measures, DOJ may not be able to effectively gauge its progress in upholding the rights afforded by the CVRA.

Although performance measures related to victims' rights do not exist at the department level, one DOJ component—the Office for Justice Programs (OJP)—has developed goals, objectives, and measures that are aligned with DOJ's strategic objective regarding victims' rights. While OJP does not directly carry out law enforcement activities, or have any direct role in providing victims their rights, DOJ's Strategic Plan tasks OJP with the responsibility to develop and implement strategies to increase victim participation.[65] In its fiscal year 2007-2012 strategic plan, OJP includes a strategic goal to "reduce the impact of crime and hold offenders accountable" and a related strategic objective to "increase participation of victims in the justice process." The performance measure OJP identified to assess progress in achieving that objective is the percent increase in the number of notifications sent to victims through the Victim Notification System. According to our analysis of VNS data provided by EOUSA, the total number of USAO VNS notifications more than doubled from fiscal year 2004, when CVRA was signed into law, through fiscal year 2007—from more than 2.7 million to nearly 7 million notifications. However, more victims being notified of additional case events does not necessarily mean there will be an increase in the number of victims participating in the criminal justice process, which is OJP's objective.

OJP uses EOUSA notification data as a proxy measure for victim participation; however, EOUSA has made efforts to collect some data—although limited—on actual victim attendance at court proceedings. Specifically, EOUSA requests—but does not require—that when USAO victim-witness professionals attend a court proceeding, they count the number of victims in attendance at the proceeding and enter the number into a spreadsheet. EOUSA then collects this information from victim- witness staff annually, and presents this information in an annual compliance report submitted to the Office for Victims of Crime (OVC). According to EOUSA, during fiscal years 2006 and 2007, the estimated number of victims nationwide who attended court proceedings along with victim-witness professionals was 14,000 and 12,000, respectively. Considering that victim-witness professionals do not consistently track victim attendance at court proceedings and are only tracking attendance at court proceedings that they themselves attend, EOUSA data on victim participation may not be very accurate, and therefore not useful in measuring progress towards OJP's objective. When asked about formalizing the tracking of victim participation, EOUSA officials expressed concern that requiring victim-witness professionals to systematically gather this information would overburden them, particularly the ones located in USAOs with heavy caseloads.

DOJ Components Have Collected Data Regarding the Provision of Victims' Rights, but Lack of Standard and Timely Data Collection and Analysis Limits DOJ's Ability to Make Meaningful Assessments of Performance

Similar to EOUSA, as required by the Attorney General Guidelines for Victim and Witness Assistance, most DOJ components have been collecting data and submitting annual reports to the Office for Victims of Crime outlining their compliance with the Attorney

General Guidelines' requirements regarding the provision of rights and services to victims. However, OVC has not analyzed this information since the CVRA was implemented. OVC has the statutory responsibility to monitor DOJ compliance with the Attorney General Guidelines for Victim and Witness Assistance.[66] According to the guidelines, responsible officials are required to submit an annual compliance report to OVC. OVC officials said that they have received compliance reports from all but three DOJ components since the guidelines were revised in 2005 to incorporate CVRA, but they have not analyzed the data or produced a report for the Attorney General. Internal control standards state that information should be made available on a timely basis in order to allow effective monitoring of activities and allow a prompt reaction. OVC officials said that they had lacked the resources to analyze and report the compliance information. However, in August 2008, OVC officials stated that they had received the necessary funding and were in the process of producing the first report summarizing DOJ components' efforts to afford victims' rights and services since the enactment of the CVRA. These officials expect the report to be issued by the end of 2008.

In addition to not analyzing and reporting on compliance data in a timely manner, OVC provides no standard format for compliance reports submitted by component agencies, thus limiting the usefulness of the data. In a letter to DOJ components requesting their annual compliance reports for fiscal year 2007, OVC acknowledged that there is no standard format. The letter included a list of general recommendations regarding the information that should be included in the component agencies' submissions, but components are not required to include them in their reports. As a result, the compliance reports submitted by the component agencies have varied content, making the measurement of overall DOJ compliance with the Attorney General Guidelines difficult. In its 2003-2004 Best Efforts Report, OVC noted that the variety of information included in the component agencies' best efforts reports resulted in a limited ability to compare information across DOJ. For example, some agencies submitted narrative reports describing programmatic development and best practices, while other agencies reported statistical information pertaining to victim notification with little or no narrative describing the work that was actually done. However, OVC did not make adjustments to its request for compliance data despite these concerns because, according to OVC officials, it may not be useful to collect the same type of information from each component because components have varying responsibilities related to crime victims. Although, there are similarities in victim responsibilities among certain components, such as those that do primarily investigative work like the FBI, ATF and DEA, which are responsible, among other things, for the initial identification of crime victims in a case. There are also similarities among the prosecutorial components, which are responsible, among other things, for affording victims the right to reasonably confer with the prosecutor. Therefore, these components could provide similar data to OVC regarding their efforts to afford victims their rights. We have previously reported that agencies should collect sufficiently complete, accurate, and consistent data in order to document performance and support decision making at various organizational levels.[67] Without standard reporting, OVC cannot analyze compliance information in such a way that allows for an indication of overall department compliance.

Not All DOJ Components with Victim-Related Responsibilities Have Incorporated References to Victims' Rights into Work Plans and Performance Appraisals for Certain Employees

The Attorney General Guidelines for Victim and Witness Assistance require that all components with victim-related responsibilities incorporate information on adherence with victims' rights requirements into the work plans and performance appraisals for appropriate employees. Performance appraisals and work plans are tools that are used to evaluate actual employee performance on the basis of objective, job- related criteria. Eight of the 14 relevant DOJ components have incorporated information on adherence with victims' rights requirements into the work plans and performance appraisals for all responsible employees, based on our review of performance appraisal documentation provided by DOJ.[68] The 3 investigative components and the U. S. Marshals Service (USMS) have not adhered to this requirement for their employees. EOUSA has adhered to this requirement for all but supervisory attorneys. Regarding the investigative components, according to DOJ, DEA, ATF, and USMS are in the process of incorporating references to adherence with victims' rights requirements into the investigators' performance appraisals and work plans. The FBI has not incorporated such references into its investigative agents' or victim specialists' performance appraisals and work plans, because, according to the Director of FBI's Office for Victims Assistance (OVA), this criterion is already included in the performance appraisals for special agents-in-charge—generally the highest ranking officials in FBI field offices. Nonetheless, the Attorney General Guidelines state that adherence with victims' rights should be incorporated into the work plans and performance appraisals for appropriate staff. Given that investigative agents are responsible for identifying federal crime victims, it is reasonable to consider them "appropriate" staff and hold them accountable for their victim-related responsibilities. In addition, victim specialists play a key role in helping to ensure victims receive needed services. According to FBI officials, the OVA has taken a number of steps to ensure compliance by victim specialists, including, among other things, revising the victim specialist position description to incorporate victim- related requirements and developing Victim Assistance Program and Practice Standards to require compliance with victims' rights and Attorney General Guidelines provisions. While these steps are beneficial, they do not provide criteria to evaluate employee performance with regard to victims' rights requirements. Without information regarding adherence to victims' rights in their work plans and performance appraisals, FBI investigative agents and victim specialists may not be aware of or held accountable for their CVRA responsibilities.

Both correctional components have incorporated victim-related responsibilities into the work plans of their staff. The victim-related responsibilities of officials at the Bureau of Prisons (BOP) and the U.S. Parole Commission (USPC) are to notify victims of their offender's status once they have been incarcerated. For BOP, this includes parole hearings and other decisions related to parole. USPC is responsible for notifying victims of hearings to determine whether the offender's supervised release should be revoked. Finally, six of the eight prosecutorial components within DOJ incorporated references to victim-related responsibilities in work plans and performance appraisals for all of their attorneys. The 2 other components—USAOs and the National Security Division—plan to take steps to do so, according to officials with whom we spoke. EOUSA has incorporated such references into the work plans and performance appraisals for all but the Supervisory Assistant U.S. Attorneys

(AUSA). According to the Assistant Director for EOUSA's Victim-Witness division, the work plans for these attorneys do not specifically include references to the Attorney General Guidelines because EOUSA believes Supervisory AUSAs know that adherence to the guidelines and directives are mandatory, and that they integrate these requirements into their day-to- day work. However, the Assistant Director also stated that EOUSA will modify the 2009 work plans for Supervisory AUSAs whose duties include direct or supervisory victim-related responsibilities to incorporate performance elements, including the Attorney General Guidelines. In DOJ's written comments on the draft report, the department stated that, as long as the USAO complies with the guidelines' requirement, it is within each office's discretion to adopt the work plan modifications to the extent that it deems appropriate. The National Security Division has two units that work with crime victims—the Counterterrorism Section (CTS) and the Office of Justice for Victims of Overseas Terrorism (OVT), according to the Director of OVT. While the work plan for the Chief of CTS contains references to victim-related responsibilities, those for trial attorneys in CTS, as well as OVT staff, do not. According to the Director of OVT, the National Security Division, established in 2006, is a relatively new organization, and as such, work plans are currently in the process of being developed and revised. She stated that the division will incorporate victim- related responsibilities into the work plans for CTS trial attorneys and OVT staff. See appendix V for the references to adherence with victims' rights included in the work plans and performance appraisals of responsible DOJ employees.

Several Key Issues Have Arisen as the Courts Interpret and Apply the CVRA in Cases, and Judges Have Differing Interpretations Regarding Whether the Law Applies to the District of Columbia Superior Court

As courts interpret and apply the CVRA in cases, several key issues have arisen, including, among other things, whether the CVRA applies to victims of offenses that have not been charged in court, whether individuals meet the "direct and proximate harm" definition of a victim, and what the right to be reasonably heard means. However, some judges in the District of Columbia Superior Court have differing interpretations regarding whether the CVRA applies to victims of local offenses prosecuted in the Superior Court. Without clarification of this issue, the question of whether the Superior Court has responsibility to implement the CVRA will remain and judges in the Superior Court may continue to differ in whether they apply the CVRA in their cases.

Several Key Issues Have Arisen as Courts Interpret and Apply the CVRA in Cases

Several key issues have arisen as courts interpret and apply the CVRA through federal court decisions, including:

- **whether and in what circumstances the CVRA applies to victims of uncharged offenses,**
- **whether individuals meet the "direct and proximate harm" definition of a victim,**
- **what the right to be reasonably heard means,**
- **whether victims should have access to presentence reports and other nonpublic information, and**
- **which standard should be used to review petitions for writs of mandamus.**

When new legislation is enacted, the courts typically interpret the law's provisions and apply the law as cases arise. As rulings on these cases are issued, the courts build a body of judicial decisions—known as case law— which helps further develop the law. Federal cases are often heard before U.S. district courts. The parties in the case can appeal a U.S. district court decision to the respective U.S. court of appeals, whose decisions serve as precedent for the district courts located within its circuit.[69] The U.S. Supreme Court may hear appeals of decisions of the U.S. courts of appeals, and U.S. Supreme Court decisions serve as precedent for all federal circuits. The issues discussed below have arisen as cases have come before the courts, largely via motions and petitions for writs of mandamus under the CVRA, and the rulings on these issues will likely contribute to the further development of case law related to the CVRA.

The Courts Are Interpreting the CVRA to Determine Whether It Applies to Victims of Uncharged Offenses

The courts have interpreted the CVRA in different ways regarding whether victims of offenses that have not been charged in court are entitled to the rights afforded in the law. While some courts have stated that CVRA rights do not apply unless charges have been filed, other courts have stated that certain CVRA rights, under particular circumstances, may apply to victims of offenses that are investigated but have not been charged in court.

The courts have made determinations about whether CVRA rights apply based on the circumstances of individual cases and have ruled that the law applies to victims of offenses that have not been charged in court in some instances and not in others. According to an FJC official, when a statute provides new rights, the issue of when they apply commonly arises and is interpreted by the courts as cases come before them. The courts have issued rulings regarding the applicability of the CVRA to victims of uncharged offenses in two general categories: (1) offenses that have not been investigated and (2) offenses that have been investigated but not charged.

Applicability of the CVRA to Victims of Uninvestigated Offenses

In the cases we reviewed where potential victims of uninvestigated offenses asserted CVRA rights, the courts ruled that the CVRA did not apply in these instances because either no criminal charges were filed or the defendant was not convicted. Table 6 provides additional detail on the court cases we reviewed that address whether the CVRA applies to potential victims of uninvestigated offenses.

Table 6. Cases that Address Whether the CVRA Applies to Potential Victims of Uninvestigated Offenses

Case	Description Court ruling	Court ruling
Searcy v. Skinner, No. 6:06-1418, 2006 WL 1677177 (D.S.C. June 16, 2006).	A federal inmate sued another inmate under the Racketeer Influenced and Corrupt Organizations (RICO) Act, arguing that the CVRA entitled him to petition the court and seek restitution.	The U.S. District Court for the District of South Carolina ruled that the CVRA does not grant victims any rights against individuals who have not been convicted of a crime and that the plaintiff could not use the CVRA to bring an action directly against the other inmate.
Searcy v. Paletz, No. 6:07- 1389, 2007 WL 1875802 (D.S.C. June 27, 2007).	A federal inmate sued another inmate for allegedly attacking him and hitting him in the throat, claiming that as a victim under the CVRA, he had not been treated with fairness and respect as required by the law.	The U.S. District Court for the District of South Carolina ruled that the plaintiff was not a victim under the CVRA because the alleged attacker had been neither charged nor convicted.
United States v. Merkosky, No. 1 :02-cr-01 68, 2008 WL 1744762 (N.D. Ohio Apr. 11, 2008) (order denying motion).	Defendant filed a motion asserting that he was the victim of several federal offenses committed by the prosecutor and investigative agent in his closed case.	The U.S. District Court for the Northern District of Ohio denied the motion, stating that the vast majority of CVRA rights only have meaning in the context of a criminal prosecution and noting that other district courts have found that the CVRA does not confer any rights upon a victim until prosecution has already begun.
United States v. Rubin, 558 F. Supp. 2d 411 (E.D.N.Y. 2008) (order denying motion in part and granting motion in part).	Defendant was indicted in 2004 for securities fraud. Victims of a superseding indictment for securities fraud in 2006 filed a motion asserting that their CVRA rights were denied, both in the interim between indictments and after the second indictment.	Although this case was investigated and charges were filed by the government, the U.S. District Court for the Eastern District of New York addressed the applicability of the CVRA to victims of uninvestigated offenses, noting in its decision that the CVRA "cannot be read to include the victims of uncharged crimes that the government has not even contemplated."

Source: GAO analysis of court cases in which the CVRA was raised.

Applicability of the CVRA to Victims of Investigated Offenses

The courts have issued varying rulings regarding whether the CVRA applies to victims of investigated offenses for which charges have not been filed. For example, in one case, which involved the right to restitution for offenses that were not charged, the court stated that the CVRA does not grant victims any rights against individuals that have not been convicted.[70] In another case—which addressed the timing of when CVRA rights apply in cases where charges are eventually filed—the court of appeals, quoting the district court, stated that "'there are clearly rights under the CVRA that apply before any prosecution is underway'" and that based on the circumstances of the case, the prosecution should have conferred with the victims regarding pre-indictment plea negotiations.[71] Table 7 provides additional detail on the cases we reviewed that address whether the CVRA applies to victims of investigated offenses that have not been charged.

Table 7. Cases that Address Whether the CVRA Applies to Victims of Investigated Offenses that Have Not Been Charged

Case	Description	Court ruling
United States v. Turner, 367 F. Supp. 2d 319 (E.D.N.Y. 2005) (order *sua sponte*).	The defendant was accused of conducting a fraudulent investment scheme through the mail. No victims sought to assert their CVRA rights in this case. The magistrate judge issued a decision on his own initiative (without either the victim or the prosecutor asserting CVRA rights) and discussed, among other things, the relationship between victim status and charges filed.	The magistrate judge stated that the courts must decide whether the CVRA accords rights to persons harmed by uncharged criminal conduct attributed to the defendant. He stated that the usual methods of determining the legislative intent of the CVRA produce inconsistent results. The magistrate judge stated that statements by the law's sponsors supported an interpretation of the definition that would include victims of offenses not charged. However, he also stated that Congress passed the CVRA knowing that similar language in a prior law related to crime victims had been interpreted not to refer to uncharged conduct. Despite the ambiguity in the law, the magistrate judge stated that he will take an inclusive approach and, absent an affirmative reason to think otherwise, accord any person self-identified as a victim the rights set forth in the CVRA.
In re Dean, No. 08-201 25 (5th Cir. May 7, 2008).	An explosion occurred at the BP refinery in Texas, killing 15 contractor employees and injuring more than 170 others. The victims petitioned for a writ of mandamus, stating that the prosecution's exclusion of the victims in reaching a pre-indictment plea agreement with BP violated their rights to notification, confer with the prosecutor, and fairness under the CVRA. Victims' petition cites the law's language stating that CVRA rights shall be asserted in the district in which the crime occurred if "no prosecution is underway" to indicate that victims' rights apply prior to charges being filed. The government disagreed, stating in its responses to the victims' motion that the CVRA does not give victims an unqualified right to notice before any charges are filed. The government also stated that, per the Attorney General Guidelines, the prosecutor's responsibility to confer with victims begins when charges are filed.	The U.S. Court of Appeals for the Fifth Circuit did not issue the writ ordering the U.S. District Court for the Southern District of Texas to not accept the plea agreement. However, in its decision, the court of appeals, quoting the district court, stated that "'there are clearly rights under the CVRA that apply before any prosecution is underway'" and that, based on the circumstances of the case, the prosecution should have conferred with victims about the plea negotiation.

Table 7. (Continued)

Case	Description	Court ruling
In re W.R. Huff Asset Management Co., 409 F.3d 555 (2d Cir. 2005).	Victims petitioned for a writ of mandamus to vacate the settlement agreement in a securities fraud case, which they asserted violated their right to restitution and to be treated with fairness under the CVRA.	The U.S. Court of Appeals for the Second Circuit denied the petition and noted that the settlement agreement involved some defendants who were not convicted, as well as other individuals who had not been charged. The court stated that "the CVRA does not grant any rights against individuals who have not been convicted of a crime," and does not restrict the government nor the court from "effecting reasonable settlement or restitution measures against non-convicted defendants."
United States v. Rubin, 558 F. Supp. 2d 411 (E.D.N.Y. 2008) (order denying motion in part and granting motion in part).	The defendant was initially indicted in 2004 for securities fraud. Victims of a superseding indictment for securities fraud in 2006 filed a motion asserting that their CVRA rights were denied, both in the interim between indictments and after the second indictment. The victims argued that their rights under the CVRA should have been triggered at the moment they were victimized, prior to charges being filed for the defendant's second indictment in 2006.	Although the U.S. District Court for the Eastern District of New York found that none of the victims' CVRA rights were violated, the court discussed in general when CVRA rights applied to the victims. The court stated that "it can be said" that the victims achieved covered status under the CVRA when the superseding indictment was filed and that the right to be protected from the accused cannot have ripened until the defendant is accused through a complaint, information, or indictment. However, it also stated that the victims' entitlement to the law's rights was triggered "no later" than when the indictment was filed and that the CVRA envisions the possibility of judicial enforcement of certain rights outside the context of an actual prosecution.
In re Jane Doe, No. 08- 80736 (S.D. Fla. filed July 7, 2008).	The victim filed a petition asserting that her CVRA rights were violated when the USAO failed to confer with her regarding pre-indictment plea negotiations that would defer federal prosecution of sex trafficking of children and other crimes if the defendant entered	As of September 12, 2008, the U.S. District Court for the Southern District of Florida had not issued a ruling on the victim's petition.
	guilty pleas to various state charges. The victim also asserted that the USAO failed to notify her of her CVRA rights, notify her of court proceedings, and provide information regarding her right to restitution. In the petition, the victim argued that CVRA rights apply during the investigation of the crime, before charges are filed. The government noted in its response that nothing in the CVRA supports the position that the victim had a right to be consulted before the government could enter into a non- prosecution agreement that defers federal prosecution in exchange for state court resolution of criminal liability.	

Source: GAO analysis of court cases in which the CVRA was raised.

In implemen... the CVRA, DOJ has also made a determination about when CVRA rights apply ...ng in the Attorney General Guidelines that CVRA rights do not apply unless ch... ...iled. The Attorney General Guidelines use the same definition of crime victim ... RA—"a person directly and proximately harmed as a result of the ... Federal offense or an offense in the District of Columbia"—but with the ...ne offense is charged" in court. DOJ's policy regarding when CVRA rights co... ...ed on, among other things, the department's initial analysis of the law. For ...rding to informal guidance provided to DOJ Criminal Division officials in 2005 ...e of Legal Counsel, the identification of a "federal offense" under the CVRA's ...f a victim occurs when charges are filed, which requires a sworn written statement ...e cause to link the defendant with a federal offense. The guidance states that it is ...o identify who has been harmed by a federal offense, as opposed to some other type ...onduct, before charges are filed.

Because DOJ requires provision of CVRA rights only to those who are victims of charged offenses, some individuals identified as victims during the investigative stage who are later not included as part of the charged criminal case are not entitled to and may not receive CVRA rights.[72] For example, in a large computer intrusion initiative in 2007, the FBI identified over one million victims whose computers had become infected with a virus. DOJ included approximately 40 victims among the charged cases. Officials told us that it would be impractical to include one million victims in the charges and stated that, while the department did not provide individual CVRA rights to those who were not included as victims of the offenses charged, the FBI and the prosecutors did send notices to the internet service providers of those individuals, with the understanding that the providers would notify their customers of the intrusion as appropriate. In addition, according to DOJ, prosecutors may and often do obtain plea agreements or sentencing conditions that require defendants to provide restitution to all victims, whether or not they were part of the charged case. Also, as discussed earlier in this chapter, during the investigative stage, DOJ mandates compliance with the Victims' Rights and Restitution Act, 42 U.S.C. § 10607, which requires federal officials to, among other things, identify victims, protect victims, arrange for victims to receive reasonable protection from suspected offenders, and provide information about available services for victims. Therefore, even though DOJ may not afford CVRA rights to victims if charges have not been filed in their cases, the department may provide certain services to victims that may serve the same function as some CVRA rights.

Victims' attorneys with whom we spoke expressed concerns about the impact of DOJ's policy that CVRA rights do not apply unless charges are filed. They stated that certain CVRA rights should take effect prior to charges being filed, including, among others, the rights to confer with the prosecutor and to be treated with fairness and with respect for the victim's dignity and privacy. In their analysis of the CVRA, the law applies before charges are filed, based on, among other things, the statement that "if no prosecution is underway," CVRA rights shall be asserted in the district court in the district where the crime occurred.

Victims have also filed complaints with the VRO regarding their CVRA rights in cases where offenses were investigated but not charged. Victims are informed of their rights and the complaint process through, among other things, brochures provided during the investigation of a case. According to the VRO, however, in instances where an individual filed a complaint related to a case where charges have not been filed, she would have to close the complaint because the complainant would not be considered a victim under the CVRA, based on the

Attorney General Guidelines. For example, in one complaint, the compla had received notice that she was a crime victim under the CVRA and allege afforded multiple CVRA rights. The VRO's response to the complainant ted that she careful review, the complaint was closed without further action because crimin was not not been filed in the matter and the complainant had not been established as a f victim as required by DOJ regulations. In another complaint in which the VR similar determination, the complainant responded that the FBI led him to believe tha a crime victim under the CVRA during the investigation but the VRO stated that he wa Therefore, under DOJ's current policy, individuals who are informed that they are vic during the investigation of their case and file complaints regarding the provision of th rights are not considered crime victims by the VRO if charges have not been filed.

Victims also filed a complaint in June 2008 in which the alleged violation occurred before charges were eventually filed.[73] This complaint addresses the timing of when CVRA rights apply in such cases. A copy of the complaint was provided to GAO by one of the attorneys who filed it on the victims' behalf. In the complaint, the victims stated that prosecutors failed to notify, confer, and treat them with fairness prior to reaching a pre-indictment plea agreement in the case. While the complaint was submitted to the VRO after charges were filed in the case, the alleged violations pertained to plea agreement negotiations that occurred before charges were filed. As of October 2008, the VRO had not made a determination on whether DOJ employees involved in this case complied with the provisions in the CVRA pertaining to the treatment of victims.

The courts have ruled that the law applies to victims of uncharged offenses in some instances and not in others, based on the circumstances of individual cases, and DOJ's Attorney General Guidelines state that CVRA rights apply when charges are filed. DOJ officials and a federal judicial official told us that this issue will likely be further developed as cases arise in the courts. In a September 2008 interview, EOUSA officials stated that the department is reviewing the *In re Dean* decision in the U.S. Court of Appeals for the Fifth Circuit—discussed in table 7—and assessing the implications of the case on the department's policy.[74] In its ruling, the court of appeals, quoting the district court, stated that "'there are clearly rights under the CVRA that apply before any prosecution is underway.'" As of September 2008, DOJ could not provide an estimated date of when the review of its policy would be completed.

The Courts Are Applying the "Direct and Proximate Harm" Definition of a Victim

The CVRA defines a crime victim as a person "directly and proximately harmed" as a result of the commission of a federal offense or an offense in the District of Columbia. The courts are applying this definition to determine who qualifies as a victim under the CVRA. Judges have used such measures as the foreseeability of harm by the defendant and the strength of the causal link between the crime committed and the harm inflicted to determine if an individual was directly and proximately harmed and therefore entitled to rights as a victim under the CVRA. In three of the four cases we reviewed that discussed this issue, the courts found that the individuals who filed motions were not victims under the CVRA. The courts will continue to address this issue as additional cases arise. Table 8 provides additional detail on the cases we reviewed that address the CVRA's "direct and proximate harm" definition of a victim.

Table 8. Cases that Address the CVRA's "Direct and Proximate Harm" Definition of a Victim

Case	Description	Court ruling
In re Jane Doe, No. 07- 1705 (4th Cir. Aug. 9, 2007).	The defendant pleaded guilty to falsely marketing a prescription painkiller as "less addictive" than other pain medications. An individual who considered herself a victim because of her addiction to the painkiller filed a motion to assert the right to restitution under the CVRA. After the U.S. District Court for the Western District of Virginia denied the motion, she petitioned for a writ of mandamus to order the district court to reopen the defendant's sentencing and enforce her right to restitution.	The U.S. Court of Appeals for the Fourth Circuit denied the petition for a writ of mandamus, stating that the individual was not a victim under the CVRA and Victim Witness and Protection Act because she could not demonstrate that she was directly and proximately harmed as a result of the conduct underlying one of the elements of the offense; that is, the chain of causation between the defendant's actions and the petitioner's addiction was too attenuated to support application of restitution law.
In re Antrobus, No. 08- 4002 (10th Cir. Jan. 11, 2008).	The defendant pleaded guilty to the illegal sale of a hand gun to a juvenile, who several months after the sale (and after turning 18) used the gun to kill several people at a shopping center. After the U.S. District Court for the District of Utah denied their motion, the parents of one of the shooting victims petitioned the court of appeals to have their daughter recognized as a victim of the gun dealer under the CVRA so that they could speak at the defendant's sentencing hearing and seek restitution.	The U.S. Court of Appeals for the Tenth Circuit denied the parents' petition for a writ of mandamus, ruling that the petitioners' right to the writ was not clear and indisputable. The court of appeals found that the U.S. District Court for the District of Utah was not clearly wrong in determining that the petitioners' daughter was not "directly and proximately" harmed by the defendant's illegal firearm sale and therefore not a victim under the CVRA. The district court had found that the daughter was not a victim of the offense because the offense and the shooting were "too factually and temporally attenuated."
United States v. Wood, No. 05-00072 (D. Haw. July 17, 2006) (order granting motion).	Defendant was found guilty of defrauding a corporation. The prosecution moved to continue sentencing to allow the victims, who were previously scheduled to be out of the country, to attend and be reasonably heard.	The U.S. District Court for the District of Hawaii granted the motion. It found that although the defendant directly harmed the corporation, the President and Senior Director of Operations of the corporation were proximately harmed because they continue to suffer the effects of the fraud in their personal and business relationships.
United States v. Sharp, 463 F. Supp. 2d 556 (E.D. Va. 2006) (order granting motion).	The defendant pleaded guilty of conspiracy to possess marijuana with the intent to distribute. The girlfriend of one of the defendant's former customers asserted that her boyfriend abused her after using marijuana sold by the defendant. She requested to be recognized as a victim under the CVRA so that she could give a victim impact statement at the defendant's sentencing hearing, and the defendant filed a motion requesting that the court exclude her testimony.	The U.S. District Court for the Eastern District of Virginia granted the defendant's motion to exclude the testimony of the purported victim, stating that the nexus between the sale of marijuana and the woman's abuse was too far removed to confer victim status under the CVRA.

Source: GAO analysis of court cases in which the CVRA was raised.

The Courts Are Interpreting the Meaning of the Right to Be Reasonably Heard

The CVRA provides victims with the right to be reasonably heard at public proceedings in the district court involving release, plea, sentencing, or parole. The courts are interpreting what "to be reasonably heard" means under the law. The courts held in two cases—one at the appellate level and one at the district court level—that the right to be heard means the right to speak.[75] The appellate level case set a precedent for all subsequent cases regarding this issue in the Ninth Circuit. In a third case at the district court level, the court held that the right to be heard would be satisfied by a written statement, based on the circumstances of the case.[76] The courts will continue to address this issue as additional cases arise. Table 9 provides additional detail on the court cases we reviewed that address the meaning of the right to be reasonably heard.

Table 9. Cases that Address the Meaning of the Right to Be Reasonably Heard

Case	Description	Court ruling
Kenna v. U.S. District Court for the Central District of California, 435 F.3d 1011 (9th Cir. 2006).	The defendants—a father and son— swindled numerous victims out of almost $100 million. One of the victims petitioned for a writ of mandamus after the U.S. District Court for the Central District of California refused to allow him to speak at the son's sentencing, after he had already spoken at the father's. The petitioner sought an order to reopen the sentence and allow him to speak at the resentencing hearing.	The U.S. Court of Appeals for the Ninth Circuit granted the petition, directing the U.S. District Court for the Central District of California to consider the victim's motion to reopen the sentence and conduct a new hearing to allow the victim to speak. The court of appeals ruled that the right to be heard gives victims the right to speak at sentencing and is not limited to victim impact statements.
United States v. Marcello, 370 F. Supp. 2d 745 (N.D. Ill. 2005).	At a pretrial detention hearing for two defendants accused of murder, the prosecutor moved to allow the son of the murder victim to give an oral statement in court, opposing the release of the defendants.	The U.S. District Court for the Northern District of Illinois ruled that the right to be reasonably heard did not mandate an oral presentation and would be satisfied by a written statement under the circumstances of the case. The court stated that the victim's proposed statement was not material to the detention hearing, in that, among other things, there was no doubt as to the seriousness of the crime and no claim that the victim's welfare would be endangered if the defendant were released. The court acknowledged that "reasonable minds" may differ on the meaning of the right to be reasonably heard.
U.S. v. Degenhardt, 405 F. Supp. 2d 1341 (D. Utah 2005).	In a criminal fraud case, the government advised the court that several victims wished to speak at the defendant's sentencing hearing.	The U.S. District Court for the District of Utah granted the request, stating that the CVRA supersedes the current rules of criminal procedure, which only give victims of violence or sexual abuse a right to allocution. The judge stated that the right to be heard "gives victims the right to speak directly to the judge at sentencing."

e: GAO analysis of court cases in which the CVRA was raised.

The Courts Are Determining Whether Victims Should Be Granted Access to Presentence Reports and Other Nonpublic Case Information

The courts have issued a number of rulings on victims' requests for access to presentence reports and other nonpublic case information under the CVRA. Presentence reports are prepared by probation officers and used to assist the courts in determining the appropriate sentence to impose on a defendant convicted of a crime. They contain sentencing guidelines, victim impact statements, and such potentially confidential information as the defendant's family history, prior criminal record, financial status, and medical condition. Victims requested the information to, among other reasons, verify its accuracy for sentencing or restitution calculations and enable them to speak knowledgeably when they exercised their right to be heard.[77] Other nonpublic case information has also been requested under the CVRA. In one case, for example, individuals asserted that they were victims under the CVRA and filed a petition for a writ of mandamus to compel the prosecution to disclose nonpublic information that supported their position.[78]

We reviewed eight cases that addressed the disclosure of presentence reports and other nonpublic information under the CVRA. In six of these cases, the court denied the victims' request for information and in one case, the court did not rule on the victims' request because it determined the request to be moot. One court issued an opinion on its own initiative, without either the victim or the prosecutor asserting CVRA rights, stating that there is nothing in the CVRA that requires the disclosure of presentence reports in the absence of a request from the victim. In the rulings denying the victims' motions and petitions, the courts stated, among other things, that victims do not have a general right under the CVRA to access these materials and that the victims failed to demonstrate that their need for the information outweighed the need for confidentiality. Table 10 summarizes the cases we reviewed that address the disclosure of presentence reports and other nonpublic information under the CVRA.

Table 10. Cases that Address the Disclosure of Presentence Reports and Other Nonpublic Information under the CVRA

Case	Description	Court ruling
Disclosure of presentence reports		
In re Kenna, 453 F.3d 1136 (9th Cir. 2006).	After the U.S. District Court for the Central District of California denied the victim's motion, the victim petitioned for a writ of mandamus to order the district court to release the presentence report. A brief filed in the case by the National Crime Victim Law Institute argued that the victim's rights to be heard, to restitution, and to be treated with fairness could not be fully enforced without disclosure of the presentence report.	The U.S. Court of Appeals for the Ninth Circuit denied the petition, stating that the U.S. District Court for the Central District of California did not abuse its discretion or commit legal error when it found that the CVRA did not confer a general right for crime victims to obtain disclosure of a defendant's presentence report. In addition, the court of appeals noted that the district court found that Mr. Kenna did not demonstrate that his reasons for requesting the presentence report outweighed the confidentiality of the report.

Table 10. (Continued)

Case	Description	Court ruling
Disclosure of presentence reports		
	disclosure of presentence reports.	for a hearing on the issue
Disclosure of other nonpublic information		
United States v. Ingrassia, No. CR-04-0455, 2005 WL 2875220 (E.D.N.Y. 2005) (report and recommendations).	The magistrate judge issued a report and recommendations that discussed the CVRA. While the case primarily pertained to victim notification of proceedings, the judge also discussed the	The magistrate judge stated that there is nothing in the CVRA that requires the disclosure of presentence reports, at least in the absence of any request from the victim and an opportunity
In re Antrobus, No. 08-4002 (10th Cir. Jan. 11, 2008).	After the U.S. District Court for the District of Utah denied their motion, individuals petitioned the court of appeals for a writ of mandamus to compel the prosecution to release investigative information—specifically, grand jury information and discovery files—that supported their position that they were crime victims under CVRA.	The U.S. Court of Appeals for the Tenth Circuit held that the U.S. District Court for the District of Utah did not abuse its discretion when it denied the request for investigative information. The district court had stated that granting rights to the prosecution's investigative files to establish individuals as victims would be a significant right to append to the CVRA. It had added that it did not want to create a right not provided in the statute that may have the effect of interfering with the prosecution of criminal matters. The district court had also stated that the CVRA does not grant rights to individuals with respect to grand jury materials and concluded that the petitioners did not demonstrate that their needs outweigh the interests in maintaining grand jury secrecy.
In re Brock, No. 08-1086 (4th Cir. Jan. 31, 2008).	The victim petitioned for a writ of mandamus, asserting that he had not been afforded the rights to be reasonably heard and be treated with fairness because the U.S. District Court for the District of Maryland did not disclose parts of the presentence report. The victim stated that, without the report, he had insufficient knowledge of the issues relevant to sentencing to meaningfully exercise his right to be reasonably heard.	The U.S. Court of Appeals for the Fourth Circuit denied the petition, stating that the U.S. District Court for the District of Maryland did not abridge the victim's CVRA rights by denying him access to parts of the presentence report. The court of appeals stated that the victim had sufficient information to make a victim impact statement without the release of the presentence report.

Table 10. (Continued)

Case	Description	Court ruling
Disclosure of presentence reports		
	disclosure of presentence reports.	for a hearing on the issue
Disclosure of other nonpublic information		
United States v. Sacane, No. 3:05-cr-325, 2007 WL 951666 (D. Conn. Mar. 28, 2007) (order denying motion).	Several victims requested access to nonpublic investigative materials provided by the prosecution to the defendant during discovery in the criminal trial for use in their pending civil suits.	The U.S. District Court for the Eastern District of Virginia granted the victims' request, but the U.S. Court of Appeals for the Fourth Circuit overturned the decision on other grounds, holding that the district court did not have the authority to order the disclosure of the information and noting that CVRA is silent and unconcerned with victims' rights to file civil claims against their assailants. United States v. Moussaoui, 483 F.3d 220 (4th Cir. 2007).
United States v. Citgo Petroleum Corp., No. C-06-563 (S.D. Tex. Aug. 8, 2007) (order denying motion).	The government filed a motion requesting the U.S. District Court for the Southern District of Texas to unseal its submission of sentencing information to the	The U.S. District Court for the Southern District of Texas denied the motion, stating that the CVRA does not require disclosure of presentence report
	U.S. probation office to, among other reasons, assist the government in identifying victims of CITGO's criminal conduct.	or other documents of a similar nature. In addition, it found that the government had not demonstrated a "compelling, particularized need for the disclosure."
United States v. Rubin, 558 F. Supp. 2d 411 (E.D.N.Y. 2008) (order denying motion in part and granting motion in part).	Victims filed a motion requesting the U.S. District Court for the Eastern District of New York to order the government to provide investigative information (grand jury records) in order for them to pursue restitution and exercise their right to be heard.	The U.S. District Court for the Eastern District of New York stated that the CVRA does not authorize an "unbridled gallop" to any and all information in the government's files. It added, however, that conferring with and seeking information from the prosecution regarding restitution in a criminal proceeding would appear to be well within the bounds of the statute. Because the government began to make efforts to provide victims with the information requested and pledged to continue to do so, the court stated that the issue of access appeared to be moot and declined to rule on the motion.

Source: GAO analysis of court cases in which the CVRA was raised.

Note: The function of a grand jury is to review information provided by the prosecutor to determine whether there is probable cause to indict, or accuse, the defendant of a crime. The information provided to the grand jury is generally confidential and not released to the public. Discovery is the formal process by which the defense and prosecution exchange information relevant to the criminal investigation and trial preparation.

Table 11. Cases that Address the Standard of Review for Deciding Petitions for Writs of Mandamus under the CVRA

Case	Description	Court ruling
Cases that applied the ordinary appellate standard of review to decide petitions for writs of mandamus		
In re W.R. Huff Asset Management Co., 409 F.3d 555 (2d Cir. 2005).	Victims petitioned for a writ of mandamus to vacate the settlement agreement in a securities fraud case, which they asserted violated their right to restitution and to be treated with fairness under the CVRA.	Although the U.S. Court of Appeals for the Second Circuit denied the petition, it stated that because the CVRA designates a writ of mandamus as a mechanism by which a victim may appeal a district court's decision denying relief, petitioners asserting CVRA rights did not need to overcome the "high hurdles" typically faced by those seeking traditional writs of mandamus.
Kenna v. U.S. District Court for the Central District of California, 435 F.3d 1011 (9th Cir. 2006).	The defendants—a father and son— swindled numerous victims out of almost $100 million. One of the victims petitioned for a writ of mandamus after the U.S. District Court for the Central District of California refused to allow him to speak at the son's sentencing, after he had spoken at the father's. The petitioner sought an order to reopen the sentence and allow him to speak at the resentencing.	The U.S. Court of Appeals for the Ninth Circuit stated that the CVRA creates a unique enforcement mechanism that provides for routine appellate review when assertions of rights are denied. It added that the court of appeals must issue a writ whenever it finds that the district court's order reflects abuse of discretion or legal error under the CVRA without regard to the balancing of factors designed to ensure that petitions for writs of mandamus do not become a vehicle for appealing routine cases before the court has issued a final decision. The court of appeals granted the petition.
Cases that applied the traditional standard of review to decide petitions for writs of mandamus		
In re Antrobus, No. 08-4002 (10th Cir. Jan. 11, 2008).	The defendant pleaded guilty to the illegal sale of a handgun to a juvenile, who several months after the sale (and after turning 18) used the gun to kill several people at a shopping center. After the U.S. District Court for the District of Utah denied their motion, the parents of one of the victims petitioned the court of appeals to have their daughter recognized as a victim under the CVRA so that they could speak at the defendant's sentencing hearing and seek restitution.	The U.S. Court of Appeals for the Tenth Circuit stated that petitions for writs of mandamus—and the strict standard of review that applies—are the subject of long-standing judicial precedent, and that Congress was aware of this when it authorized the term "mandamus," which it used instead of providing for other forms of appellate review. Accordingly, mandamus is a "drastic remedy," to be invoked in "extraordinary situations," and petitioners must show that their right to the writ is "clear and indisputable." The court denied the petition.

Table 11. (Continued)

Case	Description	Court ruling
In re Dean, No. 08-201 25 (5th Cir. May 7, 2008).	An explosion occurred at the BP refinery in Texas, killing 15 contractor employees and injuring more than 170 others. The victims petitioned for a writ of mandamus, stating that the prosecution's exclusion of the victims in reaching a pre-indictment plea agreement with BP violated their rights to notification, confer with the prosecutor, and fairness under the CVRA.	The U.S. Court of Appeals for the Fifth Circuit stated that it was in accord with the Tenth Circuit in using the stricter standard for deciding petitions for mandamus for reasons stated in the Tenth Circuit's opinion. The court denied the petition. In June 2008, the victims' attorneys in the case requested that the U.S. Supreme Court order a stay, or postponement, of plea agreement proceedings in the U.S. District Court for the Southern District of Texas to allow time for the U.S. Supreme Court to resolve the standard of review issue before the case concluded. The U.S. Supreme Court denied the request for a
		stay of proceedings, thereby allowing the district court to rule on the proposed plea agreement.
Cases that applied the ordinary appellate standard of review to decide petitions for writs of mandamus		
		If the district court accepts the proposed plea agreement, a subsequent petition requesting the U.S. Supreme Court resolve the standard of review issue may not be considered.
Cases in which the standard of review is discussed but not applied in the court's decision		
In re Jacobsen, No. 05-7086, 2005 U.S. App. LEXIS 13990 (D.C. Cir. July 8, 2005).	The defendant was indicted for first-degree murder while armed. The victim's sister petitioned for a writ of mandamus, alleging that the District of Columbia Superior Court had denied her CVRA rights by not allowing her to speak at the defendant's plea hearing before accepting the plea agreement.	The U.S. Court of Appeals for the District of Columbia Circuit stated that even if the petitioner is entitled to a writ of mandamus under the CVRA using the less stringent standard of review, which requires showing an abuse of discretion by the trial court, the petitioner failed to make that showing. The court ruled that the petition was moot because the Superior Court judge had not yet accepted the plea agreement.

Table 11. (Continued)

Case	Description	Court ruling
In re Miller, No. 06-151 82 (11th Cir. Sept. 28, 2006).	A civil plaintiff petitioned for a writ of mandamus under the CVRA to order the U.S. District Court for the Middle District of Florida or another entity to investigate the alleged criminal acts of a communications company and requested restitution in the amount of $1.3 million. He also stated that the district court failed to protect him from actions he believes were unlawful.	The U.S. Court of Appeals for the Eleventh Circuit stated that mandamus is not a substitute for appeal and is only appropriate when "no other adequate means are available to remedy a clear usurpation of power or abuse of discretion." It added that the petitioner must show that his right to the issuance of a writ is both "clear and indisputable." The court stated that it doubts that the CVRA applies to the petitioner, but even assuming that it does, found that he was not entitled to a writ.
In re Jane Doe, No. 07-1705 (4th Cir. Aug. 9, 2007).	The victim petitioned for a writ of mandamus to order the U.S. District Court for the Western District of Virginia to reopen the defendant's sentencing and enforce her right to restitution for injuries caused by the	The U.S. Court of Appeals for the Fourth Circuit stated that petitions for writs of mandamus are normally subject to an extraordinarily stringent standard in order to prevent them from becoming a substitute for appeal,
	defendant's fraudulent marketing of a prescription painkiller.	but that mandamus petitions filed under the CVRA are "not necessarily subject to this
Cases in which the standard of review is discussed but not applied in the court's decision		
		stringent standard of review." It added that the law is "not clear" on this issue. However, the court stated that it need not decide the issue at present because the petitioner would not be entitled to relief even under the lower standard.
In re Walsh, No. 06-4792, 2007 WL 1156999 (3d Cir. Apr. 19, 2007).	The victim petitioned for a writ of mandamus, asserting that military officers burglarized his house and attempted to poison him.	The U.S. Court of Appeals for the Third Circuit stated that "while mandamus relief is under a different and less demanding standard" under the CVRA, it is not available to the petitioner because, even under the generous assumption that he is a crime victim, he applied for relief in the wrong court.
In re Brock, No. 08-1086 (4th Cir. Jan. 31, 2008).	The victim petitioned for a writ of mandamus, asserting that he had not been afforded the rights to be reasonably heard and be treated with fairness because the U.S. District Court for the District of Maryland did not disclose parts of the defendant's presentence report.	The U.S. Court of Appeals for the Fourth Circuit discussed the standard of review issue, stating that it normally would apply an "extremely stringent" standard of review for mandamus petitions but that the petitioner argued, and at least two other circuits have agreed, that petitions filed under the CVRA would function in a manner similar to ordinary appeals. However, the court stated that it need not decide this issue at present, because it has concluded that the petitioner is not entitled to relief under even the more relaxed standard.

Source: GAO analysis of court cases in which the CVRA was raised.

The Courts Are Interpreting the CVRA to Determine which Standard Should Be Used for Reviewing Petitions for Writs of Mandamus

Typically, when a party appeals a district court decision to a court of appeals, the court of appeals reviews the district court decision using what may be called the ordinary appellate standard of review. Under this standard of review, the court of appeals reviews the district court decision for a legal error or abuse of discretion. A court would have committed a legal error if, for example, it applied the incorrect law or incorrectly interpreted the law. A court would have committed an abuse of discretion if, for example, it made a discretionary decision that is arbitrary or with which no reasonable person could agree. In contrast to an appeal, a petition for a writ of mandamus is a request that a superior court order a lower court to perform a specified action, and courts of appeals review these petitions under a standard of review that is stricter than the ordinary appellate standard of review. Under the standard traditionally used to review petitions for writs of mandamus, petitioners must show that they have no other adequate means to attain the requested relief, that the right to the issuance of the writ is clear and indisputable, and that the writ is appropriate under the circumstances. As of July 2008, 4 of the 12 circuits are split on which standard of review should be used to review petitions for writs of mandamus under the CVRA.[79] The U.S. Courts of Appeals for the Fifth and Tenth Circuits have applied the traditional writ of mandamus standard, asserting that because the CVRA uses the term "writ of mandamus," courts should apply the standard of review traditionally used to decide whether to issue writs of mandamus.[80] The two petitions filed by victims that were reviewed under this standard were both denied. The U.S. Courts of Appeals for the Ninth and the Second Circuits have applied the ordinary appellate standard of review, asserting that because the CVRA provides for routine appellate review of district court decisions regarding victims' rights, courts should apply the ordinary appellate standard of review.[81] One petition was granted and another denied under this standard. These four court of appeals decisions set a precedent for their respective circuits, in that the same standard would be used to review all subsequent mandamus petitions in the circuit. Such conflicting U.S. court of appeals rulings—or circuit splits—are typically resolved by the Supreme Court. Other circuits have issued rulings that discussed the appropriate standard of review under the CVRA but did not apply one of the standards in deciding the case at hand. Table 11 provides further detail on the cases at address the standard of review for deciding petitions for writs of mandamus under the CVRA.

Judges in the District of Columbia Superior Court Have Differing Interpretations Regarding Whether the CVRA Applies to Victims of Offenses Prosecuted in Their Court

Some judges in the District of Columbia Superior Court have issued different rulings regarding whether the CVRA applies to victims of local offenses prosecuted in the D.C. Superior Court.[82] Unlike the 50 states, the District of Columbia does not have autonomy over its local budget and laws; instead, Congress has ultimate authority over local governance issues. The CVRA clearly assigns responsibility to DOJ and the federal courts to implement the law's provisions for victims of federal offenses. However, the law is not explicit about whether the Superior Court, which has jurisdiction over local offenses committed in the District of Columbia, is also responsible for implementing its provisions and affording victims CVRA rights. The CVRA's definition of a crime victim includes persons "directly and proximately harmed as a result of the commission of a federal offense or an offense in the District of Columbia," which may be interpreted to mean that the law applies to victims of local offenses prosecuted in the D.C. Superior Court. However, the CVRA refers to "district courts" throughout the rest of the statute, which do not include the D.C. Superior Court. For instance, the law states that "victims have the right to be heard at any public proceeding in the district court" and states that "victims' rights... .shall be asserted in the district court" in which a defendant is being prosecuted for the crime. According to the General Counsel of the D.C. Superior Court, some Superior Court judges are applying the CVRA in their courtrooms while others are not. The former Chief Judge of the D.C. Superior Court stated that the law's reference to offenses in the District of Columbia could be interpreted to apply only to those cases where a defendant is charged with both federal and local offenses in the U.S. District Court for the District of Columbia. In these cases, local offenses would be prosecuted in federal district court.[83] The District of Columbia has its own victim's rights statute, enacted in 2001, which according to the former Chief Judge and EOUSA officials, both the D.C. Superior Court and USAO implement.[84]

We are aware of three instances where victims asserted CVRA rights in the D.C. Superior Court as of June 30, 2008. In one, the U.S. Court of Appeals for the District of Columbia Circuit denied the victim's petition as moot and, as a result, did not rule on whether the CVRA applies to proceedings in the Superior Court. The Superior Court took conflicting views on the applicability of the CVRA in the other two instances. In the first case, the judge denied the victim's request to be heard regarding the defendant's plea agreement, stating that the court was not bound by the CVRA provision. However, in another case, the D.C. Superior Court granted the victim's motion not to be excluded from proceedings and stated that there is "no dispute that the CVRA applies to the District of Columbia." Table 12 provides additional detail on the cases we reviewed that address the applicability of the CVRA to the D.C. Superior Court.

In implementing the CVRA, DOJ provides in the Attorney General Guidelines that the CVRA applies to victims of local offenses prosecuted in the D.C. Superior Court and is operating as such. Under the Attorney General Guidelines, victims of offenses charged "in Federal district court or the Superior Court of the District of Columbia" are entitled to CVRA rights.

While the question of CVRA applicability to victims of local offenses charged in the D.C. Superior Court could potentially be resolved through the appeals process, both DOJ and the Superior Court would like Congress to clarify the issue. The General Counsel of the Superior Court stated that, given the differences in the application of the CVRA among Superior Court judges, it would be beneficial for Congress to clarify whether the statute applies to victims of local offenses prosecuted in the Superior Court. He added that, if the law applies, Congress should also clarify the appropriate court of appeals in which victims' petitions for writs of mandamus should be filed.[85] DOJ would like Congress to resolve the question of the applicability of the CVRA to victims of offenses charged in the D.C. Superior Court as well, and unlike the Superior Court, has taken a position on the issue. In July 2005, DOJ proposed legislation to amend the CVRA to make explicit that the statute covers offenses prosecuted in the D.C. Superior Court and that petitions for writs of mandamus should be filed with the D.C. Court of Appeals.[86] As of October 23, 2008, Congress had yet to pass legislation to clarify this issue. In addition, unlike the other issues related to CVRA implementation that are being interpreted by DOJ and federal courts, this issue addresses the question of whether an institution has responsibility to implement the act. Without clarification on whether CVRA rights apply to victims of local offenses in the District of Columbia, the question of whether the Superior Court has responsibility to implement the CVRA will remain and individual judges in the Superior Court will continue to differ in whether they apply the CVRA in their cases. As a result, victims may be told they are entitled to CVRA rights by DOJ but whether they are afforded these rights in Superior Court proceedings will depend on which judge is presiding over their case.

Table 12. Cases that Address the Applicability of the CVRA to the D.C. Superior Court

Case	Description	Court ruling
In re Jacobsen, No. 05-7086, 2005 U.S. App. LEXIS 13990 (D.C. Cir. July 8, 2005).	The victim's sister petitioned for a writ of mandamus in the U.S. Court of Appeals for the D.C. Circuit, alleging that the Superior Court had denied her CVRA rights by not allowing her to speak at the defendant's plea hearing.	The U.S. Court of Appeals for the District of Columbia Circuit ruled that the petition was moot because the Superior Court judge had not yet accepted the plea and, as a result, did not address the jurisdictional issue of whether the CVRA applies to criminal proceedings in the D.C. Superior Court.
Transcript of Record, United States v. Mack, No. 2004-FEL6798 (D.C. Super. Ct. Aug. 30, 2006).	The prosecutor informed the D.C. Superior Court judge that the victim's family would like to be heard regarding the defendant's plea agreement. He added that it is his responsibility under the Attorney General Guidelines to bring this to the attention of the court.	The D.C. Superior Court judge stated that he was new to the CVRA. After reviewing the statute, he stated that the court was not bound by this particular statutory provision. He added that hearing the views of the victim's family would not change his ruling on the plea agreement and that the victim's family would be able to be heard at sentencing.
Transcript of Record, United States v. Blades, No. 2006CF114741 (D.C. Super. Ct. Mar. 26, 2008).	A victim-witness filed a motion in the D.C. Superior Court not to be excluded from any trial proceedings, even though she was testifying.	The D.C. Superior Court judge granted the motion, stating that there is "no dispute that the CVRA applies to the District of Columbia."

Source: GAO analysis of court cases in which the CVRA was raised.

PERCEPTIONS VARY REGARDING AWARENESS OF AND SATISFACTION WITH VICTIMS' RIGHTS AND PARTICIPATION AND TREATMENT OF CRIME VICTIMS, AND THE POTENTIAL FOR CONFLICTING INTERESTS BETWEEN VICTIMS AND DEFENDANTS IS A CONCERN

We asked various participants in the criminal justice system—namely, victim-witness professionals, prosecutors, defense attorneys, judges, and crime victim advocates—what constituted effective implementation of the act and what effects they expect to ensue as a result of CVRA implementation. In general they responded that CVRA implementation is effective if victims report being satisfied with the provision of their rights. They also responded that CVRA implementation should result in increased awareness of victims' rights among participants in the criminal justice system, increased participation of crime victims in court proceedings, and overall improvement in the treatment of crime victims. Defense attorneys also cautioned that CVRA implementation could conflict with defendants' interests, such as when victims who are testifying are able to observe the entire trial and when victims request access to presentence reports. We made various efforts to assess the effect and efficacy along the aforementioned factors and found mixed indications regarding the success of CVRA implementation. While a majority of federal crime victims who responded to our survey reported that they were aware of most of their CVRA rights, less than half reported that they were aware of their right to confer with the prosecutor. Furthermore, victims who responded to our survey reported varying levels of satisfaction with the provision of individual CVRA rights.[87] In addition, although general perceptions indicate that the treatment of crime victims has improved, CVRA implementation is perceived to have yielded mixed results regarding victims' participation in court proceedings and to have the potential for conflicting with defendants' interests.

The Majority of Victims Who Responded to the Survey Reported That They Were Aware of Each of the CVRA Rights, Except the Right to Confer with the Prosecutor

More than half of the victims who responded to survey questions regarding awareness of CVRA rights reported being aware of each of the rights, with the exception of the right to confer with the prosecutor. One hundred sixteen of the 242 victims who responded to the question regarding the right to confer with the prosecutor reported being aware of it. The victims were most aware of their right to be treated with fairness and with respect for their dignity and privacy—190 of the 244 victims who responded to the question regarding this right reported being aware of it. Figure 4 shows the level of awareness victims reported for each of the eight CVRA rights.

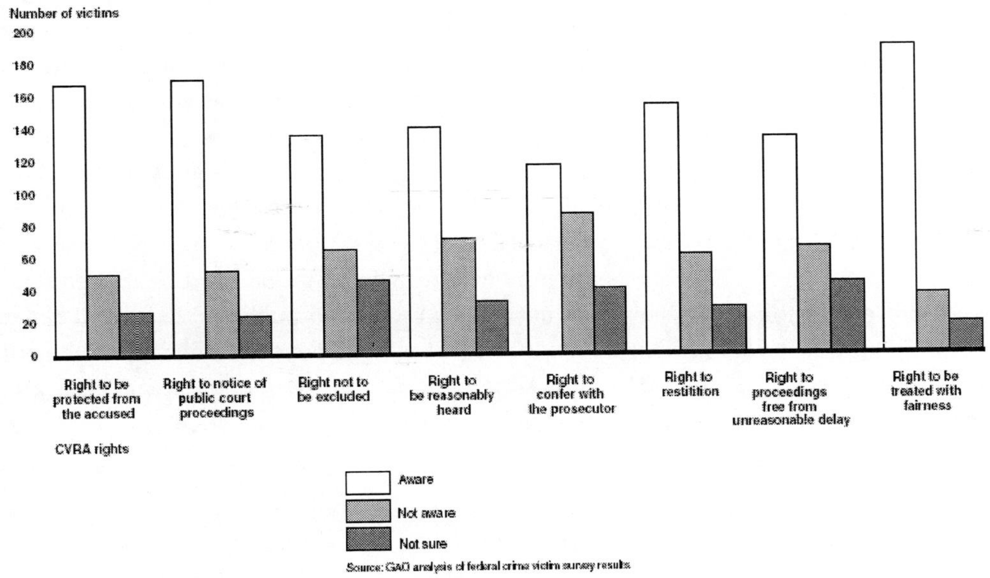

Figure 4. Awareness of CVRA Rights among Victims Who Responded to the GAO Survey Number of victims 200
Source: GAO analysis of federal crime victim survey results.

The CVRA requires DOJ to make best efforts to inform all federal crime victims of their CVRA rights. DOJ makes several efforts to do so, including through a brochure that is provided to victims during the investigative stage and in the initial letters sent to victims by the investigative agency and USAO. Most DOJ Web sites also include information on victims' rights, although 39 of the 93 USAO sites either did not list victims' rights under the CVRA or listed them incorrectly. For example, one USAO Web site listed an outdated victims' bill of rights, and did not include the rights to be reasonably heard and to proceedings free from unreasonable delay. In addition to informing victims of their eight CVRA rights in the initial notification letters, DOJ also reminds victims in the letters notifying them of sentencing proceedings that they have the right to be heard at the proceeding. However, DOJ does not remind victims of rights that may be applicable in the notification letters for other court proceedings. According to victim advocates with whom we spoke, victims may be experiencing emotional and physical trauma during the beginning of their cases, which is when they are generally informed of their CVRA rights. One victim advocate stated that reminding victims of their rights when they have the opportunity to exercise them may help to increase awareness. Despite this, the majority of victims who responded to our survey reported that they were generally aware of most of their CVRA rights.

Victims Who Responded to the Survey Reported Varying Levels of Satisfaction with the Provision of Individual CVRA Rights

One hundred thirty-two of the 169 victims who responded to the survey question regarding satisfaction with their right to notice of public court proceedings reported being satisfied with the provision of this right. In contrast, 72 of the 229 victims who responded to the survey question regarding satisfaction with the right to confer with the prosecutor reported being satisfied with the provision of this right. Survey respondents were most satisfied with the right to reasonable, accurate, and timely notice of public court proceedings, but reported the greatest dissatisfaction with the right to full and timely restitution as provided in law. Of the 232 victims who responded to the question regarding satisfaction with the right to restitution, 50 reported being very or somewhat dissatisfied. While we did not ask victims about their level of satisfaction with the provision of the right not to be excluded from certain public court proceedings, none of the victims who responded to the survey reported that the judge or prosecutor told them they were not allowed to attend public proceedings related to their case. Figure 5 shows the satisfaction of victims who responded to our survey regarding the provision of seven of the eight CVRA rights. For each of the seven rights, a greater number of victims reported being satisfied with their rights than dissatisfied.

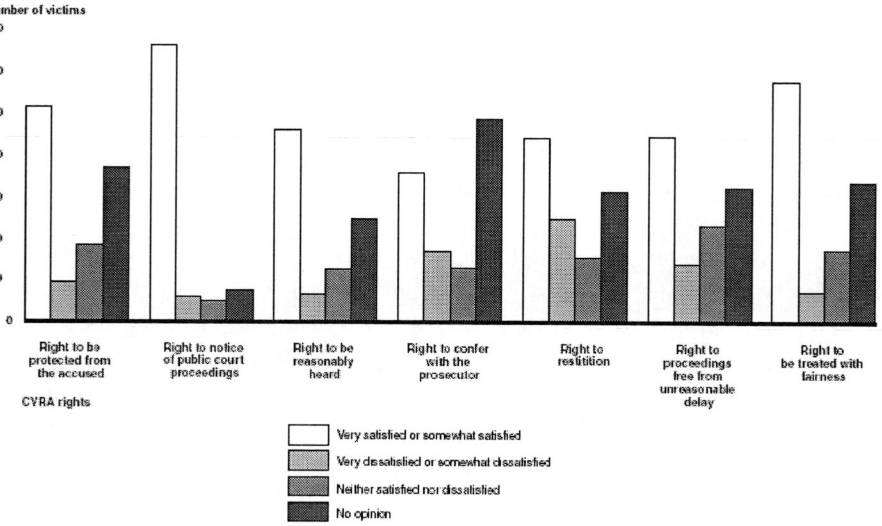

Figure 5: Satisfaction with the Provision of CVRA Rights among Victims Who Responded to the GAO Survey

Number of victims 140

Source: GAO analysis of federal crime victim survey results.

Perceptions Indicate Increased Awareness about Victims' Rights among USAO staff, Investigative Agents, and Judges

Perceptions generally indicate that the CVRA has resulted in increased awareness of victims' rights among USAO staff, investigative agents, and judges. This is due, in large part, to the education and training efforts of DOJ and the federal judiciary.

USAO Staff and Investigative Agents' Awareness of Victims' Rights under the CVRA

Perceptions generally indicate that the CVRA has resulted in increased awareness of victims' rights among USAO staff and investigative agents. For examplee, 87 percent of the USAO victim-witness professionals who responded to our survey perceived that the CVRA has increased the awareness of victims' rights among participants—which includes prosecutors and investigative agents—in the criminal justice system. In addition, as noted earlier in the report, prosecutors filed motions asserting victims' rights under the CVRA in 18 of the 43 instances in which the law's rights were asserted in district court, which indicates that they are aware of the law.

As discussed earlier in this chapter, DOJ has made a number of efforts to train and provide guidance to its employees on the CVRA, including revising the Attorney General Guidelines and sending victim-witness coordinators and investigative agents to CVRA training at the National Advocacy Center. In our survey, 95 percent of USAO victim-witness professionals reported that the CVRA-related training or written guidance provided by DOJ has been at least somewhat useful in helping to carry out their duties in assisting crime victims. Sixty-nine percent reported that the training or written guidance was very or extremely useful. In addition, many of the prosecutors and investigative agents we contacted stated that they have received sufficient training on the CVRA.

Judges' Awareness of Victims' Rights under the CVRA

The perceptions of victim-witness professionals and judicial decisions in court cases indicate that the CVRA has resulted in increased awareness of victims' rights among judges as well. In our survey of USAO victim-witness professionals, we asked how much, if at all, judges' attentiveness to the rights of federal crime victims has increased since the enactment of the CVRA. In response, 77 percent reported at least some increase in judges' attentiveness to victims' rights and 40 percent reported that judges' attentiveness had greatly or very greatly increased, based on their perceptions. Furthermore, judges have issued court opinions based on the CVRA and discussed the CVRA in decisions on their own initiative, without either the victim or the prosecutor asserting CVRA rights. As of June 30, 2008, we found 26 cases in which judges issued decisions regarding the CVRA on their own initiative.

As discussed earlier in this chapter, the AOUSC, FJC, and Judicial Conference have made a number of efforts to educate and train judges on the CVRA, including issuing memoranda on the law, revising the Benchbook for U.S. District Court Judges, discussing the CVRA in judicial workshops and orientations, developing a CVRA guidance document, producing a training video, and proposing amendments to the Federal Rules of Criminal Procedure. Although judges had varying opinions on which of the training and education efforts would be most effective in increasing CVRA awareness, 10 of the 26 district judges with whom we spoke stated that amendments to the Federal Rules of Criminal Procedure would be most helpful in increasing awareness of CVRA rights because, according to some judges, they will be mandatory for use and judges expect to refer to them on a regular basis. The amendments took effect on December 1, 2008.

Perceptions Generally Indicate That the Treatment of Federal Crime Victims Has Improved, but Some Believe It Has Not Changed Very Much because Victims Have Always Been Treated Well

Although 69 percent of USAO victim-witness professionals who responded to our survey reported, based on their perceptions, that victims were treated reasonably or very well prior to the CVRA, 67 percent of them also reported that the treatment of crime victims has at least moderately improved as a result of the CVRA. On the other hand, officials at 4 of the 9 USAOs and 4 of the 18 investigative agency field offices we visited, and 7 of the 26 judges with whom we spoke stated that CVRA has not had an impact on the treatment of crime victims. Some said that this was because they, and their respective offices, had been treating victims well prior to the enactment of CVRA, and others noted that they worked in states that had victims' rights laws that were similar to the act.

Perceptions Differ Regarding Victim Participation in Court Proceedings

One hundred forty-one of the 167 victims who responded to our survey question regarding participation in court proceedings reported that they did not attend any of the proceedings related to their cases for which they received notice. The most common reason respondents gave for not attending hearings was that the location of the court was too far for them to travel. The second most common reason was that they were not interested in attending. In addition, 167 of the 180 victims who responded to questions regarding speaking at proceedings reported that they did not speak at detention or plea hearings, and 168 of the 182 victims who responded to a related question about speaking at proceedings reported that they did not speak at sentencing hearings. The most common reason for this was their lack of interest in doing so.

From the USAO victim-witness professional perspective, 72 percent of those who responded to our survey believed that the CVRA has resulted in at least some increase in victim attendance at public court proceedings related to their cases, with 27 percent reporting that attendance among victims greatly or very greatly increased. Similarly, 77 percent of victim- witness professionals reported, based on their perceptions, at least some increase in victims submitting written statements or speaking at court proceedings, with 37 percent reporting a great or very great increase.

Defendants' Interests Are Perceived to Potentially Be in Conflict with Victims' Rights to Participate and to Be Treated Fairly

The CVRA provides victims, including those who are witnesses, with the right not to be excluded from public court proceedings, unless the court, after receiving clear and convincing evidence, determines that testimony by the victim would be materially altered if the victim heard other testimony at that proceeding. Federal defenders with whom we spoke stated that if victim-witnesses are able to observe the entire trial, their testimony may be influenced by the testimony of other witnesses, which may increase the likelihood that the defendant will be found guilty. They expressed concerns that this could potentially violate the defendant's right to a fair trial. In addition, 5 of the 9 federal defenders as well as 6 of the 19 district judges we met with said that it would be very difficult, if not impossible, to provide clear and convincing evidence—in advance of victims delivering their testimony—that the victims' testimony would be materially altered if they heard the testimony of others. For instance, one federal defender stated that such evidence could only be provided after the victim testified, by comparing statements the victim made during the investigation to those made during his or her testimony and identifying inconsistencies related to testimony that the victim observed. According to one judge, this issue is a clear example of where the CVRA and traditional criminal law, which is mainly concerned with the rights of the defendant, may come into conflict. In the two federal cases we reviewed that addressed this issue, the courts ruled that the defense did not provide clear and convincing evidence that the victims' testimony would be materially altered and allowed the victims to observe trial proceedings.

Federal defenders also expressed concerns regarding victims making false statements or introducing new evidence when speaking in court proceedings. They stated that victims are not under oath or subject to cross examination when speaking at detention, plea, or sentencing hearings. As a result, any claims the victim makes regarding the defendant may go unchallenged. In addition, according to one federal defender, the defense is not notified in advance of victims speaking in court proceedings and may be caught off guard by victims' statements, without time to counter claims that may adversely affect the defendant.

Victims have requested access to presentence reports in order to be treated fairly and fully exercise their right to be heard. However, victims accessing presentence reports may conflict with defendant interests because the report may contain confidential information about the defendant. The Judicial Conference has a long-standing policy that treats the presentence report as a confidential document. According to officials, presentence reports routinely include confidential information related to the defendant's substance abuse treatment, medical condition, and financial status. While victim advocates have suggested redacting—or removing—confidential information, both judges and federal defenders have stated that this would be administratively burdensome and cannot guarantee that all confidential information would be omitted from the presentence report provided to the victim. According to court officials, confidential information about the defendant is dispersed throughout the presentence report, which is a lengthy document, and redaction of the information is risky because it could be inadvertently disclosed to the public. The courts denied victims' requests for access to presentence reports in all three cases we reviewed.

Finally, we reviewed three cases in which defendants appealed their convictions or sentences, claiming that their due process rights were violated because individuals identified as victims were afforded CVRA rights in court proceedings. As shown in table 13, the courts denied the defendants' appeals in all three cases.

CONCLUSIONS

DOJ as well as the cosponsors of the act have suggested that the purpose of the CVRA is to increase victim participation in the criminal justice process. DOJ and the courts have made multiple efforts to implement the provisions of the CVRA. In addition, DOJ has taken actions to overcome challenges that have impeded the provision of victims' rights. However, our work has shown that if crime victims believe that their CVRA rights have been violated, they may not be aware of the mechanisms available for them to enforce their rights—the complaint process and victims' ability to file motions in court. To ensure that the victim complaint process and victims' ability to assert their rights in federal court are effective methods for enforcing victims' rights, as Congress intended, victims must be made aware of these mechanisms, particularly considering victims are generally the initiators of these processes. To maintain victims' confidence in the complaint investigation process, it is also important that the process is structured in such a way that ensures that complaint investigators are independent so that they may remain impartial and does not give the appearance that the complaint investigation is biased.

Table 13. Cases in which Defendants Appealed Convictions or Sentences Based on the CVRA

Case	Description	Court ruling
United States v. Poole, 241 F. App'x 153 (4th Cir. 2007).	The defendant pleaded guilty to possession of a firearm by a convicted felon after he had removed a police officer's gun from the holster and struck her on the head. The defendant appealed his sentence, claiming that the U.S. District Court for the Eastern District of North Carolina violated the CVRA, as well as his due process rights, by allowing the police officer, as well as another involved police officer, to make victim impact statements at sentencing.	The U.S. Court of Appeals for the Fourth Circuit affirmed the decision of the U.S. District Court for the Eastern District of North Carolina, stating that even if the police officers were not victims under CVRA and the district court had erred in admitting their statements, the error did not affect defendant's rights because it was not so unduly prejudicial as to render the defendant's sentence unfair.
United States v. Eberhard, 525 F.3d 175 (2d Cir. 2008).	The defendant appealed his conviction, stating that he received a longer sentence than he otherwise would have received because victims spoke at his sentencing, as authorized by the CVRA, which violated his due process and other rights.	The U.S. Court of Appeals for the Second Circuit affirmed the decision of the U.S. District Court for the Southern District of New York, finding that nothing in the plea agreement prevented the government from presenting victim information at sentencing.
United States v. Edwards, 526 F.3d 747 (11th Cir. 2008).	The defendant appealed his sentence, stating, among other things, that his due process rights were violated when the U.S. District Court for the Northern District of Georgia, relying on CVRA, denied his motion to sequester all witnesses during the case.	The U.S. Court of Appeals for the Eleventh Circuit affirmed the district court decision, holding that the U.S, District Court for the Northern District of Georgia had not abused its discretion and stating that defendants have no constitutional right to exclude witnesses from courtrooms.

Source: GAO analysis of court cases in which the CVRA was raised.

DOJ also has opportunities to improve its efforts to monitor progress toward achieving the objective of upholding the rights of crime victims as well as components' and the department's adherence to victims' rights. Without victim-related performance measures, DOJ and its components with victim-related responsibilities may not be able to monitor their progress towards the departmental objective of upholding the rights of crime victims. Also, without requiring DOJ components that have similar victim-related responsibilities to report the same type of information regarding compliance with these responsibilities, it will be difficult to determine how well the department is performing overall regarding CVRA implementation. In addition, by not incorporating adherence to victims' rights provisions in the work plans and performance plans of all DOJ investigative agents and victim specialists, as required by the Attorney General Guidelines, it will be difficult for DOJ to hold these employees accountable for their responsibilities regarding the provision of victims' rights.

While DOJ has several opportunities to strengthen the provision and enforcement of crime victims' rights, one aspect of CVRA implementation is challenging for DOJ and the federal judiciary to resolve, and may best be addressed by Congress. Specifically, this involves removing the uncertainty as to whether the CVRA applies to victims of local offenses charged in the District of Columbia Superior Court. If uncertainty remains, victims will continue to be treated inconsistently within this court, which could result in confusion and loss of confidence in the criminal justice system.

RECOMMENDATIONS FOR EXECUTIVE ACTION

To help ensure that the victim complaint process and victims' ability to file motions and petitions for writs of mandamus regarding their rights are effective methods for ensuring adherence with the provisions of the CVRA, we recommend that the Attorney General direct all component agencies with victim-related responsibilities to take the following 2 actions:

- explore opportunities to enhance publicity of the victim complaint process, such as by requiring all relevant components to incorporate this information on their Web sites, to help ensure that all victims are made aware of it; and
- establish a mechanism for informing all victims of their ability to assert their CVRA rights by filing motions and petitions for writs of mandamus, such as by incorporating this information in brochures and letters sent to victims and on agency Web sites.
- To further ensure that the victim complaint process is an effective method for DOJ to ensure that its employees are adhering to the provisions of the CVRA, we recommend that the Attorney General take the following action:
- restructure the process for investigating federal crime victim complaints in a way that ensures independence and impartiality, for example, by not allowing individuals who are located in the same office with the subject of the complaint to conduct the investigation.
- To help strengthen DOJ's ability to assess the performance of the department regarding the provision of victims' rights, we recommend that the Attorney General take the following action:

- identify performance measures regarding victims' rights that are aligned with the department's objective to "uphold the rights and improve services to America's crime victims" and the department's strategy of increasing victim participation in the criminal justice process.
- To further strengthen DOJ's ability to evaluate the performance of its component agencies, and that of the department overall, regarding the provision of victims' rights, we recommend that the Director for the Office for Victims of Crime take the following action:
- require component agencies with similar victim-related functions to report the same type of CVRA compliance information, as a means of monitoring overall department performance.
- In addition, as a means of monitoring employee compliance with victims' rights requirements, we recommend that the Director of the Federal Bureau of Investigation take the following action:
- incorporate references to adherence to victims' rights provisions in the work plans and performance appraisals of its investigative agents and victim specialists, as required by the Attorney General Guidelines for Victim and Witness Assistance.

MATTER FOR CONGRESSIONAL CONSIDERATION

Due to the differing interpretations among DOJ and some D.C. Superior Court judges as to whether the CVRA applies to victims whose cases are prosecuted in D.C. Superior Court, Congress should consider revising the language of the CVRA to clarify this issue.

AGENCY COMMENTS AND OUR EVALUATION

On November 26, 2008, we received written comments on the draft report, which are reproduced in full in appendix VI. DOJ generally concurred with our recommendations and stated that the department intends to convene a working group to consider the extent and manner in which they are implemented. In addition, both DOJ and AOUSC provided technical comments, which we incorporated as appropriate. With regard to our recommendations to explore opportunities to enhance publicity of the victim complaint process and establish a mechanism for informing all victims of their ability to assert CVRA in court, DOJ stated that it agrees that victims should be well-informed of these mechanisms and intends to take steps to enhance victim awareness of them. DOJ stated the working group will consider a number of options in determining which steps are most appropriate, including those mentioned in the report.

Regarding our recommendation to restructure the process for investigating federal crime victim complaints in a way that ensures independence and impartiality, DOJ stated that it recognizes the benefits of such an investigation process and that the working group, in consultation with the VRO, will explore several options that will minimize the risk of actual bias and ameliorate the perception of partiality, but also raised several points. First, DOJ believes it is important to design an impartial process without sacrificing speedy resolution of the complaint. DOJ stressed the importance of addressing a complaint quickly enough so that a victim whose rights have been violated may still have time to exercise them. While we acknowledge that it is reasonable to seek the victim's satisfaction when addressing a complaint, it is also important for the structure of the complaint process to ensure the independence of complaint investigators in order to maintain impartial investigations and uphold the credibility of the complaint process. Second, DOJ expressed concerns regarding our use of ombudsman standards as guidelines for improving the VRO's complaint process. First, they stated that the VRO, despite its name, is not an ombudsman because its defined functions do not match those of a classic ombudsman, in that, for example, the VRO does not have authority to mediate complaints between victims and DOJ employees. However, the United States Ombudsman Association defines a Governmental Ombudsman as "an independent, impartial public official with authority and responsibility to receive, investigate or informally address complaints about government actions, and, when appropriate, make findings and recommendations, and publish reports." Likewise, the VRO's role as defined in the CVRA is to "receive and investigate complaints relating to the provision or violation of the rights of a crime victim." It has the authority to address complaints by requiring training or recommending disciplinary sanctions in some cases for employees who have failed to comply with the CVRA. GAO continues to maintain, therefore, that the role of the VRO is largely consistent with the role of an ombudsman. Nonetheless, because DOJ officials expressed concerns about using ombudsman standards to assess the VRO's processes, we also compared the VRO's practices to those of state victims' rights enforcement offices, which similarly investigate and address victim complaints, to determine the extent to which they structured their processes in ways to ensure independence and impartiality. We found that those we reviewed have generally structured their investigative processes to help ensure these two standards are met. Third, DOJ stated that the VRO faces unique resource constraints, such as lack of a staff of full-time investigators and a budget for investigation-related travel, when addressing complaints. However, DOJ also stated that the working group will consider whether initial complaint investigations can be done effectively using telecommunications technology rather than in-person interviews. We agree that this could be an efficient alternative.

DOJ also concurred with our three recommendations relating to assessing and evaluating the performance of the department and its components. DOJ stated that department-wide performance measures are important, despite the difficulty in establishing objective measures. The department added that the working group will consider a variety of possibilities for strengthening its department-wide performance measures, which it also believes will assist OVC in assessing component compliance with the Attorney General Guidelines. Finally, regarding incorporating references to adherence to victims' rights into the work plans of department employees, DOJ stated that the guidelines only require that such references be included in the workplans of "appropriate" employees in components with victim-related responsibilities. GAO considers investigative agents, victim specialists, and others with victim-related responsibilities "appropriate" employees and revised the report to further clarify our position. DOJ stated that after reviewing the draft report, the FBI has agreed to revisit its position regarding the requirement.

We are sending copies of this chapter to the appropriate congressional committees, U.S. Attorney General, Director of the FBI, Director of the OVC, Director of the AOUSC,

Eileen R. Larence
Director, Homeland Security and Justice Issues

APPENDIX I: OBJECTIVES, SCOPE, AND METHODOLOGY

Sec. 104(b) of the Justice for All Act directs GAO to evaluate the "effect and efficacy" of the implementation of the Crime Victims' Rights Act (CVRA) on the treatment of crime victims in the federal system. The Department of Justice (DOJ), the federal judiciary, and other federal agencies that handle cases that involve crime victims are responsible for implementing the CVRA. To address this mandate, we sought answers to the following questions:

1. What efforts have been made to implement the CVRA, what factors have affected these implementation efforts, and how have these factors been addressed?
2. What mechanisms are in place to ensure adherence to the CVRA, and how well are these mechanisms working?
3. To what extent does DOJ monitor its performance and the performance of its employees regarding the provision of CVRA rights?
4. What are the key issues that have arisen as courts interpret and apply the CVRA in cases?
5. What are the perspectives of various participants in the federal criminal justice system regarding the effect and efficacy of CVRA implementation?

SCOPE

Given the scope of the mandate directed to GAO, our report focuses on the provision of the eight CVRA rights, mechanisms used to enforce these rights, and the procedures used by the Department of Justice to promote compliance of the act. Our report does not review the efforts taken by the Department of Justice and other agencies to provide victims with services or the department's use of the Crime Victims Fund.

We focused our review primarily on CVRA implementation efforts underway by federal judges and federal prosecutors and victim-witness professionals within DOJ because these individuals assume most of the responsibility for ensuring that crime victims are afforded their rights. We also evaluated the efforts underway by various DOJ components, particularly the Executive Office for U.S. Attorneys (EOUSA) and the Office for Victims of Crime (OVC), to ensure that crime victims are afforded their CVRA rights. Similarly, we assessed efforts underway by the federal judiciary, specifically the Administrative Office of the United States Courts (AOUSC), the Federal Judicial Center (FJC), and the Judicial Conference, to help federal courts ensure that crime victims are afforded their rights. In addition, we surveyed a stratified random probability sample from a select population of federal crime victims to obtain their perspectives on whether they were aware of and afforded their rights under CVRA. More details on this survey are provided below. We also obtained perspectives on the impact of the CVRA from crime victim advocacy groups, federal defenders, and defendant advocacy groups.

The federal prosecutors included in our review worked primarily in U.S. Attorneys Offices. Although there are additional criminal litigation divisions within DOJ (i.e., Civil Rights, Criminal, Tax, Natural Resources and Environment, and Anti-Trust), the vast majority of federal criminal cases are prosecuted either jointly or solely by Assistant U.S. Attorneys. We obtained the perspectives of Assistant U.S. Attorneys during site visits to select federal judicial districts. (The districts we visited and the criteria we used to select these districts are discussed in detail below.)

The victim-witness professionals involved in our review work primarily in U.S. Attorneys Offices as well as federal investigative agencies. Even though some of the other DOJ litigation divisions have personnel assigned to provide assistance to crime victims, our preliminary audit work revealed that once prosecution is underway, most federal crime victims are assisted by victim-witness professionals in the U.S. Attorneys Offices. We obtained perspectives of victim-witness professionals during site visits to select judicial districts and additional perspectives of U.S. Attorneys

Office victim-witness professionals through a Web-based survey. Details of this survey are provided below.

Our review focused only minimally on federal investigative agencies' efforts to implement the CVRA. Based on our preliminary audit work, federal investigative agencies have limited responsibilities related to affording and enforcing CVRA rights. Rather, most of the responsibilities investigative agencies have related to crime victims are outlined in other federal statutes.1 We did find that investigative agencies have assumed primary responsibility for identifying crime victims and obtaining victim contact information, as well as some responsibility for informing federal crime victims about their CVRA rights. Also, DOJ investigative agencies are involved in investigating victim complaints related to DOJ employee compliance with CVRA obligations. Our evaluation of the investigative agencies' efforts was limited to these areas. We included the following federal investigative agencies in our study: Federal Bureau of Investigation (FBI), Drug Enforcement Agency (DEA), and the Bureau of Alcohol, Tobacco, Firearms, and Explosives (ATF) within DOJ and the U.S. Postal Inspection Service (USPIS) within the U.S. Postal Service. We selected these agencies either because they were within DOJ, which has primary responsibility for implementing the CVRA, or because, according to the DOJ Inspector General, as of October 2007, they investigated cases that involved the greatest number of victims listed in DOJ's Victim Notification System (VNS). We excluded one DOJ investigative agency—the U.S. Marshals Service—because, based on our preliminary audit work, this agency generally does not interact with, or have any direct responsibilities related to, crime victims. According to the DOJ Inspector General, as of October 2007 the U.S. Secret Service had investigated cases that involved the third largest number of victims listed in VNS. However, we excluded this agency from our review because Secret Service officials informed us that it would be difficult to arrange meetings with their agents given that their agents were often deployed to provide security for events associated with the 2008 presidential election.

DOJ's corrections agency—Bureau of Prisons (BOP)—also had limited involvement in our study. We obtained information on BOP's CVRA efforts related to notifying crime victims of public court proceedings during the post-sentencing phase of a case, as well as notifying victims of the escape or release of the incarcerated offender.

Finally, the U.S. Parole Commission had limited involvement in our review. Parole was abolished for federal crimes committed on or after November 1, 1987, and for crimes committed in violation of the D.C. Code on or after August 5, 2000. However, the Parole Commission is still responsible for granting or denying parole to federal and D.C. code offenders who committed crimes before these respective dates. The CVRA grants crime victims the right to be notified of and to be heard at parole proceedings. We obtained information on the Parole Commission's efforts to afford these rights in the limited number of parole proceedings that take place. The commission also determines the conditions of supervised release for D.C. Code offenders, as opposed to federal judges who make this determination for federal offenders. We also obtained information on the Parole Commission's efforts to notify victims of proceedings regarding the violation or revocation of the terms of supervised release for a D.C. Code Offender.

METHODOLOGY

Our approach for evaluating the effect and efficacy of the implementation of the Crime Victims' Rights Act on the treatment of crime victims was comprised of various evaluation methods. Three of these methods— survey of federal crime victims, survey of U.S. Attorneys Office victim- witness professionals, and site visits—are detailed discussion than the others. We conducted this performance audit from May 2007 to December 2008 in accordance with generally accepted government auditing standards. Those standards require that we plan and perform the audit to obtain sufficient, appropriate evidence to provide a reasonable basis for our findings and conclusions based on our audit objectives. We believe that the evidence obtained provides a reasonable basis for our findings and conclusions based on our audit objectives.

Survey of Federal Crime Victims

To evaluate the effect and efficacy of CVRA implementation efforts, we determined that it was important to obtain the perspectives of federal crime victims. We reached an agreement with EOUSA officials on a systematic method for obtaining federal crime victims' perspectives without compromising victims' privacy and anonymity. We conducted a mail survey of a stratified random probability sample of federal crime victims, including individuals as well as businesses, who were listed in DOJ's Victim Notification System (VNS) and whose cases became active (i.e., charges were filed) on or after January 1, 2006, and closed (i.e., there was an acquittal or the sentencing decision was made) no later than November 30, 2007. We selected this time frame because the DOJ guidance and regulations for implementing the CVRA—the Attorney General Guidelines for Victim and Witness Assistance and procedures for addressing victim complaints against DOJ employees—were effective as of December 19, 2005. The case-closed date was selected because we drew our sample of crime victims in February 2008 and wanted to offer DOJ officials sufficient time to update the Victim Notification System database (from which we drew our sample) for cases closed by the end of November 2007.

We decided to survey only those victims whose cases were closed in order to obtain victims' perspectives over the duration of the criminal justice process, though perhaps excluding the post-sentencing phase. In addition, we decided to exclude certain crime victims from our survey (i.e. minors and victims who requested not to be contacted by DOJ about their cases). We excluded minors due to the sensitivities surrounding the types of crimes for which they were most likely victims—child pornography and human trafficking.

We selected our sample of federal crime victims from information DOJ provided to us from its Victim Notification System, which is used to notify crime victims of proceedings related to their cases. DOJ agreed to provide us with an extract of VNS data so that we could draw our own survey sample. However, given DOJ's concerns about maintaining the privacy and anonymity of the crime victims, with the exception of a unique identifying number for each victim and the classification of the type of crime involved, the data we received were devoid of any information that would identify individual victims. The universe of federal crime victims listed in VNS whose cases were open on or after January 1, 2006, and closed on or before November 30, 2007, and from which we drew our sample, was 118,013. Twenty-two different types of crime were associated with these victims. To assure that victims of all crime types were included in our sample, we selected a stratified random probability sample, where the strata—or groups—were based on the type of crime. The number of victims in our sample, by type of crime, is provided in table 14.

Prior to selecting our sample, we assessed the reliability of VNS data by reviewing DOJ's Office of the Inspector General Report on VNS,2 which was issued in January 2008. We also interviewed DOJ Office of the Inspector General officials who conducted the audit of VNS, and questioned the VNS project manager about VNS data quality procedures. According to the Office of the Inspector General report, few internal controls are in place to ensure the accuracy and completeness of VNS data, and given that there is no routine process to ensure that data entry errors were not made, the quality of VNS data is primarily dependent upon the agency official who initially entered the information into the system. The Office of the Inspector General also reported that the inaccuracy of VNS data was evident in its attempt to conduct a mail survey of federal crime victims. Specifically, of the 2,762 crime victims included in this survey, questionnaires to 498 (18 percent) were returned as undeliverable due to incorrect or incomplete addresses.

In addition to concerns regarding accuracy and completeness of VNS data, we identified other limitations in using VNS to select our sample for our survey.

Federal investigative agents have acknowledged that they may not be able to identify all crime victims for every case, particularly wide-scale fraud cases where there could be thousands of victims. Therefore, it is likely that not all crime victims whose cases were opened and closed between January 1, 2006, and November 30, 2007, are listed in VNS, and thus not all of these victims had the opportunity to be included in our sample.

Table 14. Number of Crime Victims Listed in VNS Whose Cases Were Opened and Closed between January 1, 2006, and November 30, 2007, by Type of Crime

Type of crime	Total number of victims listed in VNS	Number of victims in GAO sample
Antitrust violations	1	1
Assimilated crimesa	158	5
Bank robbery	4,186	42
Civil rights prosecution	170	5
Crimes against government property	34	5
Domestic violence	52	5
Firearms/triggerlock	1,183	5
Fugitive crimes	95	5
Government regulatory offenses	10,157	99
Immigration	980	5
Indian offenses	232	5
Interstate theft	328	5
Labor management offense	534	5
Motor vehicle theft	223	5
Narcotics and dangerous drugs	72	5
Offenses involving the administration of justice	36	5
Pornography/obscenity	153	5
Postal service crimes	20,230	198
Theft of government property	224	5
White collar crime/fraud	68,075	663
Other criminal prosecutions	9853	96
Missing (type of crime not entered into VNS)	1037	5
Total	118,013	1,179

Source: GAO analysis of VNS data.

aAssimilated crimes are violations of state laws adopted for an area within special federal jurisdiction, such as some military posts.

Our sample only included federal crime victims whose cases were prosecuted by an Assistant U.S. Attorney or Criminal Division attorney because the other litigation units within DOJ do not use VNS. However, as mentioned previously, the vast majority of federal criminal cases are prosecuted either solely or jointly by Assistant U.S. Attorneys; therefore, the vast majority of known federal crime victims would have had an opportunity to be included in our sample.

Despite concerns regarding the reliability of VNS, we still chose to select our sample of federal crime victims from VNS because it is the only database that contains both contact information and case information for the majority of known federal crime victims.

In addition to limitations specifically associated with VNS, we also faced other limitations. Considering DOJ's concerns about the sensitivities in surveying crime victims, we agreed to conduct a mail survey as opposed to a phone survey, which usually generates higher response rates, in order to honor the privacy and anonymity of the crime victims. In other mail survey efforts, we typically follow up multiple times with nonrespondents to encourage them to complete and return the questionnaire, with these follow-ups sometimes being conducted by telephone. However, considering the sensitivities in surveying crime victims, we agreed with DOJ to only follow up once with nonrespondent victims, and this follow- up was by mail. Since victims are used to receiving notifications from DOJ and are probably not familiar with GAO, the questionnaire was sent in a DOJ envelope and DOJ included a cover letter explaining the purpose of the survey and encouraging victims to participate. The completed questionnaires, however, were returned directly to GAO.

Of the 1,179 federal crime victims to whom we mailed a questionnaire, 248 (21 percent) returned completed questionnaires, 36 (3 percent) returned blank questionnaires which we excluded from our analysis, and 895 (76 percent) did not return questionnaires at all. In addition, 154 (13 percent) questionnaires were returned to DOJ as undeliverable. EOUSA staff were able to obtain current mailing addresses for some of the victims whose questionnaires were returned as undeliverable, although the exact number of victims for which EOUSA found addresses is unknown because EOUSA did not keep track of this information. Therefore, there is some overlap between the number of victims whose questionnaires were returned undeliverable and the number of victims who returned completed or partially completed questionnaires or who did not return their questionnaires at all.

Due to the low response rate to our survey, we cannot generalize the survey results to federal crime victims in our study period, and instead, limit our discussion of survey results to only those victims who responded.

Survey of U.S. Attorneys Office Victim-Witness Professionals

Victim-witness professionals, particularly those at U.S. Attorneys Offices, have the most direct interaction with crime victims during and following the prosecution phase of a case. We therefore decided to obtain their perspectives on CVRA implementation. We conducted a Web-based survey of all 201 victim-witness professionals who were located in each of the 93 U.S. Attorneys Offices as of April 2008, which is when we released the questionnaire. Each of the 201 victim-witness professionals were sent an e¬mail containing a unique user name and password to ensure that only members of the target population could respond to our survey. To encourage victim-witness professionals to complete the questionnaire, we sent a number of follow-up e-mails to those who had not yet completed their Web-based questionnaire over the course of a 5-week period. We received responses from 174 (87 percent) of the victim-witness professionals. For the survey of federal crime victims as well as the survey of victim- witness professionals, the practical difficulties of conducting such surveys may introduce errors, commonly referred to as nonsampling errors. For example, difficulties in how a particular question is interpreted, in the sources of information available to respondents, or in how data are entered into databases or analyzed, can introduce unwanted variability into the survey results. We took steps in the development of both questionnaires to minimize these nonsampling errors. For example, a social science survey specialist designed both questionnaires in collaboration with GAO staff with subject matter expertise. Then, both draft questionnaires were pretested with a number of federal crime victims and victim-witness professionals to ensure that the questions were relevant, clearly stated, and easy to comprehend. When data were analyzed for both surveys, a second independent analyst checked all computer programs that assimilated and summarized the results. In the case of the crime victim survey, data were entered by staff at a professional data entry firm and a sample of the data was verified by GAO staff. Since the victim-witness professional survey was Web-based, respondents entered their answers directly into the electronic questionnaire. This eliminated the need to key the data into a database, thus removing an additional source of error.

Site Visits to Select Federal Judicial Districts

Considering that the enforcement mechanisms—victims' ability to file motions and petition for writ of mandamus and DOJ's process for investigating and taking disciplinary action in response to victim-related complaints—are an expansion of other federal crime victim statutes, we thought it was essential to visit locations where these enforcement mechanisms had been employed. We selected a nonprobability sample of 7 federal judicial districts for site visits because these districts either had multiple instances in which individuals asserted CVRA rights in court (filed a motion for relief in district court, petitioned the court of appeals for writ of mandamus, or otherwise asserted CVRA rights in court) or a judge, on his or her own initiative, based a case-related decision on the CVRA.3 In addition, in one of these districts, several victim complaints against a DOJ employee were investigated. Also, these locations allowed us to visit courts in various federal circuits. Specifically, these 7 districts are located in 6 different federal circuits. (There are a total of 12 federal regional circuits.) The districts we visited were:

- **Central District of California (Los Angeles)**
- **District of the District of Columbia (Washington, D.C.)**
- **District of Utah (Salt Lake City)**
- **Southern District of Texas (Houston)**
- **District of Hawaii (Honolulu)**
- **Eastern District of New York (Brooklyn)**
- **Northern District of Iowa (Cedar Rapids)**

In each location, we met with district judges or magistrate judges, Federal Public Defenders or Assistant Federal Public Defenders, and USAO staff— including Criminal Division Chiefs, Assistant U.S. Attorneys, and victim- witness professionals—who were involved in cases where victims filed motions or petitioned for a writ of mandamus regarding their CVRA rights. In addition, we met with investigators and victim-witness professionals at FBI field offices in each location and at U.S. Postal Inspection Service, ATF, and DEA field offices if located in the jurisdictions we visited. We also spoke with appellate judges in Houston, Texas and Los Angeles, California who presided over cases in which victims petitioned for a writ of mandamus regarding their CVRA rights. During the design phase of our review, we met with similar officials in the District of Arizona and the District of Maryland. We selected Arizona and Maryland because these states were identified by the victim advocates we interviewed as having a long-standing history of victims' rights enforcement. Table 15 identifies the types of officials we met with or spoke to in each location.

Table 15. Types of Federal Officials GAO Met with or Spoke with at Site Visit Locations for the CVRA Review

Site visit location	Appellate judges	District judges	Magistrate judges	Clerks of courts	USAO	Federal public defender	FBI	USPIS	ATF	DEA
Central District of California	X	X		X	X		X	X		X
District of the District of Columbia		X		X	X		X	X	X	
District of Utah		X			X	X	X	X		
Southern District of Texas	X	X		X	X		X	X		
District of Hawaii		X		X	X	X	X		X	
Eastern District of New York		X			X		X		X	X
Northern District of Iowa		X	X		X		X	X	X	
District of Arizona		X			X	X				
District of Maryland		X	X		X	X				

Source: GAO summary of site visit locations and meetings.

[a]One of the individuals we included in our tally of district judges with whom we met in Utah is a retired federal judge who has now assumed a role as a crime victim advocate and attorney.

In total we met with or spoke to 3 appellate judges, 19 district judges, 2 magistrate judges, 9 Federal Public Defenders or Assistant Federal Public Defenders, and Criminal Division Chiefs, Assistant U.S. Attorneys, and victim-witness professionals at 9 U.S. Attorneys Offices. In addition, we met with federal agents and victim-witness professionals at 7 FBI field offices, 5 U.S. Postal Inspection Service field offices, 4 ATF field offices, and 3

DEA field offices. Because we selected a nonprobabiity sample of districts to visit, the information we obtained at these locations may not be generalized to all federal judicial districts across the country. However, because we selected these locations based on specific activity that had occurred concerning the CVRA, the information we obtained at these locations provided us with a good perspective on the actual use of CVRA enforcement mechanisms.

OBJECTIVE 1: EFFORTS TO IMPLEMENT THE CVRA

Department of Justice Efforts

We used various methods to identify efforts made by DOJ to implement the CVRA. First, we reviewed written guidance provided to DOJ employees on actions that could and should be taken to afford crime victims their CVRA rights. Guidance included the Attorney General Guidelines on Victim and Witness Assistance and information generated by individual U.S. Attorneys Offices.

Second, we interviewed DOJ headquarters officials—including Executive Office of the United States Attorneys (EOUSA) staff who oversee the victim-witness program for U.S. Attorneys Offices. During site visits, we interviewed victim-witness personnel and Assistant U.S. Attorneys and investigative agency field staff to determine efforts they have made—above and beyond written guidance—to afford crime victims their rights.

Third, given that the extent to which victims are afforded their right to reasonable, accurate, and timely notice of public court proceedings is measurable, we reviewed notification letters sent by select U.S. Attorneys Offices to determine whether they were timely. We reviewed notification letters sent by USAOs with large, medium, and small caseloads. We used the number of all criminal cases that were filed in judicial districts between March 2006 and March 2007, according to Administrative Office of the U.S. Courts (AOUSC) data, as the caseload measure. We reviewed notification letters sent out by: (1) the three judicial districts with the most criminal cases, (2) three judicial districts with cases close to the median number of criminal cases, and (3) the three judicial districts with close to the least number of criminal cases. Considering that VNS only maintains records of notification letters for 30 days, we requested notification letters sent out by these USAOs over a specific 30-day period. The judicial districts from which we obtained notification letters are listed in table 16, along with the total number of criminal cases filed in that district between March 2006 and March 2007. Please note that in many of these districts, the majority of criminal cases filed, such as immigration cases, do not involve victims. However, our purpose was to select districts based on overall workload as opposed to the workload solely associated with victims. Because we selected nonprobability samples of U.S. Attorney Offices and notification letters from these offices, the results of our analysis cannot be generalized either to all USAOs or to all notification letters sent by the offices we selected. However, this analysis provided us with informative examples of the timeliness of notification letters sent by USAOs.

Table 16. Number of Notification Letters Sent by Select Large, Medium, and Small U.S. Attorneys Offices during One 30-day Period from February 2008 to April 2008

U.S. Attorneys Office	Number of all criminal cases filed between March 31, 2006, and March 31, 2007	Number of notification letters sent in February 2008	Number of notification letters sent in March 2008	Number of notification letters sent in April 2008
District of Arizona	3,671	208		
Western District of Texas	5,149		51	
Southern District of Texas	5,011			52
Middle District of	444	68		
Pennsylvania				
District of Colorado	574		132	
Southern District of	451			116
Mississippi				
Eastern District of Oklahoma	69	29		
District of Guam	136		1	
District of the Virgin Islands	117			1

Source: GAO analysis of notification letters sent to crime victims.

Note: If a cell in this table has been left blank, we did not request notification letters from that particular USAO for that particular month.

Federal Judiciary Efforts

Fourth, through site visits and headquarters meetings, we obtained perspectives from DOJ officials on any challenges they have experienced in affording crime victims their rights and efforts they have made or planned to make to address these challenges. We also solicited perspectives from victim-witness personnel in affording crime victims their rights—since they have the most direct interaction with victims — through our Web-based survey. We also sought suggestions from these officials on how the challenges of affording victims their rights could be overcome.

We used various methods to identify and assess the efforts made by the federal judiciary—including AOUSC, FJC, the Judicial Conference, and select judges—to ensure that crime victims are afforded their rights under the CVRA.

First, we reviewed CVRA-related training and guidance developed by AOUSC, FJC, and the Judicial Conference for federal judges. The guidance was in the form of memoranda, training materials, videos, as well as revisions to the Federal Rules of Criminal Procedure and the Benchbook for U.S. District Court Judges. Second, during our site visits to federal judicial districts, we interviewed federal judges to obtain their perspectives on the usefulness of the guidance and training they received regarding the CVRA, and whether any additional information would be useful to help them ensure that crime victims are afforded their rights. We also interviewed AOUSC and FJC officials to inquire about additional CVRA-related efforts they have planned.

OBJECTIVE 2: MECHANISMS TO ENSURE ADHERENCE TO THE CVRA

Complaint Process

To help ensure that DOJ officials are complying with CVRA requirements, the CVRA requires DOJ to designate an administrative authority to receive and investigate complaints related to the provision or violation of the rights of a crime victim. The CVRA also required DOJ to train or impose disciplinary actions on employees who fail to comply with the provisions of federal law pertaining to the treatment of crime victims.

First, we evaluated the extent to which victims are aware of the complaint process. In order for the complaint process to be an effective method for ensuring that DOJ officials are compliant with CVRA, victims need to be aware of the process and understand its purpose. During our data collection phase, we interviewed DOJ officials, such as victim-witness personnel and prosecutors, regarding the methods used by DOJ to inform victims about the complaint process. Also, we reviewed various DOJ components' brochures and Web sites to determine what complaint process information was being provided to crime victims. We used our Victim-Witness Personnel Survey to determine whether staff inform any or all victims about the complaint process. Additionally, we incorporated questions into our crime victim survey in an attempt to determine whether they were aware of the victim complaint process.

Second, we reviewed 141 of the 144 files related to victim complaints received by DOJ's Victims' Rights Ombudsman (VRO) from December 2005 to April 20084 to obtain information on the nature of the complaints and the VRO's decisions as to whether the DOJ office or employees cited in the complaints had not afforded victims their CVRA rights. We selected December 2005 as the start date for our review of victim complaints because this was when the first person filed a complaint with the VRO. While DOJ's regulations regarding the complaint process did not take effect until December 19, 2005, While DOJ's regulations regarding the complaint process did not take effect until December 19, 2005, the VRO accepted a complaint filed before the effective date and responded to it after the regulations took effect.5 We chose April 2008 as the end date of our review to allow us enough time to analyze the complaint information prior to issuing our report. We summarized the complaint file information in a data collection instrument. Information collected includes (a) a summary of the concerns raised by the complainant, (b) CVRA rights the complainant alleged were not afforded, (c) the title of the individual whom the complainant claimed denied them their CVRA rights, and (d) actions taken by DOJ officials to investigate and resolve the complaint.

Third, we determined whether the VRO's protocol for investigating and responding to victim-related complaints is consistent with professional ombudsman standards6 and standards for internal control in the federal government. For example, we determined whether the VRO is recording the basis for its decisions and whether the selection of individuals to investigate complaints allows for an independent and impartial review. To make this determination, we conducted interviews with the VRO and reviewed documentary evidence outlining VRO procedures for addressing victim complaints. We also conducted in-person or phone interviews with U.S. Attorney "points-of-contact" who investigated complaints from federal crime victims. In this discussion, we inquired about actions taken to conduct the investigation, and if relevant, why these officials may have deviated from guidance. Further, we reviewed two studies that assessed the practices of state victims' rights enforcement offices—located in Alaska, Arizona, Connecticut, Colorado, Maryland, Minnesota, South Carolina, and Wisconsin—regarding their efforts to address victim complaints against state officials. We also interviewed representatives from each of these offices to obtain additional information on their process for investigating victim complaints.

Filing Motions and Petitions for Writ of Mandamus

We also obtained information on instances in which crime victims asserted their CVRA rights in court by filing a motion for relief in the district court, petitioning the appellate court for a writ of mandamus, or otherwise asserting CVRA rights in court. Specifically, we described instances in which federal crime victims asserted their rights in court, the specific rights they were asserting, and the courts' decisions on these assertions. We also identified any differences in judges' interpretations of CVRA provisions when deciding these cases. However, we are not in a position to make an evaluative judgment on the courts' decisions. We coordinated with the National Crime Victims' Law Institute (NCVLI), which maintains a database of instances in which the CVRA is cited in court decisions, to help ensure that we captured as many cases in which federal victims file CVRA motions and petitions as possible. (We were not able to identify all instances in which victims may have asserted their rights, particularly instances in which the victims' motions or courts' orders were made verbally or not published in a searchable database.) In addition, we incorporated questions into our crime victim survey in an attempt to determine the extent to which victims were aware of their rights and aware that they could assert their rights in federal court.

During site visits, we obtained perspectives from various participants in the federal criminal justice process on how victims asserting their rights affected court proceedings and whether they had any concerns or would like additional clarification or guidance to help the victim assertion process run more smoothly. Specifically, we interviewed select appellate, district, and magistrate judges, prosecutors, victim-witness personnel, and federal defenders who have experienced a situation where a crime victim filed a motion for relief, petitioned for a writ of mandamus, or otherwise asserted CVRA rights.

We also assessed whether AOUSC had met the CVRA requirement to report to Congress annually the number of times that a CVRA right is asserted in a criminal case and the relief requested is denied, the reason for the denial, as well as the number of times a mandamus action is brought pursuant to the CVRA. We reviewed AOUSC memoranda regarding the CVRA reporting requirement that was distributed to the courts and interviewed clerks in the district courts about how they identified cases to submit to AOUSC. We also interviewed AOUSC officials about the process used for preparing the annual reports and the steps taken to ensure that the reports are complete. In addition, we obtained AOUSC's annual reports for fiscal years 2005 to 2007—that is, each report that had been issued since the enactment of the CVRA—and compared AOUSC's list of denied motions and victim petitions to the list we generated through our own searches. We discussed any discrepancies between the two lists with the AOUSC officials responsible for preparing the annual report, district judges who ruled on the motions over which there was a discrepancy, and the clerks of the courts where the judges are located.

OBJECTIVE 3: DOJ PERFORMANCE REGARDING PROVISION OF CVRA RIGHTS

To address this objective, we first reviewed DOJ's 2007-2012 Strategic Plan to identify any department-wide performance measures regarding the provision of victims' rights. We determined the extent to which these measures were consistent with Government Performance and Results Act of 1993 (GPRA) requirements.7

Second, we reviewed the strategic plans and other performance measurement materials of all DOJ component agencies identified by the Attorney General Guidelines as having responsibilities regarding the provision of crime victims' rights to determine whether the components had performance goals and measures that were aligned with the department's objective regarding the provision of crime victims' rights.

Third, we assessed DOJ's efforts to ensure agency compliance with victims' rights provisions by requesting and reviewing the annual compliance reports each DOJ agency with victim-related responsibilities is supposed to prepare in accordance with the Attorney General Guidelines. We also interviewed OVC officials about the process they used to analyze and summarize each of the component compliance reports to determine overall departmental compliance with victims' rights provisions and how OVC uses the results to help component agencies improve their victims' rights efforts. We used the internal control standards for the federal government as the basis for evaluating the effectiveness of DOJ's victims' rights compliance monitoring efforts.

Finally, we reviewed DOJ's performance appraisal process to determine whether it is an effective measure for evaluating DOJ employees' compliance with CVRA, as intended. The Attorney General Guidelines require DOJ agencies to incorporate—in their annual work plans and performance appraisals—the implementation of and evaluation of employee adherence or non-adherence to victims' rights standards set forth in the Attorney General Guidelines. To determine if agencies are complying with Attorney General Guidelines, we obtained and reviewed the performance expectations for investigative agents, prosecutors, victim- witness personnel, corrections officers, and parole officers, and determined how well these performance expectations aligned with the standards set forth in the Attorney General Guidelines.

OBJECTIVE 4: FEDERAL COURTS' INTERPRETATION OF THE CVRA

We employed various methods to identify and analyze the key issues that have arisen in the interpretation of the CVRA by the federal courts. First, we reviewed and analyzed motions and petitions for writs of mandamus under the CVRA, as well as cases in which the courts based a decision on the CVRA on its own initiative, without either the victim or the prosecutor asserting CVRA rights. We obtained these cases through legal search engines, court dockets, interviews, and case compilations by the FJC and the National Crime Victims Law Institute to help ensure that we performed as comprehensive a review as possible. We searched for all cases in which CVRA had been discussed. We conducted our final electronic search on June 30, 2008. The cases included in this chapter are those that were available in legal databases as of that date.8 We chose this date to allow us enough time to review and summarize the cases prior to issuing this chapter. However, we may not have identified all instances in which victims asserted CVRA rights, particularly if the motion and court ruling were made verbally, or not published within a searchable database. We analyzed the cases to identify key CVRA provisions that are being interpreted by the courts and any differences in the way in which the courts have interpreted them. However, we are not in a position to make an evaluative judgment on the courts' decisions.

Second, during our site visits, we interviewed judges, prosecutors, defense attorneys, and victim attorneys who were involved in CVRA-related cases to discuss the interpretation issues that arose in their cases and how court decisions have contributed to the development of case law. We also conducted phone interviews and in-person meetings with representatives of crime victim advocacy associations to obtain their perspectives on what they considered to be the key CVRA provisions that are being interpreted by the courts. These associations included the National Crime Victims Law Institute, Arizona Voice for Victims of Crime, and Maryland Crime Victims' Resource Center. We chose these organizations because they have assisted victims in filing motions and petitions for writs of mandamus to assert their CVRA rights in court.

Third, we analyzed DOJ policies, in the Attorney General Guidelines and other guidance, that address key CVRA provisions and obtained perspectives from DOJ officials regarding why these policies were enacted. We also reviewed FJC guidance on the CVRA to capture issues that were discussed and interviewed FJC and AOUSC officials to obtain their perspectives on these issues.

Finally, we reviewed files for victim complaints that were submitted to the VRO to identify concerns raised related to the interpretation of CVRA provisions.

OBJECTIVE 5: PERSPECTIVES ON CVRA IMPLEMENTATION

In order to understand the impact that the CVRA has had on participants in the federal justice system, we asked a range of federal participants about outcomes associated with implementing this act.

First, we incorporated questions into our crime victim survey in an attempt to determine the extent to which DOJ and federal courts' efforts to afford victims CVRA rights are effective. Specifically, the survey results, though not generalizable, helped to provide some indication about victims' awareness of their rights and their reported satisfaction with the extent to which they were afforded those rights. The survey results also provided an indication about the extent to which victims reportedly exercised their rights by attending, speaking, or submitting written statements at court proceedings. However, we did not use victims' level of participation in court proceedings to provide an indication of the effectiveness of DOJ and the courts' efforts to afford crime victims' their rights, since victims may choose not to participate in court proceedings for a variety of reasons (e.g., wanting to put the case behind them and move on).

Second, during site visits, we obtained the perspectives of federal judges, Assistant U.S. Attorneys, victim-witness personnel, and federal defenders regarding the impact the CVRA has had on the treatment of crime victims as w ell as defendants, and the impact the CVRA has had on court proceedings. Perspectives of victim-witness personnel were also obtained through the Web-based survey.

Third, we conducted phone interviews and in-person meetings to obtain the perspectives of representatives of major national crime victim advocacy associations regarding the impact the CVRA has had on the treatment of crime victims. These associations include the: National Center for Victims of Crime; Justice Solutions; National Organization for Victim Assistance; National Criminal Justice Association; Joint Center on Violence and Victim Studies; Parents of Murdered Children; and the National Crime Victim Law Institute and its three federal clinics located in Arizona, Maryland, and South Carolina.

Fourth, we conducted phone interviews and in-person meetings to obtain the perspectives of defendant advocate associations regarding the impact of the CVRA on the treatment of defendants. These associations include the American Civil Liberties Union and the National Association of Criminal Defense Lawyers.

We identified these organizations based on publications they issued regarding crime victims' rights.

The information obtained to answer this objective is limited to the opinions we collected from federal employees and others, and cannot be generalized to the attitudes of all participants in the federal criminal justice system regarding the impact of the act.

APPENDIX II: FEDERAL STATUTES ENACTED PP FERAL STE AC BETWEEN 1982 A 2004 THA ADDRESS SIMIL TH CVA BETWEEN 1982 AND 2004 THAT ADDRESS SIMILARISSUES AS THE CVRA

Table 17. Federal Statutes Enacted from 1982 to 2004 that Address Similar Issues as the CVRA

Crime Victims' Rights Act of 2004	Victim and Witness Protection Act of 1982	Victims of Crime Act of 1984	Victims' Rights and Restitution Act of 1990	Violent Crime Control and Law Enforcement Act of 1994	Mandatory Victims Restitution Act of 1996	Victim Rights Clarification Act of 1997
The right to be reasonably protected from the accused.			Provided that federal crime victims have the right to be reasonably protected from the accused offender.			
The right to reasonable, accurate, and timely notice of any public court proceeding, or any parole proceeding, involving the crime or of any release or escape of the accused.	Required the Attorney General, when developing DOJ guidelines, to consider that victims of major serious crimes should receive prompt advance notification, if possible, of judicial proceedings related to their cases, including arrest, initial appearance, release, and proceedings of prosecution.	Amended the 1982 law to require the Attorney General to consider that victims of serious crimes, rather than victims of major serious crimes, should receive prompt advance notification, if possible, of arrest, initial appearance, release, and proceedings in the prosecution and punishment of the accused.	Provided that federal crime victims have the right to be notified of court proceedings and the right to information about the conviction, sentencing, imprisonment, and release of the offender; also requires responsible officials to provide victims with the earliest possible notice of investigation, arrest, filing of charges, certain court proceedings, release or detention status, acceptance of plea of guilty or rendering of verdict, sentencing, scheduling of parole hearing, and any form of release of the offender.			

Table 17. (Continued)

Crime Victims' Rights Act of 2004	Victim and Witness Protection Act of 1982	Victims of Crime Act of 1984	Victims' Rights and Restitution Act of 1990	Violent Crime Control and Law Enforcement Act of 1994	Mandatory Victims Restitution Act of 1996	Victim Rights Clarification Act of 1997
The right not to be excluded from any such public court proceeding, unless the court, after receiving clear and convincing evidence, determines that testimony by the victim would be materially altered if the victim heard other testimony at that proceeding.			Provided that federal crime victims have the right to be present at all public court proceedings related to the offense, unless the court determines that testimony by the victim would be materially affected if the victim heard other testimony at trial.			
The right to be reasonably heard at any public proceeding in the district court involving release, plea, sentencing, and any parole proceeding.				Amended Rule 32 of the Federal Rules of Criminal Procedure to require the judge, if a sentence is to be imposed for a crime of violence or sexual abuse, to address the victim personally if the victim is present at the sentencing hearing and determine if the victim wishes to make a statement or present any information in relation to the sentence.		Provided that federal crime victims may not be excluded from the trial related to the offense because the victim may, during a sentencing hearing, make a statement or submit information related to the sentence.

Table 17. (Continued)

Crime Victims' Rights Act of 2004	Victim and Witness Protection Act of 1982	Victims of Crime Act of 1984	Victims' Rights and Restitution Act of 1990	Violent Crime Control and Law Enforcement Act of 1994	Mandatory Victims Restitution Act of 1996	Victim Rights Clarification Act of 1997
The reasonable right to confer with the attorney for the Government in the case.	Required the Attorney General, when developing DOJ guidelines, to consider that victims of serious crimes should be consulted by the attorney for the government in order to obtain the the victim's views about the disposition of any federal criminal case brought as a result of such crime, including the views of the victim about dismissal, release of the accused pending judicial proceedings, plea negotiations, and pretrial diversion program.		Provided that federal crime victims have the right to confer with the attorney for the government in the case			
The right to full and timely restitution as provided in law.	Provided for discretionary restitution in cases arising out of Title 18 of the U.S. Code or in air piracy cases.		Provided that federal crime victims have the right to restitution.	Provided for mandatory restitution in certain cases, including cases involving sexual abuse, sexual exploitation of children, and domestic abuse.	Provided for mandatory restitution in certain cases involving violent crimes and property crimes arising under Title 18 of the U.S. Code.	
The right to proceedings free from unreasonable delay.						
The right to be treated with fairness and with respect for the victim's dignity and privacy.			Provided that federal crime victims have the right to be treated with fairness and respect for the victim's dignity and privacy.			

Source: GAO analysis of federal statutes

Appendix III: Complaints Submitted to the pp Cpls itte th Vctims Rights Ombudsman by ndiviual Ded B Fdl Ci Viti Victims' Rights Ombudsman by Individuals Determined to Be Federal Crime Victims

Table 18 includes a summary of the 11 complaints submitted to the Department of Justice (DOJ) Victims' Rights Ombudsman (VRO) from December 2005 to April 2008 by individuals whom the VRO determined to be federal crime victims.[1] The VRO determined that in none of these instances was a DOJ employee noncompliant with his or her obligations regarding the provision of victims' rights. We are not in a position to separately assess the validity of these complaints or the truthfulness of any of the allegations therein because we did not conduct an independent investigation of the complaints. We also did not obtain additional information on the VRO's decisions related to these complaints, other than the final determination. Therefore, the information included in the table below only represents the victims' perspectives regarding the complaints.

Table 18. Complaints Submitted to the Victims' Rights Ombudsman from December 2005 to April 2008 by Individuals Determined to Be Federal Crime Victims

Number	Date received by the VRO	Complaint summary
1	October 2006	The complainant, a victim-witness, did not feel she was reasonably protected from the accused. She also claimed that she did not receive timely notice of hearing dates or of plea negotiations with some of the defendants. The complainant stated that the prosecutors tried to exclude her from observing the trial, but the judge permitted her to participate. Although the complainant stated that she was able to meet with the prosecutor on several occasions, she stated that the prosecutor eventually became nonresponsive and called her derogatory names in court. She also claimed that the trial was unreasonably delayed.
2	October 2006	The complainant did not feel like she was reasonably protected from an inmate against whom she had testified, as she had received letters from him. She also asserted that she was not notified of instances in which the inmate was transferred to a different facility.
3	December 2006	The complainant stated that she was dissatisfied that there was no federal indictment, after the federal prosecutor told her that he would bring the case to a federal grand jury. The complainant also raised concerns that the federal prosecutor did not respond to her attempts to contact him and claimed that the prosecutor did not attend the hearing that had been scheduled.
4	March 2007	The complainant believed that one of the defendants in a fraud case should have been charged for additional counts of

		fraud and that the defendant's sentence was inadequate compared to the damage caused by the crime. (Seven victims in this case submitted complaints.)
5	May 2007	No summary was provided by the complainant; however, in the "Other Relevant Information" section of the complaint form, the victim provided information on how being defrauded by the defendant led to significant financial hardship and may have had a negative impact on her health. (Seven victims in this case submitted complaints.)
6	May 2007	The complainant believed that the plea agreement negotiated for the individual who defrauded him was too lenient, noting that the defendant could have been charged with more counts. The complainant wanted an explanation of the plea agreement and an investigation of whether there was collusion between the parties that negotiated the plea agreement. (Seven victims in this case submitted complaints.)
7	May 2007	The complainant believed that the defendant in a fraud case should have been subjected to greater punishment that adequately reflected the damage caused by the crime. (Seven victims in this case submitted complaints.)
8	May 2007	The complainant believed that the defendant in a fraud case should have been subjected to greater punishment that adequately reflected the damage caused by the crime. (Seven victims in this case submitted complaints.)
9	June 2007	The complainant believed that the defendant in a fraud case should have been subjected to greater punishment for his crime, stating that he had suffered significant hardship as a result of his victimization. (Seven victims in this case submitted complaints.)
10	June 2007	The complainant believed that the plea agreement for one defendant did not match the crime or the hardship caused to the victims, and that the defendant should have been charged with additional counts of fraud. The complainant claimed that as a result of the crime, her family's financial condition has been dramatically changed. Although the complainant did not specify which CVRA right she felt she had been denied, she underlined text for the right associated with full and timely restitution. (Seven victims in this case submitted complaints.)
11	January 2008	Complainant was the executor of the victim's estate and had to pay the bank money because the deceased's account was overdrawn

Source: GAO analysis of federal crime victim complaint files.

APPENDIX IV: SUMMARY OF CASES IN WHICH A PP Y ES N WH COURT ISUED A DCISION BAED N TE CVRA COURT ISSUED A DECISION BASED ON THE CVRA.

Table 19. Summary of Cases in which a Court Issued a Decision Based on the CVRA that We Reviewed, as of June 30, 2008a

United States v. Tobin, No. 04-cr-21 6-01, 2005 WL 1868682 (D.N.H. July 22, 2005) (order granting motion).	The crime victim objected to a joint motion to continue the trial for 90 days, arguing, among other things, that a continuance would violate the victim's right to proceedings free from unreasonable delay. The U.S. District Court for the District of New Hampshire granted the motion for a continuance, finding that the continuance was reasonable, but the court noted that, based on its obligation to ensure that crime victims are afforded their rights, no further continuance would be granted absent extraordinary circumstances.	The right to proceedings free from unreasonable delay
United States v. Sacane, No. 3:05-cr-325, 2007 WL 951666 (D. Conn. Mar. 28, 2007) (order denying motion).	The crime victims moved for an order directing the defendant to provide the victims with detailed financial information in advance of a restitution hearing. The U.S. District Court for the District of Connecticut denied the motion, stating that if the CVRA does not provide victims with a right to disclosure of presentence reports, then it would not provide victims with the right to obtain such disclosures directly from the defendant; rather, if the victims believe that disclosure of the information is necessary, they may seek the assistance of the government.	The right to full and timely restitution, as provided in law
Rzayeva v. United States, The plaintiffs brought a civil suit alleging that certain federal agencies had None	492 F. Supp. 2d 60 (D. Conn. violated the CVRA by failing to investigate the death of a medical patient. 2007). The U.S. District Court for the District of Connecticut held that it did not have jurisdiction to order federal officials to initiate a prosecution.	None
United States v. Turner, 367 F. Supp. 2d 319 (E.D.N.Y. 2005).	After discovering that victims had not received adequate notice of the initial appearance and detention hearing, the U.S. District Court for the Eastern District of New York ordered the government to provide victims with a summary of the earlier proceedings and notice of future proceedings. The court also approved a joint written request for a Speedy Trial Act waiver, stating that it would not cause unreasonable delay and noting that a public hearing on the matter	The right to reasonable, accurate, and timely notice The right to be reasonably protected from the accused The right not to be excluded from any public court proceeding The right to be reasonably heard The right to proceedings free from unreasonable delay

Table 19. (Continued)

	would have required victim notification. The opinion also discusses other CVRA provisions in general.	The right to be treated with fairness and with respect for dignity and privacy
United States v. GuevaraToloso, No. 04-1 455, 2005 WL 1210982 (E.D.N.Y. May 23, 2005) (order *sua sponte*).	In a case involving a defendant arrested for illegally reentering the United States after being convicted of a felony and subsequently being deported, the U.S. District Court for the Eastern District of New York asked the prosecutor whether the victims of the predicate offense, which was the initial felony, had been notified of the proceedings. The prosecutor opined that he did not think that the CVRA required such notification, and the court agreed, stating that because the predicate conviction was for a state offense, the victims of the predicate crime were not victims under the CVRA.	The right to reasonable, accurate, and timely notice
United States v. Ingrassia, 392 F. Supp. 2d 493 (E.D.N.Y. 2005).	In a securities fraud case involving at least 200 victims, the government provided notification to victims through a publication and a mailed notification that informed victims that further information would be provided through the VNS Web site. In the report and recommendations, the magistrate judge found that reliance on the VNS Web site in this case did not satisfy the CVRA notification requirement. The magistrate judge recommended that the judge accept the guilty pleas of the defendants once the government provided notification to all identified victims by first-class mail of the defendants' pleas, release status, sentencing date, and the victims' right to be heard with regard to the plea and sentence. The district judge accepted the magistrate judge's report and recommendation.	The right to reasonable, accurate, and timely notice
United States v. Saltsman, No. 07-cr-641, 2007 WL 4232985 (E.D.N.Y. Nov. 27, 2007) (order granting motion).	In a securities fraud case potentially involving tens of thousands of victims, the government moved for an order authorizing it to provide notice to victims through a publication that directs victims to a Web site providing further information about the case. The U.S. District Court for the Eastern District of New York granted the motion, noting that the CVRA authorizes the court to fashion a reasonable procedure to give effect to the CVRA when the number of victims makes it impracticable to accord all of the victims all of the CVRA rights.	The right to reasonable, accurate, and timely notice
United States v. Rubin, 558 F. Supp. 2d 411	In a case in which the defendant was indicted for securities fraud first in 2004	All CVRA rights

Table 19. (Continued)

(E.D.N.Y. 2008).	and then by a superseding indictment in 2006, victims of the superseding indictment filed a motion asserting that multiple CVRA rights had been violated. The U.S. District Court for the Eastern District of New York held that although the government did not meet its CVRA obligation to inform victims of their CVRA rights, no substantive CVRA rights had been violated.	
United States v. Rigas, 371 F. Supp. 2d 474 (S.D.N.Y. 2005).	In a securities fraud case potentially involving tens of thousands of victims, the government proposed a settlement agreement in which the defendants would forfeit certain assets and establish a victim compensation fund, and in order to receive funds from the forfeited assets and fund, victims would forgo most civil actions against the defendants. Two sets of victims opposed the settlement agreement, arguing that it violated their rights to full and timely restitution and to be treated with fairness. The U.S. District Court for the Southern District of New York accepted the settlement agreement, finding that the agreement was fair and equitable and in the best interest of all the parties.	The right to full and timely restitution, as provided in law The right to be treated with fairness and with respect for dignity and privacy
In re W.R. Huff Asset Management Co., 409 F.3d 555 (2d Cir. 2005).	Crime victims in United States v. Rigas filed a petition for a writ of mandamus, seeking to vacate the settlement agreement approved by the U.S. District Court for the Southern District of New York on the basis that the government violated the victims' right to full and timely restitution, right to fairness, right to notification, and right to confer with the prosecutor. The U.S. Court of Appeals for the Second Circuit held that the district court did not abuse its discretion in approving the settlement agreement, as the settlement agreement was in accordance with applicable restitution law and the government's actions with respect to notice and conferral were reasonable.	The right to reasonable, accurate, and timely notice The reasonable right to confer with the prosecutor The right to full and timely restitution, as provided in law The right to be treated with fairness and with respect for dignity and privacy
United States v. Blumhagen, No. 03-cr-56s, 2006 U.S. Dist. LEXIS 15380 (W.D.N.Y. Apr. 3, 2006) (order *sua sponte*).	The U.S. District Court for the Western District of New York required the government to notify victims of an upcoming plea hearing and include in its notice a statement of its reasons for entering a plea agreement with one defendant and for moving to dismiss the indictment against the other.	The right to reasonable, accurate, and timely notice The right to be reasonably heard The right to be treated with fairness and with respect for dignity and privacy

Table 19. (Continued)

United States v. Kopp, No. 00-cr-1 89A, 2007 WL 1747165 (W.D.N.Y. June 18, 2007) (order denying motion).	The government opposed the defendant's motion for assignment of new counsel, citing in part the victim's right to a prompt disposition of the case. The U.S. District Court for the Western District of New York, relying in part on the CVRA, denied the defendant's motion for new counsel.	The right to proceedings free from unreasonable delay
Third Circuit		
In re Walsh, No. 06-4792, 2007 WL 1156999 (3d Cir. Apr. 19, 2007).	After petitioner's civil case against the United States, the Navy, and eight military officers was dismissed by the U.S. District Court for the Middle District of Pennsylvania, the petitioner filed a petition for a writ of mandamus requesting a broad range of relief, including a restraining order and the arrest of specified military officers. The U.S. Court of Appeals for the Third Circuit denied the petition, stating that, even assuming that the petitioner was a victim under the CVRA, the petitioner applied for relief in the wrong court.	The right to full and timely restitution, as provided in law
Fourth Circuit		
United States v. Bermudez, No. 1:06-cr-00135 (D. Md. Jan. 17, 2008) (order denying motion).	The crime victim filed a motion requesting to be granted access to certain portions of the presentence report. The U.S. District Court for the District of Maryland allowed the victim to speak at the sentencing hearing but denied the motion, concluding that the victim had enough information to make a victim impact statement, and did not allow the victim to present information about the Federal Sentencing Guidelines calculation.	The right to be reasonably heard The right to full and timely restitution, as provided in law The right to be treated with fairness and with respect for dignity and privacy
In re Brock, No. 08-1086 (4th Cir. Jan. 31, 2008).	The crime victim in United States v. Brock filed a petition for a writ of mandamus, requesting the U.S. Court of Appeals for the Fourth Circuit to order the U.S. District Court for the District of Maryland to reopen the sentencing, grant the victim access to the presentence report, and allow the victim to be heard regarding the Federal Sentencing Guidelines calculation. The U.S. Court of Appeals for the Fourth Circuit denied the petition, without deciding on the standard of review, finding that the district court did not abuse its discretion or violate the victim's CVRA rights because the district court considered the victim's written statement and allowed the victim to speak at the sentencing hearing.	The right to be reasonably heard The right to be treated with fairness and with respect for dignity and privacy

Table 19. (Continued)

Searcy v. Skinner, No. 6:06- 1418, 2006 WL 1677177 (D.S.C. June 16, 2006).	Plaintiff, a federal inmate, filed a complaint against a fellow inmate, arguing that the CVRA creates a right to petition the court and that the CVRA entitles him to restitution. The U.S. District Court for the District of South Carolina dismissed the complaint, stating that the government declined to bring charges against the defendant and that the plaintiff could not use the CVRA as a mechanism to bring an action against the defendant directly.	The right to full and timely restitution, as provided in law
In re Searcy, No. 06-7703 (4th Cir. Oct. 6, 2006).	After the U.S. District Court for the District of South Carolina dismissed his civil complaint, petitioner filed a petition for a writ of mandamus claiming that he was entitled to restitution under the CVRA. The U.S. Court of Appeals for the Fourth Circuit denied the petition, stating that the petitioner was not entitled to relief under the CVRA in his civil case, and that if he were dissatisfied with the district court's dismissal of his case, he could seek review through appeal.	The right to full and timely restitution, as provided in law
Searcy v. Paletz, No. 6:07- 1389, 2007 WL 1875802 (D.S.C. June 27, 2007).	Plaintiff, a federal inmate, filed a complaint under the CVRA against a fellow inmate and several federal agencies, alleging that the inmate assaulted him and that the agencies failed to protect him. The U.S. District Court for the District of South Carolina dismissed the complaint for failure to state a claim upon which relief can be granted, stating that the government declined to bring charges against the defendant and that the plaintiff could not use the CVRA as a mechanism to bring an action against the defendant directly.	The right to full and timely restitution, as provided in law The right to be treated with fairness and with respect for dignity and privacy
United States v. Sharp, 463 F. Supp. 2d 556 (E.D. Va. 2006).	The former domestic partner of a man to whom the defendant distributed marijuana requested to give a victim impact statement at the defendant's sentencing hearing, arguing that she suffered abuse as a result of the marijuana use of her former domestic partner. The U.S. District Court for the Eastern District of Virginia denied the request, holding that she was not a victim of the defendant because she was not directly and proximately harmed as a result of the offense, as the harm to her was not foreseeable by the sale of the marijuana and the sale of the marijuana was not a "but for" cause of the abuse that she suffered.	The right to be reasonably heard

Table 19. (Continued)

United States v. Moussaoui, No. 1:01-cr-00455 (E.D. Va. Apr. 7, 2006) (order granting motion).	Crime victims, also plaintiffs in a related civil case, requested access to nonpublic discovery information provided by the government to the defendant. The U.S. District Court for the Eastern District of Virginia granted the motion, based on the CVRA and the Air Transportation Safety and System Stabilization Act. (The government appealed the decision, and the U.S. Court of Appeals for the Fourth Circuit reversed the district court decision, based on grounds other than the CVRA, as the crime victims abandoned the CVRA argument at the appellate level. United States v. Moussaoui, 483 F.3d 220 (4th Cir. 2007).)	The right to be treated with fairness and with respect for dignity and privacy
United States v. Purdue Frederick Co., Inc., No. 1:07- cr-00029 (W.D. Va. July 23, 2007).	Crime victims opposed a plea agreement, arguing that they were not provided sufficient notice of proceedings and that restitution provided for in the plea agreement was insufficient. The U.S. District Court for the Western District of Virginia held that sufficient notice was provided, as information was posted on the court's Web site, and accepted the plea agreement, finding under relevant restitution law that, due to the difficulty of establishing causation, the restitution process would unduly complicate and prolong the sentencing process.	The right to reasonable, accurate, and timely notice The right to full and timely restitution, as provided in law
In re Jane Doe, No. 07-1705 (4th Cir. Aug. 9, 2007).	In United States v. Purdue Frederick Co., Inc., a case in which the defendant pleaded guilty to misbranding Oxycontin with the intent to defraud or mislead, petitioner, an Oxycontin addict, filed a petition for a writ of mandamus requesting the U.S. Court of Appeals for the Fourth Circuit to order the U.S. District Court for the Western District of Virginia to reopen the sentencing and enforce the petitioner's right to restitution under the CVRA. Without deciding on the standard of review, the court of appeals held that the district court did not abuse its discretion in denying the petitioner's motion because the petitioner was not a victim under restitution law. The court of appeals found that the petitioner was unable to demonstrate that she was directly and proximately harmed as a result of the conduct underlying one of the elements of the offense; that is, the chain of causation between the defendant's actions and the petitioner's addiction was too attenuated to support application of restitution law.	The right to full and timely restitution, as provided in law

Table 19. (Continued)

Fifth Circuit		
United States v. Lay, 456 F. Supp. 2d 869 (S.D. Tex. 2006).	When the defendant died before his sentencing hearing and while his appeal was pending, the defendant's estate moved to dismiss the indictment and vacate the conviction, and the crime victim opposed the motion, requesting the U.S. District Court for the Southern District of Texas to issue an order of restitution under the CVRA and restitution law. The district court granted the estate's motion and denied the victim's motion, stating that restitution only applies when the defendant is convicted of an offense, and the abatement doctrine provides that a conviction is to be vacated when a defendant dies while an appeal is pending.	The right to full and timely restitution, as provided in law
United States v. Lay, 456 F. Supp. 2d 869 (S.D. Tex. 2006).	When the defendant died before his sentencing hearing and while his appeal was pending, the defendant's estate moved to dismiss the indictment and vacate the conviction, and the crime victim opposed the motion, requesting the U.S. District Court for the Southern District of Texas to issue an order of restitution under the CVRA and restitution law. The district court granted the estate's motion and denied the victim's motion, stating that restitution only applies when the defendant is convicted of an offense, and the abatement doctrine provides that a conviction is to be vacated when a defendant dies while an appeal is pending.	The right to full and timely restitution, as provided in law
In re Butler, No. 06-20848 (5th Cir. Nov. 1, 2006).	A crime victim in United States v. Lay filed a petition for a writ of mandamus requesting the U.S. Court of Appeals for the Fifth Circuit to order the U.S. District Court for the Southern District of Texas to reverse its decision to vacate the defendant's conviction and dismiss the indictment. The court of appeals denied the petition, finding that the district court correctly applied the abatement doctrine and that the CVRA right to restitution is subject to, and not exempt from, the abatement doctrine.	The right to full and timely restitution, as provided in law
United States v. Citgo Petroleum Corp., No. C-06- 563 (S.D. Tex. Aug. 8, 2007) (order denying motion); United States v. Citgo Petroleum Corp., No. C-06- 563 (S.D. Tex. May 12, 2008) (order	The government filed a motion requesting that the U.S. District Court for the Southern District of Texas to unseal the government's submission to the probation office in aid of sentencing, arguing in part that the information may assist the government in identifying victims and thereby assist the government in making its best efforts to ensure that victims are	The right not to be excluded from public court proceedings

Table 19. (Continued)

granting motion).	notified of and afforded their CVRA rights. The district court denied the motion, finding that the submission is similar to a presentence report and that the government did not overcome the presumption against disclosure of such information by demonstrating a compelling, particularized need for disclosure. Later in the same case, the government filed a motion requesting the district court to reconsider its decision to exclude victim-witnesses from the initial phase of the sentencing hearing after they have testified, arguing that the court had received no evidence that the testimony of the victim- witnesses would be materially altered if they heard other testimony. The district court granted the motion without opinion, allowing the victim- witnesses to attend the hearing.	
United States v. BP Products North America Inc., No. 4:07- cr-434, 2008 U.S. Dist. LEXIS 12893 (S.D. Tex. Feb. 21, 2008) (order denying motion)	Crime victims filed a motion requesting the U.S. District Court for the Southern District of Texas to reject a plea agreement because their CVRA rights had been violated. The district court found proper the district court's prior ruling granting permission to the government to delay notifying victims and conferring with victims about plea negotiations until after the plea agreement had been reached, under the CVRA provision that authorizes the court to fashion a reasonable alternative to give effect to the CVRA when the number of crime victims makes it impracticable to afford all of them the CVRA rights.	The right to reasonable, accurate, and timely notice The reasonable right to confer with the prosecutor The right to be treated with fairness and with respect for dignity and privacy
In re Dean, No. 08-201 25 (5th Cir. May 7, 2008).	Crime victims in United States v. BP Products filed a petition for a writ of mandamus, requesting that the U.S. Court of Appeals for the Fifth Circuit order the U.S. District Court for the Southern District of Texas to reject the plea agreement because of CVRA violations. The court of appeals, applying the writ of mandamus standard of review, found that the victims' rights had been violated, as the court should have fashioned a reasonable way to inform victims of the likelihood of criminal charges and to ascertain the victims' views on the proposed plea agreement before the plea agreement was reached. However, the court of appeals declined to issue a writ of mandamus, finding that such a writ was not appropriate under the circumstances because victims were able to participate in	The right to reasonable, accurate, and timely notice The reasonable right to confer with the prosecutor The right to be treated with fairness and with respect for dignity and privacy

Table 19. (Continued)

	the sentencing hearing and the district court would be able to consider their objections before deciding whether to accept the plea agreement.	
Sixth Circuit		
United States v. Gallion, No. 07-39 (E.D. Ky. Aug. 14, 2007) (order denying motion); United States v. Gallion, No. 07-39 (E.D. Ky. Aug. 20, 2007) (order *sua sponte*).	In a case involving charges of conspiracy to commit wire fraud with approximately 440 victims, the government filed a motion requesting that the U.S. District Court for the Eastern District of Kentucky authorize the government to provide notice to the victims by an initial letter that informs victims about the VNS Web site and call center, under the CVRA provision that authorizes the court to fashion a reasonable alternative to give effect to the CVRA when the number of crime victims makes it impracticable to afford all of them the CVRA rights. The district court denied the motion, stating that the victims are entitled to the full extent of notice provided by statute and that the proposed alternatives may be inadequate to ensure complete and timely notice. Later in the case, the district court, concerned about the victims' right to proceedings free from unreasonable delay and right to restitution, found that if the proceedings were to be continued, as requested by the defendant and government, it would be necessary for the court to revoke the defendant's bond. After appeals had been filed, the district court set aside its revocation order and deferred the hearing until the appeal had been decided.	The right to reasonable, accurate, and timely notice The right to full and timely restitution, as provided in law The right to proceedings free from unreasonable delay
United States v. Merkosky, 1 :02-cr-01 68, 2008 WL 1744762 (N.D. Ohio Apr. 11, 2008) (order denying motion).	A convicted defendant filed a motion asserting that he was a victim of several federal offenses and requesting that he be declared a crime victim under the CVRA. The U.S. District Court for the Northern District of Ohio denied the motion, finding that the defendant failed to establish that he had been denied any CVRA right and that the law prevents a person accused of the crime from obtaining any relief under the CVRA.	None
United States v. Stokes, No. 3:06-00204, 2007 WL 1849846 (M.D. Tenn. June 22, 2007) (order granting motion).	In a case involving an alleged embezzlement scheme with an estimated 35,000 victims, the government filed a motion requesting that the U.S. District Court for the Middle District of Tennessee authorize the government to provide notice to victims by proxy and by publication, under the CVRA provision that authorizes the court to fashion a	The right to reasonable, accurate, and timely notice

Table 19. (Continued)

	reasonable alternative to give effect to the CVRA when the number of crime victims makes it impracticable to afford all of them their CVRA rights. The district court granted the motion, finding that it would be impracticable to identify and notify all of the potential victims and that the proposed means of notification were reasonable.	
Seventh Circuit		
United States v. Marcello, 370 F. Supp. 2d 745 (N.D. Ill. 2005) (order denying motion).	The government requested that a crime victim be permitted to offer an oral statement opposing the release of the defendants at a detention hearing. The U.S. District Court for the Northern District of Illinois denied the motion, finding that because the CVRA provision providing that victims have the "right to be reasonably heard" includes a reasonableness requirement and a legal term of art (to be heard), it does not require courts to allow oral statements, particularly when the victim's statement is not material to the decision at hand.	The right to be reasonably heard
United States v. Croteau, No. 05-cr-30104 (N.D. Ill. Mar. 16, 2006) (order granting motion); United States v. Croteau, No. 05-cr-30104, 2006 U.S. Dist. LEXIS 23684 (N.D. Ill. Apr. 27, 2006) (order granting motion).	In a case involving thousands of victims, the government filed a motion requesting permission to send a one-time individualized mailing to all of the victims and establish a Web site with information about the case, under the CVRA provision that authorizes the court to fashion a reasonable alternative to give effect to the CVRA when the number of crime victims makes it impracticable to afford all of them their CVRA rights. The U.S. District Court for the Northern District of Illinois granted the motion. Later in the case, the government filed a motion requesting permission to publish a scheduled change of plea hearing on the Web site, noting that such publication may conflict with a local rule prohibiting public disclosure of the possibility of a plea of guilty or not guilty. The district court granted the motion, finding that disclosure would not cause the harm that the local rule was meant to prevent and that there was a strong interest in fulfilling Congress' mandate to notify victims of court proceedings.	The right to reasonable, accurate, and timely notice
United States v. Ballinger, No. 3:04-cr-0141, 3:05-cr-0002 (N.D. Ind. Jan. 13, 2005) (order granting	In a case with over 1,000 victims, the government filed a motion requesting that the U.S. District Court for the Northern District of Illinois find that due to the large number of victims, it was impracticable to	The right to reasonable, accurate, and timely notice

Table 19. (Continued)

motion).	afford them all of their rights by notifying them prior to a plea hearing. The district court granted the motion, finding that the number of victims made it impracticable to afford the victims their notification rights, but provided that the government may notify the victims as soon as practicable but prior to sentencing.	
United States v. Koetz, No. 05-cr-234 (E.D. Wis. Mar. 13, 2006) (order denying motion).	The government filed a motion to reopen the sentencing after it discovered that one of the victims had not been notified of a schedule change and was not able to speak at the hearing, noting that it would not seek a change in the sentence and that the defendant had no objection to the reopening. The U.S. District Court for the Eastern District of Wisconsin denied the motion.	The right to be reasonably heard
In re Oak Brook Bank, No. 06- 2331 (7th Cir. May 12, 2006).	The crime victim filed a petition for a writ of mandamus, requesting that the U.S. Court of Appeals for the Seventh Circuit order the U.S. District Court for the Northern District of Illinois to vacate its order denying the victim standing under relevant restitution law to object to the magistrate judge's recommendations regarding restitution. The court of appeals denied the petition, finding that the district court had not yet denied the victim any CVRA rights, as the court had not yet made a final determination about restitution and had invited all interested parties, including the victim, to file arguments regarding who should be considered a victim.	The right to full and timely restitution, as provided in law
In re Sabbia, No. 07-1368 (7th Cir. Feb. 21, 2007).	Petitioner filed a petition for a writ of mandamus asserting that the Department of Justice had denied him CVRA rights because three individuals had committed fraud against him through state court proceedings. The U.S. Court of Appeals for the Seventh Circuit denied the petition, finding that the filing was frivolous and forbidding the petitioner from filing any further legal papers in the circuit.	Not known
Eighth Circuit		
United States v. Johnson, 362 F. Supp. 2d 1043 (N.D. Iowa 2005).	The government filed a motion requesting that the U.S. District Court for the Northern District of Iowa allow victims to attend the trial. The district court granted the motion, citing the CVRA provision that victims have a right not to be excluded from the proceeding, unless the court finds that their testimony would be materially altered by hearing the testimony	The right not to be excluded from public court proceedings

Table 19. (Continued)

	of others, and finding that the defendant had provided no evidence that the testimony of any of the victims would be altered.	
United States v. L.M., 425 F. Supp. 2d 948 (N.D. Iowa 2006).	In a juvenile case, the government filed a motion requesting that the U.S. District Court for the Northern District of Iowa permit the government to notify the victim of proceedings and to allow the victim to attend any proceedings related to the case. The district court granted the request to notify the victim of proceedings and denied in part the request to attend proceedings, finding that the CVRA provides the right to attend public court proceedings, that federal law provides that district judges have discretion in determining whether juvenile proceedings should be public, and that the upcoming transfer hearing should be closed to the public.	The right to reasonable, accurate, and timely notice The right not to be excluded from public court proceedings
Ninth Circuit		
United States v. Leichner, No. 2:03-cr-00568 (C.D. Cal. May 23, 2005); United States v. Leichner, No. 2:03-cr-00568 (C.D. Cal. June 19, 2006) (order denying motion).	In a case with two defendants, victims spoke at the sentencing hearing of the first defendant, and a victim requested to speak at the sentencing of the second defendant. The U.S. District Court for the Central District of California did not allow the victim to speak, stating that the victim had spoken at the first sentencing hearing and that nothing that the victim would say would have any impact on the court's decision. Later in the case, the victim filed a motion requesting access to the presentence report, and the district court denied the motion.	The right to be reasonably heard
Kenna v. U.S. District Court for the Central District of California, 435 F.3d 1011 (9th Cir. 2006).	The victim in United States v. Leichner filed a petition for a writ of mandamus, requesting that the U.S. Court of Appeals for the Ninth Circuit order the U.S. District Court for the Central District of California to vacate the defendant's sentence and allow the victim to speak at the defendant's resentencing. The court of appeals, using the ordinary appellate standard of review, granted the petition, finding that although the language of the CVRA providing the right to be reasonably heard is ambiguous, an examination of the legislative history supports an interpretation of the law that provides victims the right to speak at sentencing hearings.	The right to be reasonably heard
In re Kenna, 453 F.3d 1136 (9th Cir. 2006).	The victim in United States v. Leichner filed a petition for a writ of mandamus,	The right to be reasonably heard The right to full and timely

Table 19. (Continued)

	requesting that the U.S. Court of Appeals for the Ninth Circuit order the U.S. District Court for the Central District of California to release to the victim the presentence report. The court of appeals denied the petition, holding that the district court did not abuse its discretion or commit legal error when it found that the CVRA did not confer a general right to disclosure of the presentence report and that the victim did not show that his reasons for disclosure outweighed the reasons for keeping the report confidential.	restitution, as provided in law The right to fairness and to be treated with dignity and privacy
United States v. Mikhel, No. 02-cr-220 (C.D. Cal. June 13, 2006).	The government requested that victims be allowed to attend the trial, and the U.S. District Court for the Central District of California denied the request, stating that victims who would be testifying would not be allowed to attend the trial until after they had testified	The right not to be excluded from public court proceedings
In re Mikhel, 453 F.3d 1137 (9th Cir. 2006).	In response to the district court order in United States v. Mikhel, the government filed a petition for a writ of mandamus, requesting that the U.S. Court of Appeals for the Ninth Circuit order the U.S. District Court for the Central District of California to permit crime victims to attend the trial. The court of appeals granted the petition in part and remanded to the district court to determine whether clear and convincing evidence showed that the victims' testimony would be materially altered by hearing the testimony of others during the trial.	The right not to be excluded from public court proceedings
United States v. Crompton Corp., 399 F. Supp. 2d 1047 (N.D. Cal. 2005).	In response to a government motion to unseal a plea agreement, the defendant filed a motion requesting that his name be redacted from the plea agreement. The U.S. District Court for the Northern District of California denied the defendant's motion, stating that redacting the defendant's name would conceal information from the victims and violate the CVRA.	The right not to be excluded from public court proceedings
Williamson v. U.S. District Court for the Northern District of California, No. 06-74584 (9th Cir. Sept. 29. 2006).	Petitioner filed a petition for a writ of mandamus, alleging crimes of multiple federal officials and seeking a broad range of relief, including an injunction requiring respondents not to use microwaves against him. The U.S. Court of Appeals for the Ninth Circuit denied the petition, stating that the petitioner identified no order in which a district court denied him rights under the CVRA.	None

Table 19. (Continued)

United States v. Lee, No. 01- cr-00132 (D. Haw. June 17, 2005) (order denying motion).	Crime victims, who were foreign nationals, filed a motion requesting that the U.S. District Court for the District of Hawaii order the government to authorize their entry to attend the sentencing hearing. The district court denied the motion but provided that the victims could submit their views to the court in writing and participate in the hearing by telephone.	The right not to be excluded from public court proceedings
United States v. Wood, No. 05-cr-00072 (D. Haw. July 17, 2006) (order granting motion).	The government filed a motion requesting to continue sentencing so that the employees of a corporation that had been defrauded by the defendant could attend and speak at the hearing. The U.S. District Court for the District of Hawaii granted the motion, finding that the employees were victims under the CVRA because although the corporation was directly harmed, the individuals were proximately harmed as a result of the fraud and that continuing the sentencing would afford the victims their right to be reasonably heard and would not unduly prolong the proceedings.	The right to be reasonably heard
United States v. Patkar, No. 06-cr-00250, 2008 WL 233062 (D. Haw. Jan. 28, 2008) (order denying motion).	The Associated Press, as intervenor, filed a motion requesting to dissolve a stipulation and order between the government and the defendant that sealed certain e-mails that formed the basis of the extortion charge against the defendant. The U.S. District Court for the District of Hawaii denied the motion, finding that the crime victims' right to be treated with fairness and with respect for the victim's privacy and dignity was sufficient good cause to limit disclosure of the e-mails.	The right to be treated with fairness and with respect for dignity and privacy
United States v. W.R. Grace, 401 F. Supp. 2d 1057 (D. Mont. 2005); United States v. W.R. Grace, 408 F. Supp. 2d 998 (D. Mont. 2006).	The defendant filed a motion to compel the government to comply with rules regarding public statements, and the government objected on the grounds that the statements were necessary to comply with the CVRA. The U.S. District Court for the District of Montana denied the motion, stating that the government was aware of the rules regarding public statements and an order would be superfluous; the court noted that although some of the government's statements were arguably necessary to comply with the CVRA requirement to provide timely notification of proceedings, others were not necessary under the CVRA and subject to the rules governing such statements. Later in the case, the defendant filed a	The right to reasonable, accurate, and timely notice The right not to be excluded from public court proceedings

Table 19. (Continued)

	motion for a change of venue, due to pretrial publicity. The district court denied the motion, noting that the CVRA provides victims with the right not to be excluded and requires courts to make every effort to permit the fullest attendance possible by the victims.	
Tenth Circuit		
United States v. Degenhardt, 405 F. Supp. 2d 1341 (D. Utah 2005).	The government notified the U.S. District Court for the District of Utah that victims wanted to speak at the defendant's sentencing hearing. The district court granted the request, finding that the CVRA superseded the rule providing that only victims of crimes of violence or sexual abuse may speak at sentencing. The district court also stated that an examination of the legislative history of the act supports a construction that requires courts to allow victims to personally address the court during sentencing.	The right to be reasonably heard
United States v. Heaton, 458 F. Supp. 2d 1271 (D. Utah 2006).	The government filed a motion to dismiss charges against a defendant. The U.S. District Court for the District of Utah ordered that the dismissal would not be approved by the court until the government provided the court with the victim's views on the dismissal, stating that the CVRA right to be treated with fairness and right to confer with the prosecutor extended to the decision to dismiss.	The reasonable right to confer with the prosecutor The right to be treated with fairness and with respect for dignity and privacy
United States v. Wilson, 350 F. Supp. 2d 90 (D. Utah 2005).	The U.S. District Court for the District of Utah declined to delay sentencing to ponder a decision that the Supreme Court had made the previous day on the Federal Sentencing Guidelines, finding that the sentencing had already been delayed and crime victims have a right to proceedings free from unreasonable delay.	The right to proceedings free from unreasonable delay
United States v. Hunter, No. 2:07-cr-307, 2008 WL 53125 (D. Utah Jan. 3, 2008) (order denying motion); United States v. Hunter, No. 2:07-cr-307, 2008 WL 110488 (D. Utah Jan. 8, 2008); United States v. Hunter, No. 2:07-cr-307, 2008 WL 153785 (D. Utah Jan. 14,	In a case in which the defendant pleaded guilty to unlawfully selling a handgun to a juvenile, the family of the victim who was shot and killed by the recipient of the handgun filed a motion requesting that they be considered victims under the CVRA. The U.S. District Court for the District of Utah denied the motion, finding that the victim was not directly and proximately harmed as a result of the offense, as the sale of the firearm to the juvenile and the shooting of the victim 8 months later were 'too factually and	The right to be reasonably heard The right to full and timely restitution, as provided in law

Table 19. (Continued)

2008).	temporally attenuated" and the shooter's conduct was an intervening factor that broke the chain of causation. Later in the case, the victims filed a motion requesting the district court to compel the government to disclose information supporting their position that they were crime victims under the CVRA or to release grand jury documents on the subject. The district court denied the motion, stating that if Congress had intended to afford members of the public access to prosecution files to determine their victim status, it would have stated so clearly in the law, and that the victims have not demonstrated that their need for grand jury documents outweighs the interests in maintaining grand jury secrecy. The victims filed a subsequent motion requesting the district court to reconsider its decision on the prosecution information and requesting a stay of the sentencing. The district court denied the motion, relying on the CVRA provision providing that in no event shall proceedings be stayed or subject to a continuance of more than 5 days for the purposes of enforcing this chapter and stating that the victims may be able to reopen the sentence if the court of appeals determined that they were victims under the CVRA because they had asserted their rights in the district court and had petitioned for a writ of mandamus within 10 days.	
In re Antrobus, No. 08-4002 (10th Cir. Jan. 11, 2008).	The purported victims in United States v. Hunter filed a petition for a writ of mandamus requesting that the U.S. Court of Appeals for the Tenth Circuit direct the U.S. District Court for the District of Utah to recognize them as victims under the CVRA. The court of appeals denied the petition, under the writ of mandamus standard of review, finding that the area of law regarding whether a sale of a gun to a minor is a proximate cause of any injury to a third person is not well-developed and that it could not say that the district court was clearly wrong in its decision.	The right to be reasonably heard The right to full and timely restitution, as provided in law
In re Antrobus, No. 08-4013 (10th Cir. Feb. 1, 2008).	The purported victims in United States v. Hunter filed a petition for a writ of mandamus requesting that the U.S. Court of Appeals for the Tenth Circuit order the U.S. District Court for the District of Utah to require the government to certify whether it had information to support their	The right to be treated with fairness and with respect for dignity and privacy

Table 19. (Continued)

	position that they should be recognized as victims under the CVRA and to release such information from the grand jury transcript and government files. The court of appeals denied the petition, under the writ of mandamus standard of review, finding that the district court had not clearly abused its discretion in denying the purported victims' motion.	
United States v. Kaufman, No. 04-40141, 2005 WL 2648070 (D. Kan. 2005).	A television station filed a motion requesting that sketch artists be allowed in the courtroom during a trial, and the victims did not oppose the motion but requested that the sketch artists not be allowed to sketch the faces of the victims. The U.S. District Court for the District of Kansas granted the motion and ordered that the sketch artists not be allowed to sketch the faces of the victims, stating that the CVRA right to be treated with fairness and with respect for the victims' dignity and privacy requires such restrictions.	The right to be treated with fairness and with respect for dignity and privacy
Eleventh Circuit		
In re Jane Doe, No. 08-80736 (S.D. Fla. July 7, 2008) (victim petition).	In a case in which the defendant had pleaded guilty to several charges in a state court and the federal government was engaged in plea negotiations with the accused that may have deferred federal prosecution, the victim filed a petition requesting that the U.S. District Court for the Southern District of Florida ensure that the government respect her CVRA rights, including the right to confer regarding the plea agreement. The district court has not yet decided this case.	The reasonable right to confer with the prosecutor
United States v. Williams, No. 1:06-cr-313 (N.D. Ga. Jan. 8, 2007).	The corporate victim filed a motion requesting an appearance to respond to the defendant's motion requesting to interview the victim's employees, asserting the CVRA rights to be protected from the accused and to be treated with fairness. The U.S. District Court for the Northern District of Georgia denied the motion.	The right to be reasonably protected from the accused The right to be treated with fairness and with respect for dignity and privacy
In re Searcy, No. 06-1 4951 (11th Cir. Sept. 15, 2006).	Petitioner filed a petition for a writ of mandamus seeking an injunction against multiple companies and the Attorney General to prohibit them from using certain software. The U.S. Court of Appeals for the Eleventh Circuit dismissed the complaint, finding that the U.S. District Court for the Middle District of Florida had not abused its discretion in dismissing the petitioner's claim on the grounds of res judicata.	None

Table 19. (Continued)

In re Miller, No. 06-15182 (11th Cir. Sept. 28, 2006).	Petitioner filed a petition for a writ of mandamus complaining of the actions of a communications company and requesting restitution from the company. The U.S. Court of Appeals for the Eleventh Circuit denied the petition, stating that it doubted that the CVRA applied to the petitioner's claims, and even if the CVRA did apply, relief such as directing an investigation and providing restitution is not available via mandamus.	None
District of Columbia Circuit		
United States v. Gooch, No. 04-128-23, 2006 WL 3780781 (D.D.C. Dec. 20, 2006).	The government requested that victims of the defendant's noncapital offenses be able to speak at the penalty phase of the defendant's capital trial. The U.S. District Court for the District of Columbia denied the request, finding that the Federal Death Penalty Act authorizes victim impact information only from victims of the capital offenses and that the victims of the noncapital offense did not have an independent right under the CVRA to be heard at the penalty phase for the capital offenses because the right to be heard only includes proceedings involving offenses against the crime victim.	The right to be reasonably heard
In re Jacobsen, No. 05-7086, 2005 U.S. App. LEXIS 13990 (D.C. Cir. July 8, 2005).	The victim in United States v. Hall, a case in the D.C. Superior Court, filed a petition for a writ of mandamus requesting that the U.S. Court of Appeals for the District of Columbia Circuit direct the D.C. Superior Court to reopen the plea and provide victims with reasonable notice and opportunity to be heard before accepting the plea. The court of appeals denied the petition as moot, stating that the D.C. Superior Court had not yet accepted the plea agreement.	The right to reasonable, accurate, and timely notice The right to be reasonably heard
Sieverding v. American Bar Assoc., No. 07-51 26, 2007 U.S. App. LEXIS 13756 (D.C. Cir. June 8, 2007).	Petitioners filed a petition for a writ of mandamus, requesting to be declared victims of extortion, witness intimidation, and related federal crimes. The U.S. Court of Appeals for the District of Columbia Circuit denied the petition, stating that the individuals failed to first file a motion with the district court and that the petitioners' allegations do not show that they qualify as crime victims under the CVRA.	The right to be reasonably protected from the accused The right to be treated with fairness and with respect for dignity and privacy

Table 19. (Continued)

D.C. Superior Court		
Transcript of Record, United States v. Mack, No. 2004- FEL-6798 (D.C. Super. Ct. Aug. 30, 2006).	During a plea hearing, the government informed the D.C. Superior Court that the victim's family wanted to address the court regarding the plea agreement. The D.C. Superior Court denied the request, stating that it was not bound by the CVRA, but noted that the victims would be allowed to speak at the sentencing hearing.	The right to be reasonably heard
Transcript of Record, United States v. Blades, No. 2006CF114741 (D.C. Super. Ct. Mar. 26, 2008).	The victim-witness filed a motion requesting to be allowed to attend the trial the defendant. The D.C. Superior Court granted the motion, finding that. there was no evidence that suggested that the victim-witness' testimony would be materially altered after hearing other testimony.	The right not to be excluded from public court proceedings

Source: GAO analysis of court cases in which the CVRA was raised.

Cases in which the court did not base its decision on the CVRA were not included. We conducted our final electronic search on June 30, 2008. The cases included are those that were available in legal databases as of that date.

APPENDIX V: REFERENCES TO ADHERENCE WITH APP ADE WH VICTIMS' RIGHT REQUIREMES IN DJ WORK PL D PF AIL VICTIMS' RIGHTS REQUIREMENTS IN DOJ WORK PLANS AND PERFORMANCE APPRAISALS

Table 20. Examples of References to Victim-Related Responsibilities in Performance Appraisals and Work Plans of Investigators, Attorneys, and Other DOJ Staff Positions

DOJ component	Excerpts and descriptions of staff performance appraisals and work plans related to providing federal crime victims their rights
Alcohol Tobacco and Firearms	*Agents* According to the ATF, they are ... in the process of placing critical elements into the Bureau's performance appraisals for special agents, supervisors, and other appropriate personnel that will include the evaluation of their adherence or non-adherence with the victims' rights and witnesses' services provisions.
Federal Bureau of Investigation	*Special Agents and Victim Specialists* Standard performance appraisal records for special agents and victimspecialists do not include references to victims' rights.
Drug EnforcementAdministration	*Agents* AdministrationAccording to the DOJ, the "DEA plans to incorporate the Victim Witness reference in investigators' workplans by the end on the second quarter of FY 09."
Executive Office of the U.S. Attorneys' Offices	*Assistant United States Attorneys* From the performance work plan and appraisal record: "As necessary, communicates pertinent information to andconsults with supervisors, agencies, victims, and others."

Table 20. (Continued)

Antitrust Division	*Attorneys* From the performance work plan: "Routinely identifies victims of crime in assigned matters and provides them with appropriate victim services. "Notifies as appropriate both victims and witnesses of their rights under federal law and Attorney General Guidelines for Victim and Witness Assistance and provides such rights within one week as needed or requested. Keeps victims/witnesses appropriately informed as to the status of the investigation, litigation, and sentencing. Consults with them as appropriate concerning charging and plea decisions, restitution rights, and appropriate litigation decisions."
Tax Division	*Trial Attorneys* From the performance appraisal record: "Handling of cases and other assignments including awareness of and adherence to Department guidelines and policies with respect to victim and witness protection, including the Attorney General's Guidelines on Victim and Witness Assistance."
Environmental and Natural Resources Division	*Attorneys* From the performance work plan: "Uses best efforts to afford victims their legal rights in compliance with Department policy by identifying victims of crimes; in cooperation with investigators; informing victims of case events, in cooperation with victim/witness coordinators at U.S. Attorney's Offices; consulting with victims if requested; seeking appropriate restitution; and informing victims of victim impact statement options prior to sentencing."
Civil Division	*Trial Attorneys* From the performance work plan: "Communicates and coordinates with witnesses and victims of crime, clients, Justice Department Personnel, and others." "Keeps witnesses and victims of crime, clients, and other appropriate individuals informed of the status of litigation and relevant developments in a timely manner."
Civil Rights Division	*Associate Deputy Chiefs* From the performance plan agreement: "Complies fully with statutory and Departmental rules regarding victims."
Criminal Division	*Associate Deputy Chiefs* From the performance work plan and appraisal record: "Complies with the Attorney General's guidelines on Victim Witness issues." "Interacts with superiors, co-workers, support staff and members of the public (victim and witnesses) in a constructive manner concerning victim witness issues." "Ensures that the rights and needs of victims are appropriately addressed by Fraud Section personnel by, among other things, supporting the implementation of related policies." "Ensures that the rights and needs of crime victims and witnesses are upheld. Provide necessary victim information to the coordinator/liaison in a timely fashion." "Supervises and supports the Fraud Section's requirement in mentoring and training new employees with information concerning Criminal Division's obligation

Table 20. (Continued)

National Security Division	*Trial Attorney, Chief of the Counterterrorism Section* From the performance work plan: Ensures that the rights and needs of victims are appropriately addressed by Counterterrorism Section personnel. Goals include ensuring that victim-witness issues are addressed in Counterterrorism Section cases. Measures include description of efforts to (1) develop and expand training and educational opportunities in order to improve emergency response procedures and systems and (2) ensure that the rights and needs of victims are appropriately addressed by CTS personnel. According to an NSD official, victim-related responsibilities will be incorporated into the performance work plans for trial attorneys in the Counterterrorism Section and all Office of Justice for Victims of Overseas Terrorism staff.
Bureau of Prisons	*Managers and Department Heads* From the performance appraisal record, their performance may be rated "outstanding" if the official: "Create(s) procedures to implement, monitor, and evaluate the practices/procedures associated with the Attorney General's victim/witness guidelines." *Office Support Staff* From the performance appraisal record, their performance may be rated "outstanding" if the official: "Create(s) innovative forms of implementing, monitoring, and evaluating the practices/procedures associated with the Attorney General's victim/witness service guidelines in accordance with current policies and procedures."
U.S. Marshal Service	According to the USMS, USMS does not currently address victim-related responsibilities in performance work plans. However, procedures are being updated to include these responsibilities in performance work plans where appropriate. It is anticipated that we will have this accomplished, as directed by OPM, by June 2009.
U.S. Parole Commission	*Hearing Examiners* From the performance plans - successful elements include: "Consistently works with the Victim/Witness Section to ensure that victims/witnesses are provided with the right to participate in the hearing process including the right to be reasonably heard at any parole proceeding. *Post Release Analysts, Pre Release Analysts, Case Service Assistants, and Victim-Witness Coordinators* From the performance plans - successful elements include: Consistently works to protect the privacy rights of victims/witnesses including removing/redacting any personal information regarding victims that is confidential and ensuring that any personal information regarding a victim is not discussed with any parties that do not have the need to know such information.

Source: GAO analysis performance appraisals and work plans for DOJ staff positions.

APPENDIX VI: COMMENTS FROM THE PP TS TH P OF JUSTC DEPARTMENT OF JUSTICE

U.S. Department of Justice

NOV 2 6 2008

Washington, D.C. 20530

Ms. Eileen R. Larence
Director, Homeland Security and Justice
U.S. Government Accountability Office
Washington, DC 20510-1501

Re: Government Accountability Office Draft Report GAO 09-54

Dear Ms. Larence:

Thank you for the opportunity to review the Government Accountability Office (GAO) draft report entitled *Crime Victims' Rights Act: Increasing Awareness, Modifying the Complaint Process, and Enhancing Compliance Monitoring Will Improve Implementation of the Act.* The draft report recognizes that since its enactment the Department of Justice (Department) has taken a number of steps to implement and ensure compliance with the Crime Victims' Rights Act (CVRA, or the Act), codified at 18 U.S.C. §3771. The draft report acknowledges that, for example, the Department has revised its internal guidelines on providing victim assistance, conducted training for employees on both the revised guidelines and the CVRA, and created a process to examine victim complaints against its employees. The draft report also makes several recommendations designed to improve compliance with the Act.

With respect to the Department, the draft report recommends that the Attorney General take steps to ensure that victims are more aware of the enforcement mechanisms available to them to assert their CVRA rights in court, and the complaint process afforded to them if they believe their rights have been violated by a Department employee. The draft also recommends that the complaint process be restructured to ensure independence and impartiality during the investigation phase. The draft recommends that the Department identify suitable performance measures to evaluate how fully and well victims are being accorded their rights and services, and uniform information reporting requirements focused on component compliance. Finally, the draft report recommends that the Federal Bureau of Investigation (FBI) make adherence to victims' rights a formal part of its agents' work plans and performance appraisals.

The comments below address the draft report's recommendations as well as language that should be clarified or modified to more accurately reflect the Department's views. As an initial matter, however, we note that the Department intends to convene a working group comprising

Ms. Eileen R. Larence Page 2

representatives from its components with victim-related responsibilities for purposes of considering the recommendations contained in the final GAO report. Those recommendations are likely to have value but, for the reasons articulated below, the extent and manner in which they are implemented requires input from the affected components.

With respect to GAO's first recommendation, the draft report acknowledges that neither the CVRA nor the existing Attorney General Guidelines for Victim and Witness Assistance (the Guidelines) require Department components to inform victims of their ability to file motions or petitions for writs of mandamus to enforce their rights, and their ability to submit complaints against Department employees for alleged violations of the CVRA. Nevertheless, the draft report recommends that Department components with victim-related responsibilities be directed by the Attorney General to explore ways to increase victim awareness of these potential remedies. We agree that victims should be well informed about the various enforcement mechanisms available to them under the CVRA, and about their right to initiate complaints against Department employees. We intend to take steps to enhance victim awareness of these rights. In deciding which steps are most appropriate, the working group will consider a number of options, including those mentioned in the report.

With regard to GAO's recommendation that the complaint process be restructured, the working group will consider that as well. We recognize the salutary benefits of an investigation process that avoids both actual and apparent bias. Removing responsibility for conducting initial complaint investigation from the local office, however, has drawbacks. Principal among them is the additional delay it will almost certainly impose upon the process. We continue to believe that addressing a complaint at a point when a victim whose rights have been violated may still have time to exercise them is at least as important as punishing the violation.

As a result, in consultation with the Victim's Rights Ombudsman (VRO), we intend to explore several options that will minimize the risk of actual bias and ameliorate the perception of partiality, without sacrificing speed. It may be inadvisable, moreover, to fashion a one-size-fits-all remedy. What works in a large U.S. Attorney's Office (USAO) may not work in a small one. What works in a litigation division at Main Justice may not work in a USAO. What works best for complaints against prosecutors may not work well for complaints against employees of investigative or corrections components. In considering possible options the working group will examine whether initial complaint investigations can be done effectively by using telecommunications technology rather than in-person interviews.

Although we are committed to re-examining this issue, we do disagree with GAO's decision to evaluate the VRO-administered complaint investigation process by referring to outside standards generally applicable to Ombudsmen, or practices used by other investigative bodies. First, unlike the Office of Professional Responsibility (OPR), the VRO has no staff of full-time investigators at her disposal. She must, by necessity, rely upon employees for whom the complaint investigation process is a collateral duty. Also unlike OPR, the VRO has no budget for investigation-related travel. Finally, and as we described to the GAO auditors during the review,

Ms. Eileen R. Larence Page 3

the VRO is not an Ombudsman in the manner envisioned by either the *Governmental Ombudsman Standards* or the American Bar Association's Standards for the Establishment and Operation of Ombuds Offices. The VRO is a Department employee appointed by the Attorney General, who also has operational and administrative control over the programs that are subject to the VRO's jurisdiction. The VRO's defined functions, moreover, do not match those of a classic Ombudsman. The VRO does not have authority, for example, to mediate complaints between victims and DOJ employees. Instead, the VRO determines whether a victim's CVRA rights have been violated by a Department employee, and if so recommends either training or discipline for the employee. The responsibility to resolve victim complaints and implement VRO recommendations remains with the employee's local office.

The draft report discusses the use of employee work plans as a means of evaluating whether individuals are complying with their obligations under the CVRA. In so doing, the draft report should clarify both what the Guidelines require and what responsible Department components have done and are doing to comply with those requirements.

Employee work plans (a generic term used here to encompass all written records of employee performance) are put in place each year for each employee, and individual performance is evaluated at the end of the rating period based upon how well an employee has performed the tasks identified in his or her work plan. The Guidelines dictate, moreover, that work plans for "each appropriate" Department employee include reference to the employee's obligations under the CVRA and the Guidelines, so that their performance in meeting those obligations will be part of their annual review. At several places, however, the draft report suggests that some reference to the CVRA is or soon will be part of every work plan for every employee within all but one of the many Department components with victim-related responsibilities. And, in particular, the draft report indicates that the Executive Office for United States Attorneys (EOUSA) has already incorporated references to the Guidelines in all non-supervisory Assistant U.S. Attorney (AUSA) work plans, and will incorporate such references into the 2009 work plans for supervisory AUSAs.

In fact, the Department believes that work plan references to the CVRA and the Guidelines are only required and desirable for "appropriate" employees, that is, for employees whose job actually entails victim-related responsibilities. The fact that a Department component has victim-related responsibilities does not mean that all of its employees have such responsibilities, and it is contrary to sound personnel management principles to encumber an employee's work plan with tasks he or she is not expected or likely to perform.

Similarly, EOUSA creates model work plans and makes them available to the field, but EOUSA does not dictate their use. Within some broad parameters, each USAO is free to put work plans in place for its employees that most accurately describe an employee's actual duties. As a result, it's likely that USAOs have employee work plans in place (including for non-supervisory AUSAs) that appropriately make no mention of the CVRA or the Guidelines. EOUSA will provide model work plan language for 2009 for Supervisory AUSAs whose duties include direct

Ms. Eileen R. Larence Page 4

or supervisory victim-related responsibilities. However, as long as it complies with the Guidelines requirement, each USAO will remain free to use that language, some other language, or in appropriate situations no language at all.

The draft report singles out the FBI as the lone Department component that has yet to adequately commit to incorporating CVRA compliance in the work plans of all employees with victim-related responsibilities. After reviewing the draft report, however, the FBI has agreed to revisit its position.

The draft report recommends that the Department establish performance measures to gauge whether the Department, as a whole, is meeting its stated goal of ensuring that victim participation in the criminal justice system is consistent with the CVRA. At the same time, GAO acknowledges that objective measurements are difficult to define. The raw number of Victim Notification System (VNS) letters mailed each year is a measure of effort, but may say little about effectiveness. In fact, because VNS is not used by all Department components (e.g., ATF) with victim-related responsibilities, it has significant limitations as a Department-wide performance measure. So too, victim attendance at public court proceedings is impossible to track with any degree of accuracy.

Nevertheless, we agree that Department-wide performance measures are important, and the working group will consider a variety of possibilities in making recommendations to the Attorney General. We believe this process will also assist the Office of Victims of Crime in assessing component compliance with the Guidelines.

Our final comment focuses on GAO's recognition that there can be tension between the interests of the victim and the interests of the United States in a particular prosecution. The draft report describes, for example, a situation where a victim's presence at a plea hearing for a cooperating defendant could undermine what the report refers to as a successful prosecution. There is no single test for what constitutes a successful prosecution. We believe Congress appreciated this tension, and addressed it by allowing victims to assert their rights in court – with or without counsel of their choosing – independent of the prosecutor. The appropriate balance between the interests of the United States, the victim's rights under the CVRA, and the defendant's rights must then be struck by the court.

Ms. Eileen R. Larence Page 5

We appreciate the substantial time and effort involved in GAO's examination of the CVRA and the manner in which it has been implemented by the Department and the courts. Thank you, again, for the opportunity to provide comments on the report.

Sincerely,

Lee J. Lofthus
Assistant Attorney General
for Administration

ACKNOWLEDGMENTS

In addition to the contact named above, Kristy Brown, Assistant Director, managed this assignment.

Lisa Berardi Marflak, David Schneider, Matthew Shaffer, and Johanna Wong made significant contributions to the work.

Tracey King provided significant legal support and analysis.

David Alexander, Stuart Kaufman, Carl Barden, and Minette Richardson provided significant assistance with design and methodology, as well as the analysis of survey results.

Adam Vogt provided assistance in report preparation.

Amber Edwards, Benjamin Jordan, and Jessica Wintfeld made contributions to the work during the preliminary phase of the review.

RELATED GAO PRODUCTS

Human Trafficking: A Strategic Framework Could Help Enhance the Interagency Collaboration Needed to Effectively Combat Trafficking Crimes. GAO-07-915. Washington, D.C.: July 26, 2007.

Services Provided to Victims of Domestic Violence, Sexual Assault, Dating Violence, and Stalking. GAO-07-846R. Washington, D.C.: July 19, 2007.

Identity Theft: Some Outreach Efforts to Promote Awareness of New Consumer Rights Are Under Way. GAO-05-710. Washington, D.C.: June 30, 2005.

Criminal Debt: Court-Ordered Restitution Amounts Far Exceed Likely Collections for the Crime Victims in Selected Financial Fraud Cases. GAO-05-08. Washington, D.C.: January 31, 2005.

GAO'S MISSION

The Government Accountability Office, the audit, evaluation, and investigative arm of Congress, exists to support Congress in meeting its constitutional responsibilities and to help improve the performance and accountability of the federal government for the American people. GAO examines the use of public funds; evaluates federal programs and policies; and provides analyses, recommendations, and other assistance to help Congress make informed oversight, policy, and funding decisions. GAO's commitment to good government is reflected in its core values of accountability, integrity, and reliability.

ENDNOTES

[1] Pub. L. No. 108-405, 118 Stat. 2260 (2004).

[2] Relief is a generic term for all types of benefits or redress that a party asks of a court.

3 Most motions must include a written statement of the relief sought and the grounds for seeking the relief. The motion must be served on all parties, and a judge may hold a hearing for oral arguments on the motion. During a trial or a hearing, an oral motion may be permitted.

4 A writ of mandamus is an order from a higher court directing a lower court to perform a specified action.

5 Nonprobability sampling is a method of sampling where observations are selected in a manner that is not completely random, generally using specific characteristics of the population as criteria. Results from a nonprobability sample cannot be used to make inferences about an entire population because some elements of the population being studied had no chance or an unknown chance of being selected as part of the sample.

6 VNS only maintains records of notification letters for 30 days.

7 We did not review the three additional complaints received by the VRO during this time period because the complaints were still under investigation and the VRO had yet to make a determination regarding them.

8 28 C.F.R. § 45.10.

9 The ombudsman standards against which we compared DOJ's victim complaint process include United States Ombudsman Association, *Governmental Ombudsman Standards*, (Dayton, OH: October 2003) and American Bar Association, *Revised Standards for the Establishment and Operation of Ombuds Offices* (February 2004). The other offices that conduct similar investigations as the VRO include DOJ's Office of Professional Responsibility and state offices that review victim complaints located in Alaska, Arizona, Connecticut, Colorado, Maryland, Minnesota, South Carolina, and Wisconsin.

10 *In re* Dean, No. 08-20 125 (5th Cir. May 7, 2008).

11 The District of Columbia Superior Court handles all local trial matters in the District of Columbia.

12 Pub. L. No. 97-291, 96 Stat. 1248 (1982).

13 Pub. L. No. 98-473, ch. XIV, 98 Stat. 1837 (1984).

14 Pub. L. No. 10 1-647, tit. V, 104 Stat. 4789 (1990).

15 Pub. L. No. 103-322, 108 Stat. 1796 (1994).

16 Pub. L. No. 104-132, tit. II, 110 Stat. 1214 (1996).

17 Pub. L. No. 105-6, 111 Stat. 12 (1997).

18 Pub. L. No. 108-405, tit. I, 118 Stat. 2260 (2004). The federal government has passed other laws that provide benefits and services to certain classes of crime victims including the Trafficking Victim Protection Act (for victims of human trafficking crimes) and the Justice for Victims of Terrorism Act (for victims of terrorism). Pub. L. No. 106-386, 114 Stat. 1464 (2000); Pub. L. No. 104-132, 110 Stat. 1214 (1996).

19 Pub. L. No. 10 1-647, § 502, 104 Stat. 4789, 4820 (1990), *repealed by* Pub. L. No. 108-405, § 102(c), 118 Stat. 2260, 2264 (2004). The rights listed in the 1990 law included: (1) the right to be treated with fairness and with respect for the victim's dignity and privacy; (2) the right to be reasonably protected from the accused offender; (3) the right to be notified of court proceedings; (4) the right to be present at all public court proceedings related to the offense, unless the court determines that testimony by the victim would be materially affected if the victim heard other testimony at trial; (5) the right to confer with the attorney for the government in the case; (6) the right to restitution; and (7) the right to information about the conviction, sentencing, imprisonment, and release of the offender.

20 *Id.* at § 503, 104 Stat. 4820-22 (codified at 42 U.S.C. § 10607).

21 Pub. L. No. 108-405, 118 Stat. 2260 (2004).

22 Id. at § 102(a) (codified at 18 U.S.C. § 3771(a)).

23 18 U.S.C. § 3771(f).

24 28 C.F.R. § 45.10.

25 18 U.S.C. § 3771(d)(3).

26 18 U.S.C. § 3771(d)(5).

27 18 U.S.C. § 3771(c)(1).

28 18 U.S.C. § 3771(c)(2).

29 The NAC is operated by EOUSA and is used to train federal, state, and local prosecutors and litigators in advocacy skills and management of legal operations.

30 Magistrate judges are judicial officers appointed by the district court to serve for 8-year terms. Their duties include, among other things, conducting most of the initial proceedings in criminal cases (including search and arrest warrants and detention hearings), trying most criminal misdemeanor cases, and conducting a wide variety of other proceedings referred to them by district judges.

31 National Sentencing Policy Institutes are biennial meetings of federal judges, prosecutors, defense attorneys, and probation officers. These meetings feature panel discussions and presentations on current sentencing issues.

32 The challenges we identify in this section are based on information we obtained from our site visits to nine federal judicial districts, where we met with a number of USAO and federal investigative staff and court officials. Not all of the officials with whom we met identified each of these factors as an impediment to CVRA implementation, in part because some of the challenges, such as those involving victims who live on Indian reservations are not relevant to all offices. Therefore, our intent is not to focus on the pervasiveness of these challenges; rather, as CVRA implementation continues, and as other DOJ offices and federal courts may encounter these same challenges, this section is intended to inform the reader of efforts that have been made in the past to overcome them.

33 Five of the nine USAOs we visited have Indian reservations within their jurisdiction.

34 FBI Legal Attaché offices work to combat crime, such as terrorism, internationally by working with their foreign counterparts and by covering international leads for domestic U.S. investigations.

35 This average was based on responses from the 45 percent of USAO victim-witness professionals who reported in our survey as working additional hours as a result of CVRA requirements.

36 CM/ECF is the federal courts' electronic case management and filing system and, as such, contains the schedule of court proceedings, as well as information about motions, court orders and parties.

37 The system is currently configured such that USAO victim-witness personnel have to manually transfer case scheduling information from CM/ECF to the USAOs' case management system—the Legal Information Office Network System (LIONS). Schedule information from LIONS is then automatically uploaded to VNS daily.

38 We calculated the ratio of cases per victim-witness personnel in each USAO by dividing the total number of victim-related cases (sex crimes, violent crimes, identity theft, etc.) filed by the USAO between March 2006 and March 2007 by the total number of victim- witness personnel in the USAO as of April 2008. We based our calculations on victim- related cases because they are generally the cases with which victim-witness personnel would be involved. In addition, we recognize that the number of victim-witness personnel in each office as of April 2008 may differ from the number in each office as of March 2007; however, at the time of our review, data on the number of victim-related cases and the number of victim-witness personnel were not available for the same periods of time. We categorized the USAOs whose ratio fell within the top third (at least 101 cases per personnel) as having the "highest" ratio; the USAOs whose ratio fell within the middle third (between 57.5 and 101 cases per personnel) as having a "middle range" ratio; and the USAOs whose ratio fell within the bottom third (less than 57.5) as having the "lowest" ratio.

39 An arraignment is a judicial proceeding where the defendant is read the charges filed against her or him and then is asked to enter a plea. A detention hearing is a judicial proceeding used to determine whether a defendant should remain in custody before her or his trial, and if released, what conditions, if any, will be in place, such as a no-contact order with a victim or witness.

40 GAO separated the USAOs into sizes based on their districts' caseloads, which were measured using AOUSC data on the number of all criminal cases that were filed in each judicial district between March 2006 and March 2007. See app. I for more details..

41 DOJ suggested revising 18 U.S.C. § 3771(c)(3) to read, "notice otherwise required pursuant to this chapter shall not be given if such notice may endanger the safety of any person or compromise an ongoing investigation."

42 We were not able to review the files associated with 3 of these 144 complaints because the complaints were still under investigation and a final determination had not been made at the time of our review. Therefore, our analysis of victim complaints is based on our review of 141 complaint files.

43 See 28 C.F.R. § 45.10(c)(3).

44 See 18 U.S.C. § 3771(d)(1).

45 See 28 C.F.R. § 45.10(a).

46 See 28 C.F.R. § 45.10(a).

47 See 28 C.F.R. § 45.10(c)(3).

48 We mailed a questionnaire to 1,179 victims, and for the reasons we mention in app. I, the response rate was low. As a result, we cannot generalize the survey results to all federal crime victims in our study period, and instead, limit the discussion of survey results to only those victims who responded.

49 These percentages do not add up to 100 due to rounding.

50 VRO internal guidelines direct investigators to attempt to resolve any complaint that can be done so reasonably and to the victims' satisfaction, and notes that no further investigation need be conducted if the victim is satisfied with the steps taken to resolve the complaint.

51 The Office of Professional Responsibility reviews allegations of professional misconduct of DOJ employees when providing investigative, litigative, or legal advice. The Office of Professional Responsibility receives allegations of misconduct against department attorneys from a variety of sources, including self-referrals and

referrals of complaints by officials in U.S. Attorneys' offices and litigating divisions, private attorneys, defendants and civil litigants, other federal agencies, state or local government officials, judicial and congressional referrals, and media reports.

[52] One study was compiled by an Arizona State Victims' Rights Enforcement Officer, and the second study was issued by the Institute for Public Research, both in 2006.

[53] The eight state victims' rights enforcement offices included in these two studies are located in Alaska, Arizona, Colorado, Connecticut, Maryland, Minnesota, South Carolina, and Wisconsin. Two other offices included in this study, located in Oregon and New Mexico, were not included in our analysis given the offices' recent transition into receiving and investigating victim complaints.

[54] We obtained CVRA-related cases through legal search engines, court dockets, interviews, and case compilations by the Federal Judicial Center and the National Crime Victims Law Institute. We conducted our final electronic search on June 30, 2008. The cases included are those that were available in legal databases as of that date.

[55] We mailed a questionnaire to 1,179 victims, and for the reasons we mention in app. I, the response rate was low. As a result, we cannot generalize the survey results to all federal crime victims in our study period, and instead, limit the discussion of survey results to only those victims who responded.

[56] The Judicial Conference Committee on Rules of Practice, Procedure, and Evidence coordinates the work of the advisory committees, considers proposals recommended by the advisory committees, and transmits such proposals with its recommendation to the Judicial Conference.

[57] Judicial Conference Advisory Committees on Rules of Practice and Procedure study the operation and effect of rules of practice and procedure and suggest recommendations with respect to the rules. The proposed amendment, which is expected to be effective in December 2009, would provide that when computing deadlines framed in terms of hours, the start time is at the occurrence of the event that triggers the deadline—in this case, the filing of the petition for writ of mandamus. The time period computation includes weekends and legal holidays, except that if the deadline expires on one of these days, it is extended to the same time on the next day that is not on a weekend or legal holiday.

[58] We did not determine the extent to which the courts complied with the 72-hour requirement for all petitions for writs of mandamus that were filed. We did not have access to all the petitions and those that we were able to obtain did not contain information on the exact time they were filed with the court. In addition, we could not ascertain the exact time that the petitions were decided from the published court decisions and did not interview all the judges and clerks who were involved with the petitions.

[59] 59 Kenna v. U.S. District Court for the Central District of California, 435 F.3d 1011 (9th Cir. 2006).

[60] United States v. Marcello, 370 F. Supp. 2d 745 (N.D. Ill. 2005).

[61] United States v. Lee, No. 01-00132 (D. Haw. June 17, 2005) (order denying motion).

[62] United States v. Williams, No. 1:06-cr-00313 (N.D. Ga. Jan. 08, 2007) (order denying motion).

[63] GAO, *Standards for Internal Control in the Federal Government*, GAO/AIMD-00-21.3.1 (Washington, D.C.: November 1999).

[64] The Crime Victims Fund was established by the Victims of Crime Act of 1984, as amended, and is comprised of fines collected from individuals convicted of offenses against the United States and donations from private entities.

[65] OJP's mission is to increase public safety and improve the fair administration of justice across the United States through innovative leadership and programs. According to OJP, it strives to achieve its mission by providing and coordinating information, research and development, statistics, training, and support to help the justice community build the capacity it needs to meet its public safety goals.

[66] 42 U.S.C. § 10603(c)(3)(A).

[67] GAO, *Executive Guide: Effectively Implementing the Government Performance and Results Act*, GAO/GGD-96-118, (Washington, D.C.: June 1996).

[68] The Office of the Inspector General (OIG) was excluded from our analysis because they determined that they did not need to submit an annual compliance report to OVC. According to a memo from the Assistant Inspector General for Investigations, DOJ, not an individual, is the victim in most OIG investigations and, in those cases with individual victims, the OIG is not the first responder.

[69] The 94 U.S. judicial districts are organized into 12 regional circuits, each of which has a U.S. court of appeals

[70] *In re* W.R. Huff Asset Management Co., 409 F.3d 555 (2d Cir. 2005)

[71] *In re* Dean, No. 08-20125 (5th Cir. May 7, 2008).

[72] DOJ officials stated that the department's *Principles of Federal Prosecution* outlines some considerations when deciding not to file charges or limit charges, which include the sufficiency of the evidence, the strength of the federal interest that would be served by the prosecution, and whether there are adequate non-criminal

alternatives to prosecution. In addition, they stated that department policy also indicates that once a decision to prosecute has been made, the prosecutor should charge, or recommend that the grand jury charge, the most serious readily provable offense that is consistent with the nature of the defendant's conduct, and that is likely to result in a sustainable conviction.

73 This complaint was filed after the April 2008 end date of GAO's complaint file review but is included here as an example of a complaint that addresses the issue of whether CVRA rights apply before charges are eventually filed.

74 *In re* Dean, No. 08-20 125 (5th Cir. May 7, 2008).

75 Kenna v. U.S. District Court for the Central District of California, 435 F.3d 1011 (9th Cir. 2006); U.S. v. Degenhardt, 405 F. Supp. 2d 1341 (D. Utah 2005).

76 United States v. Marcello, 370 F. Supp. 2d 745 (N.D. Ill. 2005).

77 Presentence reports contain information to help the court determine the appropriate amount of restitution under the law.

78 *In re* Antrobus, No. 08-4002 (10th Cir. Jan. 11, 2008).

79 Four of the 12 circuit courts have used one of the two standards of review to decide petitions for mandamus. Other courts have discussed the standard of review under the CVRA but did not apply either standard in deciding the case at hand.

80 *In re* Dean, No. 08-20 125 (5th Cir. May 7, 2008); *In re* Antrobus, No. 08-4002 (10th Cir. Jan. 11, 2008).

81 Kenna v. U.S. District Court for the Central District of California, 435 F.3d 1011 (9th Cir. 2006); In re W.R. Huff Asset Management Co., 409 F.3d 555 (2d Cir. 2005).

82 According to EOUSA officials, the D.C. USAO is responsible for prosecuting almost all adult criminal offenses and certain juveniles charged as adults in the D.C. Superior Court.

83 In the District of Columbia, local law provides that the U.S. District Court for the District of Columbia has jurisdiction over local offenses if a federal offense and local offense are joined in the same indictment. D.C. Code § 11-502.

84 The D.C. crime victims' statute contains rights similar to those in the CVRA. However, among other differences, the D.C. statute lacks the clear and convincing evidence standard to exclude victims from public proceedings and the right to be reasonably heard in public proceedings involving release, plea, sentencing, or any parole proceeding. D.C. Code § 23- 190 1. The statute instead gives victims the right to submit a written impact statement at sentencing and release or parole hearings. D.C. Code § 23-1904. The statute also does not establish mechanisms to ensure adherence to and enforcement of victims' rights.

85 The Assistant General Counsel of the D.C. Superior Court stated that victims would be confused about the appropriate court of appeals in which to file petitions for writs of mandamus under the CVRA. The D.C. Court of Appeals typically hears appeals of Superior Court decisions, but the CVRA states that victims are to assert their rights in the "district court," which in the District of Columbia is under the jurisdiction of the U.S. Court of Appeals for the D.C. Circuit.

86 DOJ proposed that 18 U.S.C. § 3771(e) be amended to add a new sentence at the end to read as follows:

"For cases prosecuted by the United States in the Superior Court of the District of Columbia, the terms 'court' and district court' mean the Superior Court of the District of Columbia and the term 'court of appeals' means the District of Columbia Court of Appeals for purposes of this chapter."

87 We mailed a questionnaire to 1,179 victims, and for the reasons we mention in app. I, the response rate was low. As a result, we cannot generalize the survey results to all federal crime victims in our study period, and instead, limit the discussion of survey results to only those victims who responded.

CHAPTER SOURCES

The following chapters have been previously published:

Chapter 1 – This is an edited, excerpted and augmented edition of a Federal Judicial Center publication, dated June 2, 2008.

Chapter 2 – This is an edited, excerpted and augmented edition of a United States Government Accountability Office (GAO), Report to Congressional Committees. Publication GAO-09-54, dated December 2008.

INDEX

D

E

F

G

T

U

V

W